THE WALKING DEAD
PSYCHOLOGY
Psych of the Living Dead

Edited by

TRAVIS LANGLEY

#TWDpsych

STERLING
New York

STERLING
New York

An Imprint of Sterling Publishing
1166 Avenue of the Americas
New York, NY 10036

Marylene Coitre: 244; Ryan Condron: 161, 265; Sherri Craig: 165;
Tanner Gibson: 4, 200, 219, 228, 253; Lupe Hurtado: 159; iStock: ©A-digit: 223;
©Big_Ryan: 7; ©carlacdesign: 71; ©CSA-Images: 42; ©gashish: 192; ©Gil-Design: 125;
Nick Langley: iii, vii, xii, 266, 276; Travis Langley: viii; Albert Muhlenbruch: 65;
John Russo: xiv; E. Paul Zehr: 36; Shutterstock: ©Babich Alexander: 9; ©chronicler: 246;
©chuhall: 82; ©Koshevnyk: 137; ©LHF Graphics: 93; ©Macrovector: 206; ©MaKars: 20;
©mega_spy: 57, 111, 169; ©AleksMelnik: 59, 148; ©MrBenBa: 234; ©Nikiteev_Konstantin: 225;
©RomanYa: 31; ©Ron and Joe: 171; ©rosapompelmo: 182; ©xpixel: 113

ISBN 978-1-4549-1705-2

Distributed in Canada by Sterling Publishing
c/o Canadian Manda Group, 664 Annette Street
Toronto, Ontario, Canada M6S 2C8
Distributed in the United Kingdom by GMC Distribution Services
Castle Place, 166 High Street, Lewes, East Sussex, England BN7 1XU
Distributed in Australia by Capricorn Link (Australia) Pty. Ltd.
P.O. Box 704, Windsor, NSW 2756, Australia

For information about custom editions, special sales, and premium and corporate purchases, please
contact Sterling Special Sales at 800-805-5489 or specialsales@sterlingpublishing.com.

Manufactured in Canada

2 4 6 8 10 9 7 5 3 1

www.sterlingpublishing.com

DEDICATION

to

Comics Arts Conference chair Kathleen McClancy and founders Peter Coogan and Randy Duncan, without whom I would never have met many of this book's outstanding contributors.

SPECIAL THANKS

to

Richard Matheson (*I Am Legend*, 1954 novel), George A. Romero, and John Russo (*Night of the Living Dead*, 1968 film), and Robert Kirkman, Tony Moore, and Charlie Adlard (*The Walking Dead*, comic book since 2003) for feeding our hunger for tales of undead that hunger for us.

• CONTENTS •

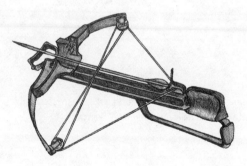

For one man, the end of the world begins in mysteriously
empty hospital halls (Arkadelphia, Arkansas).

• ACKNOWLEDGMENTS •

Brains!

Behind any book, you'll find a lot of brains.

I thank every contributor to this book for such thoughtful work. The writers, illustrator, photographers, and editorial staff put a lot into this project and put up with me. Because I met most of them at conventions or through our *Psychology Today* blogs, I must thank Matt Smith (not the timey-wimey one), whose research led me to my first Comic-Con, and Kaja Perina, my editor at PsychologyToday.com. Eddie Ibrahim, Sue Lord, Adam Neese, Gary Sassaman, and others who run Comic-Con International have provided valuable opportunities for us to meet and, through convention panels, cultivate our ideas on the psychology of popular culture. I can't thank Chris Jansen and his fellow Wizard World organizers strongly enough for all their help. Through events like theirs, New York Comic Con, and Comi-ConWay, I've gotten to discuss the psychology of a zombie outbreak with tellers of zombie tales (George A. Romero, Max Brooks, J. Michael Straczynski, Robert Kirkman, Frank Darabont, Gale Anne Hurd, S. G. Browne) and too many actors to name here. Among those actors, though, I must specifically thank Norman Reedus (Daryl) and Andrew J. West (Gareth).

Even though my graduate research under my mentor, Ed O'Neal, at Tulane University focused on media, my love of fantastic fiction stayed separate from my work in psychology for a long time. Communication professor Randy Duncan introduced comics studies at Henderson State University, where we both teach, long before I got involved. Things have grown. Now we offer a Comics Studies minor. Active, enthusiastic students in the Comics Arts Club, the Legion of Nerds, and related classes keep the educational experience exciting. Our library maintains a healthy graphic novel reading collection, so it's a good thing librarian Lea Ann Alexander welcomes my weird acquisition requests. We are truly fortunate to work at a university where administrators such as President Glen Jones, Provost Steve Adkison, and Dean John Hardee support creative teaching methods and help us meet our goals. Linda Mooney, Millie Bowden, Denise Cordova, Ermatine Johnson, Carolyn Hatley, Renee Davis, Sandra Johnson, and many other staff members make sure the essentials get done. Our faculty writers group (Angela Boswell, Martin Halpern, Vernon Miles, David Sesser, Michael Taylor) reviewed portions of this manuscript. My fellow psychology faculty members offered endless encouragement, and I enjoyed hearing my colleague Paul Williamson explain *The Walking Dead* to our department chair, Aneeq Ahmad.

A brain trust of nonpsychologists provided important perspectives and invaluable input: Jenna Busch, "Action Flick Chick" Katrina Hill, and Alan "Sizzler" Kistler. Katrina wrote some entertaining sidebars. She and Alan make fine editorial assistants. Although wikis are tricky because any idiot can edit them, I've seen no idiocy at walkingdead.wikia.com, where conscientious contributors create an outstanding, ongoing resource. We'd always go the original source, but the wiki often helped us double-check the correct issue, episode, or game.

So many others helped set me on the path toward this book's creation. My mom introduced me to comic books. My sons plotted antizombie survival strategies with me long before the zombie boom of recent years. My dad provided the weapon references for this book's illustrations. My wife Rebecca supplied caffeine, proofread drafts, and offered insight as a therapist and psychology instructor. Austin Biegert, Eric Bailey, Len

Barnhart, David Bateman, Renee Couey, Brett Culp, Christine Dickson, Kieran Dickson, Athena Finger, Danny Fingeroth, Tanner Gibson, Marko Head, Brian Keene, Elizabeth Ann Kus, Shaunna Murphy, Marc Nadel, Tom Savini, David Stoddard, Patricia Tallman, Janey Tracey, Michael Uslan, and many others deserve recognition for reasons diverse and occasionally bizarre. I do not, however, thank Noah Webster, who stuck us with the stupid-looking American spelling of the word *acknowledgments*.

Thank you, Connie Santisteban and the other fine folks at Sterling Publishing, for providing us with the opportunity to write these things—with special mention of Sterling publicist Blanca Oliviery, who promised to hurt anyone who kept her from working on this book (allegedly). Thanks also go to my agent, Evan Gregory of the Ethan Ellenberg Literary Agency, who tends to more details than most readers want me to explain.

We owe a great debt to Robert Kirkman, Frank Darabont, George Romero, their collaborators, and all of the many story-tellers who led us here, with a special note of appreciation for John Russo. We are honored to have *Night of the Living Dead*'s co-creator, the brains behind the Living Dead, write this book's foreword. When John suggested to George Romero that their flesh eaters should be the recently deceased, he invented a hungry new species of walking dead.

The Walking Dead Creators

COMIC BOOK
Writer: Robert Kirkman (all issues)
Lead Artists: Tony Moore, then Charlie Adlard
Publisher: Image Comics
Debut: October, 2003

TELEVISION SERIES
Developer: Frank Darabont
Producers: Gale Anne Hurd, David Alpert, Robert Kirkman, Charles H. Eglee,
    Greg Nicotero, Tom Luse, and the showrunners
Showrunners: Frank Darabont, Glen Mazzara, Scott Gimple
Original Network: AMC
Production Companies: AMC Studios, Circle of Confusion, Valhalla Entertainment,
    Idiot Box Productions
Debut: Halloween, 2010

• FOREWORD •

Why Don't They Die?

JOHN RUSSO
co-creator of *Night of the Living Dead*

"**J**ust as zombies can't die unless shot in the head, I guess the *fascination* with zombies won't die unless we shoot every zombie *fan* in the head!"

I made that flippant statement when I was interviewed back in 2010 by Bram Stoker Award winner Jonathan Maberry. I went on to say that somehow "this flesh-eating zombie craze has tapped into a raw atavistic dread that we all feel."[1] The dread and fascination have gone on to reach epidemic proportions in *The Walking Dead*.

The compelling question before us in this comprehensively insightful anthology assembled by Travis Langley is *why?* What is the cause in our psychological makeup of our continuing willingness—no, our actual *craving*—to be scared and entertained by the likes of *Night of the Living Dead*, *The Evil Dead*, *The Return of the Living Dead*, and on and on, right up to the present-day comic book and television blockbuster *The Walking Dead*, which keep going year after year with undiminished popular enthusiasm, booming sales, and sky-high ratings?

When we made *Night of the Living Dead*, we didn't call our flesh-eating dead people *zombies*.[2] We called them *ghouls* because, technically, not every zombie is a ghoul. A ghoul is a being, alive or dead, who eats human flesh, usually dead flesh at that. When I was in grade school and high school, I went to see all the

Russo as the first zombie to enter the house in *Night of the Living Dead* (1968).

horror films that came into town, and most of them had trite, boring, overworked plots. I saw a few zombie flicks but was not impressed with any of them. I never thought zombies were heavyweight fright material like vampires or werewolves. They mostly just shambled around trying to look scary but didn't do much except maybe toss somebody against a wall or try to strangle somebody. But when we turned them into flesh eaters, that did the trick. We struck an atavistic chord in people, an intense element of fear that probably goes back to eons ago, when we were daily prey for wild beasts. A fossilized skull of a Stone Age infant was found in Africa in the same area as was found the skull of a saber-toothed tiger with a broken-off incisor, and the matching incisor fits perfectly into the hole in the infant's head. So we can imagine the terror that Stone Age mother must have felt every day not only for her child but for herself and everyone else in her tribe. We, as humans, had to fear not only saber-toothed tigers but also cave bears, lions, tigers, hippos, vultures, alligators, and crocodiles—and that's only a partial list.

But the human being, as was said a few days ago on a true-crime show that I watch on ID Discovery, is definitely "the most dangerous animal there is." And *The Walking Dead* deals with that most dangerous animal as well as with the undead manifestations of his own kind that are coming after him as a result of a worldwide epidemic.

In *Night of the Living Dead*, we intimated that the phenomenon was happening all over the United States even though our story was confined to what was happening to a small group of people in an isolated farmhouse. But the Walking Dead are walking everywhere! And the thrust of the series is to show how all kinds of people in all kinds of circumstances must deal with the devastation, the destruction, the almost overpowering threat to their humanity.

In the very first episode, I was struck by the sequence with a big rig overturned as the result of some kind of catastrophe on the highway.[3] The police car approaches slowly and takes a long time getting there, just as Barbra and Johnny's car took an ominously long time heading toward the tombstones in the cemetery. You know something awful is going to transpire, but you don't know exactly what. The accident on the highway looks terrible but not supernatural, yet it is almost analogous to what Ben in *Night of the Living Dead* told Barbra had taken place at Beekman's Diner—the big rig crashing into the gas pumps and exploding and so on. In *The Walking Dead*, suspense and intrigue build with the revelation of the little-girl zombie, and the cop doesn't know what to make of her. Then slowly the story gets heavily into what is really happening—the dead have arisen and have turned against live people. But before we realize the full extent of the phenomenon, we meet two very ordinary, empathetic cops talking and eating in their squad car. We learn that this drama is not just going to be about a swarm of zombies tearing people apart and devouring them but is going to explore how real people might react if such a terrible worldwide cataclysm actually erupted. It is exactly the theme we had aimed to explore in *Night of the Living Dead*, albeit on a much smaller canvas.

The revelations in *The Walking Dead* accumulate slowly, with patience and restraint, so that we are captured by puzzlement and intrigue. We follow Rick Grimes, the policeman we met early on, as he gets a terrible life-threatening wound and wakes up days later in an ICU. Next we find out that the hospital is strangely abandoned. Then we see dozens of corpses outside, wrapped up, shrouded in bloody sheets. Eventually we are treated to corpses in coolers, rotting half corpses that can still crawl and come after live humans, and an undead young woman who tries to get back into the house where she used to live when she was alive and not undead so that she can see—or perhaps devour—her son Duane. And later, we experience the inner conflict of the woman's husband, Morgan, when he tries to force himself to shoot her but cannot bring himself to pull the trigger.

Similarly, Rick is driven to try to reunite with his wife and child after he manages to make it out of the ICU and back to his home, only to find them missing.

Thus, we are drawn into the very human stories behind the overall tragedy; good movies about any great calamity would not be so good if they were only about the tragedy of it all and not about the way it tugs at our humanity and demands the most of us. Basically, in *The Walking Dead* we are in a world war against a dire version of ourselves. And this theme, this powerful concept, must be explored, and *is* explored, with all the care and depth of a good war movie such as *The Longest Day*, *The Winds of War*, or *All Quiet on the Western Front*. They are not totally about the battles; they are about the people *in* the battles.

I often say that *Night of the Living Dead* is *Stagecoach* with zombies instead of Indians. We weren't thinking of it that way when we were writing the script and making the movie. But both of those movies are about human beings, with all their good qualities and all their bad qualities, having to fight for survival against tremendous odds and daunting, soul-deadening destruction. Both movies say something about all of us as human beings and how we may rise to the occasion when we are in extreme jeopardy or how we may fail.

Sometimes people ask me, "Why doesn't the zombie craze die out?" "When will it ever end?" "When will people grow tired of it?" I don't think they will as long as writers, producers, and directors keep coming up with fresh, exciting ideas. The right chords have been struck, and an enduring phenomenon has been created. From now on, it will continue to be reinvigorated by the artistic imagination.

A compelling zombie story must have the same elements as any other successful story, and *The Walking Dead* has them. It has intriguing, believable characters whom people care about. It has well-developed plots and subplots. And it has important things to say about the human condition, which is one of frailty and nobility, weakness and courage, fear and hope, good and evil. These are the enduring puzzles and enigmas of our existence, and we can delve into them and learn from them vicariously when we sit down to watch *The Walking Dead*.

 **John Russo** co-created *Night of the Living Dead* with George Romero. Russo invented the Living Dead as we know them, the flesh-eating ghouls people later called zombies, when he came up with the idea for the people attacking the film's farmhouse to be the recently deceased. His sequel novel, *Return of the Living Dead*, spawned a movie series that bears little resemblance to his book. Those films introduced the zombies that famously groan, "Brains!" John has written much more for film and print, including comic books such as *Escape of the Living Dead*. His academic endeavors include co-founding the John Russo Movie Making Program at Dubois Business College.

The Rules

1. All corpses with intact brains rise.

2. Walking corpses hunger to eat the living.

3. Damaging the brain ends reanimation.

4. Despite reanimation, walkers are dead.

5. A walker's bite is deadly.

6. The toxic bite is not what causes reanimation. Bitten or not, the dead rise.

7. Zombie gore is lethal in other ways—for example, through a deep scratch.

8. The mindless walkers can be tricked.

9. With poor physical senses, walkers do not notice whispers.

10. Romero's zombies learn, but Kirkman's do not. They just rot.

11. Whatever reanimates the corpses also slows their decay.

12. Walkers follow stimuli, especially any related to food.

13. The reason why the dead rise is utterly unknown.

— Travis Langley

References

Maberry, J. (2012, March 30). *Fresh meat: The staying power of the zombie genre.* http://sqt-fantasy-sci-fi-girl.blogspot.com/2012_03_01_archive.html.

Notes

1. Maberry (2012).
2. *Night of the Living Dead* (1968 motion picture).
3. Episode 1–1, "Days Gone Bye" (October 31, 2010).

The Uncanny Valley of the Shadow of Death

Travis Langley

"Why *The Walking Dead*?"

People keep asking. A friend asked me that mere minutes before we crossed paths with my favorite editor in the hall at New York Comic Con and had the conversation that led to this book's creation. *Night of the Living Dead* co-creator John Russo addresses the question in his foreword to this book. Our chapter authors offer an assortment of answers, and every answer can be correct. A cultural phenomenon explodes onto the scene for many reasons.

The question is multilayered: Why do many people enjoy post-apocalyptic scenarios? Why a zombie apocalypse? Why this particular zombie apocalypse?

What was it about the early issues of *The Walking Dead* that inspired me to write the only letters I ever sent that saw print in a comic book's letter column? Three times! Before the television series premiered, I asked its creator, Robert Kirkman, and developer, Frank Darabont, about the twenty-first century's zombie boom.

> *Langley:* Why are zombies so popular now? As opposed to some other time.
>
> *Kirkman:* (*with a laugh*) Once [a previous U. S. president] made this country so horrible to live in, the fiction

has to be that much more horrible and depressing to make up for how horrible and depressing life is. And what's more horrible and depressing than zombies and surviving, living from day to day in this kind of world where these ravenous monsters can attack you?

Darabont: But it's also fun. Zombies are fun.

Langley: You get to shoot people without them really being people.

Darabont: With impunity!

Kirkman: We all really just want to shoot people indiscriminately and not get in trouble.

Darabont: Exactly! To hell with the metaphors.[1]

World War Z author Max Brooks offered filmmaker George A. Romero and Dr. Steven Schlozman (who has a chapter in this book, "The Seductive Nostalgia of *The Walking Dead*") a more serious yet similar explanation.

Brooks: I think there has been a sense from 9/11 on that the system is breaking down, and we want to know what the end game is psychologically . . . what all this is leading to. The problem is if you watch a movie where the catalyst for that disaster is real, like a nuclear war . . . you will not sleep that night. So if the catalyst is something like zombies, you can say, "Ah, wow, look, neighbors are stabbing each other . . . and FEMA's incompetent and the President is flying over, going, 'That's peculiar,' but it's zombies so that's totally okay and I'm gonna go sleep."[2]

Apocalyptic narratives offer the fantasy of a worldwide do-over. With most of the world's population and technology out of the way, life becomes more savage but also simpler in many ways. "I don't even know what time it is anymore," Hershel tells Rick. "Ever since I gave Glenn my watch, it's always 'right now' to me."[3] *The Walking Dead* has a timeless quality that lets it cross generations in its appeal and in its likely longevity.

Why not a vampire apocalypse? Why not killer robots, alien invaders, or rabid turtles? Zombies scare for reasons unlike those others. Like vampires, they blend the primitive fears of ghosts, violence, and losing our own humanity or souls. Senile dementia, schizophrenia, and many other disorders make some people dread the real possibility that they or those they know might lose the special qualities they think of as *who* they are. Unlike vampires, though, mindless zombies don't talk. They aren't sexy. Zombies descend deep into the uncanny valley.

In the 1970s, robotics professor Masahiro Mori[4] noted that as robots become more human in appearance, people feel increasingly comfortable with them and the robots feel increasingly familiar—until, that is, they get too close to human-looking.

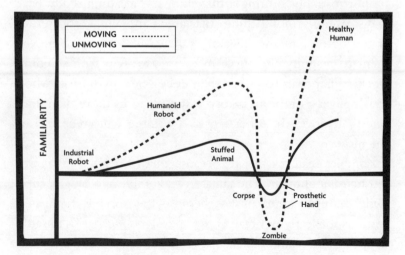

Deep in the uncanny valley, the corpse that moves may unnerve us the most.

Detached and alone, Morgan comes here to burn walkers (Grantville, Georgia).

When they're eerily human while obviously nonhuman, like human characters in early attempts at CGI animation, viewers find them creepy.[5] That's when the comfort level dips down into a valley (see the accompanying figure). A taxidermy bear is not as cute as a teddy bear that has big eyes and infantlike proportions, but putting a fully human face on a teddy bear is disturbing. Among things that aren't moving, a corpse lies at the bottom of the uncanny valley. Mori expected movement to magnify the curve in every way: A person standing stock-still appeals to us less than does a healthy human who's moving, yet a motionless corpse appeals to us more than does one that moves. In other words, a zombie will creep us out the most.

Zombies scare us in part because they're nearly human yet distinctly nonhuman. The fantasy of a zombie apocalypse, curiously enough, scares us less because the zombie-dominated world is so clearly not real. Other apocalyptic scenarios unsettle us with more realistic threats, versions of reality that fall into an uncanny valley of being realitylike. No matter how realistic a story such as *The Walking Dead* may be in depicting characters and their reactions, we know their world cannot become our own and it's clearly not close to becoming real. That lets us have fun watching characters in that world even as we worry about what the walking corpses and the living antagonists might do to them.

Why *The Walking Dead*? Those of us who write about the psychology of it get asked that question with one additional meaning: Why look at the psychology of something so clearly unreal? Largely for the reasons Max Brooks mentioned: We can talk about the best and worst aspects of human behavior without repulsing the audience. When a sheriff's deputy once showed crime scene photos to my forensic psychology students, the images disturbed them so much that some looked away. They later remembered all the gruesomeness but none of the points he was trying to make. When we talk about fictional heroes, monsters, and everyone in between, though, they listen.

Why *The Walking Dead*? My nephew knows: "Because it's awesome."

References

Mitchell, W. J., Szerszen, K. A., Lu, A., Schermerhorn, P. W., Scheutz, M., & MacDorman, K. F. (2011). A mismatch in the human realism of face and voice produces an uncanny valley. *i-Perception, 2*(1), 10–12.

Mori, M. (1970). Bukimi no tani. *Energy, 7*(4), 33–35.

TheRocketLlama (2012, November 2). *Zombie fun—Robert Kirkman and Frank Darabont on AMC's The Walking Dead.* https://www.youtube.com/watch?v=oxykW7Fasi0.

Notes

1. TheRocketLlama (2012).
2. *Doc of the Dead* documentary film (2014).
3. Episode 4–8, "Too Far Gone" (December 1, 2013).
4. Mori (1970).
5. Mitchell et al. (2011).

The dead awaken, but in body only. Their minds and souls stay gone.

A comatose police officer awakens. The life and world he knew are gone.

Apocalypse survivors awaken, at varying rates, to how this terrifying new world works. Many will wonder if hope is gone, and yet by struggling to endure, they show how strongly they hope.

How I Learned to Stop Worrying and Love the Zombie Apocalypse

FRANK GASKILL

"Oh, you're awake. We're just getting ready to have dinner."
—Morgan Jones to Rick Grimes[1]

In 1996, my wife, Elizabeth, and I were misplaced southerners far from home, family, and friends, living in a Philadelphia suburb. That January, close to four feet of snow fell over two days, leaving much of the Northeast paralyzed. Our apartment complex of over a thousand people was cut off from everything. All we had were our candles, a chess set, and some poorly supplied battery radios. Through my second floor window, beyond the trees, I could see seven-foot snowdrifts, and the once lumpy parking lot now as a smooth, snowy field. Not one of the hundreds of cars could be seen under that deep snow. Ordered not to leave their homes, any civilians who chose to go for a snowy stroll, as one of our friends did, would be picked up by the National Guard and taken to shelter.

At that time, Valley Forge Apartments was filled with young professionals beginning their careers in computer programming, psychology, and theology. Next door lived a barrel-chested, chess-obsessed Russian. Farther down the hall were computer gamers with a local area network set up between their apartments. A few musicians, actors, models, and national defense contractors rounded out the crowd.

We were a disconnected, diverse group of strangers with common interests trying to make our way in the world. In retrospect, these neighbors probably would have made a formidable group against a walker herd. Before the storm, however, my neighbors were unknown to me. Afterward, I would have chosen most of them for my zombie survival team. The blizzard of 1996 is the closest personal reference I have to a zombie apocalypse.

Why Do We Watch?

We love *The Walking Dead*. LOVE it! But why? Most readers and viewers do not consider that they are tuning in to a formula that deliberately and intensely excites their conscious and unconscious senses, hopes, and dreams. The formula created by Robert Kirkman and the writers of the television series and games provides an audience an experience deeply seated in the biology of violence, the stripping away of our technological existence, and our innate desire for intimate social connectivity. We welcome the simplicity of decluttered lives and a clear and present danger we can confront physically. Walkers offer something tangible we can kill.

Trapped in homes, a farm, a prison, and even the seemingly safe communities of Terminus and Alexandria, the characters of *The Walking Dead* face an identifiable threat to their existence. We

Walker Taxonomy

Walkers. The main characters call their world's reanimated corpses *walkers*, a term Rick picks up from Morgan. Because electronic and print communication has broken down, people everywhere develop different terms. The respective zombie names—*geeks, biters, deadheads, lamebrains, monsters, skin-eaters, rotters,* and *those people in the barn*— reflect the nature of the people who do the naming.

Lurkers. Instead of staying on the move, some linger in one spot, not walking until a stimulus snaps them into action. Every place living characters step can be minefield-dangerous. Alert for roamers, they can wander right up, ready to chomp an ankle.

Roamers. Most of the walkers the characters encounter tend to wander.

Talkers. Walkers do not talk, although a few comic book issues left fans wondering if they might. For information on what the talkers turn out to be, see Case File VII: The Whisperers.

Herds. Environment makes walkers take paths of least resistance—following pavement, ambling downhill—and appetite drives all roamers toward stimuli they associate with living food. Without remembering gunshots they heard or passing vehicles they stumbled after, they walk. They cross paths. One follows another. Groups grow. New noise redirects groups. Hundreds, even thousands, may merge into this mindless mass. It's not what social psychologists call *conformity*, which would be matching others' behavior because of real or imagined pressure. They herd themselves no more deliberately than creeks flow into rivers.

—Travis Langley

are obsessed with their relationships and their survival. Countless blogs, books, and articles attempt to answer the question "Why do we love *The Walking Dead*?" The zombie genre and specifically *The Walking Dead* can seem like the ultimate Rorschach test, allowing us to project our fears, hopes, and dreams onto the meaning of "Why do we watch?"

Do we watch because we want a simplified life with less technology or because we enjoy vicariously feeling the deeper social connections brought on by a common threat? Maybe we just like watching Michonne decapitate walkers. Once upon a time, you might have doubted my sanity if I'd said the world would obsessively watch a show in which a mother asks for a suicidal C-section and to be fatally shot by her own son. But we watch and rewatch week after week, death after death, trauma after trauma. Why do we talk about it at work? Why do we think through our zombie survival plans and contemplate who we might save or where we might go in order to survive?

I believe *The Walking Dead*. The zombie genre as a whole excites us biologically and awakens an unconscious longing. The walkers clear away what distracts us and exposes not only who we are now but who we might like to become. The zombies do more than provide the mechanism for the story. The zombie apocalypse embodies the true definition of apocalypse. The term *apocalypse* is a word generally meaning "a revelation," derived from the Greek *apokalypsis* ("to take the covering away").[2] "Anyone who watches zombie movies must be prepared for a strong indictment of life in modern America."[3] Romero's groundbreaking movies provided needed mechanisms to decry societal evils and call out the worst of us, but *TWD* is not so blatantly a social commentary.

When I think of Romero's films, I am horrified by the idea of living in the worlds he visualizes. I don't try to imagine myself in those settings. I usually feel disgust when I watch them (even though I love those films). In contrast, I often imagine and talk with my friends about living in a world similar to that of *The Walking Dead*. The zombies are just as real; the scenes of violence and gore are often worse than in the most intense zombie films to date. The uncovering process of the zombie apocalypse forces us to examine consciously and unconsciously what is hidden from our view.

Yes, Virginia, We Love Gore

Many people ask why I watch *The Walking Dead*. "It's so gross!" "All those zombies are disgusting!" My indignant reply: "It's not about the zombies! It's about people and relationships. Have you ever watched it?" In response, I get blank stares after reinforcing people's sense that I'm a weirdo. A close friend questioned the simplicity of my theory that the primary reason we watch is the imagined hope or longing for a more simplistic and possibly primitive existence. Many people are drawn to gory movies because these scenes of violence ignite primeval systems that are both stimulating and reinforcing. Violent sports, the *Rocky* movies, and many other films that stimulate our crocodile and predatory "old brains" are very popular. Our conscious and unconscious preoccupation with violence is also why the news starts off with fires and shootings.

The violence and gore typical of *The Walking Dead* comic book are exceptional for TV and cross barriers never before seen on a mainstream network such as AMC. The scene that crossed new boundaries appeared in the series premiere.[4] Rick rides into Atlanta on humankind's domesticated companion of thousands of years, the horse. Rick has lost his family and his society as he knew it but has a companion in the horse, a connection with the living, to family, a farm, and a pond. The horse is life. The symbolism of the sheriff riding into town offers us hope. Skyscrapers and an M1 Abrams tank surround him with representations of humankind's technological feats. Alas, to survive the assault by scores of zombies, Rick must abandon his horse to climb into the belly of the tank. His equine companion's cry and the walkers' ensuing antlike attack shock me to this day, a flash-bulb memory my mind can replay frame by frame. The violent and primeval carnage inflicted on the brave and helpless animal that unknowingly sacrifices itself for Rick's survival invokes a visceral response of revulsion and revenge. This scene was brutal, and I did not look away.

The level of violence elicits in the viewer a basic biological response that compels people to watch and discuss each episode. The imagery shocks and holds us in such a primitive way that we bond to the experience. The story's creators hold us hostage to our biology, innate fear, and fascination with violence. Although the violence pulls in many viewers, people also get satisfaction from watching such violence beyond the physical exhilaration.

In an exhaustive review of violent media, the social psychologist Jeffrey Goldstein suggests that we gain cathartic emotional experiences when we view violence and that we enjoy the spectacle because of our need to identify with others who are experiencing trauma and stress. The more intense the violence is, the more readily we pair ourselves with either the aggressor or the victim. Rick's role as solitary survivor finding his way allows us to identify with and root for him as he travels the hero's path. The horse gives us our victim, helpless and at the environment's mercy. The horse trusts Rick and ultimately falls prey to walkers.

Have We Lost Our Way?

"Morgan, I don't know if you're out there. . . .
My wife and son, they're alive. I wanted you to
know that. There's something else you need to know.
Atlanta isn't what we thought. It's not what they
promised. The city is—Do not enter the city."
—Rick Grimes[5]

Our technologically advanced world surrounds us with warmth, self-driving cars, and instant communication. With a few swipes of our fingers, we can download books, check the weather in New Zealand, and buy whatever we want. Through social media networks, family and friends update us minute by minute on their lives. We're always plugged in. As the human species goes, we are working harder and demonstrating the highest levels of anxiety in known human history, with people reporting more stress, worry, and panic attacks (at least 40 percent more!) than in the 1950s.[6] Have we pushed our brains past the point at which we can process all the data in our lives? And does this stress make us lose the meaningful social connections that hold us together and protect us? Rick's effort to contact Morgan symbolically addresses these questions and illustrates two more variables that cause audiences to tune in each week: (1) a need for deep feeling and human connection and (2) a desire for a simplified life.

Rick is calling out over radio waves to his first post-apocalyptic human companion, the man who nursed him to health after the horrors of the hospital. Rick reaches out to share the joy of finding his family and to tell Morgan to stay safe. He doesn't text. Through hearing the spoken word rather than reading a text, we feel both elation and survivor guilt over his reunion with his wife and son. Both are fathers striving to save their sons, but with a difference: Rick finds his wife and gains a community of social support, but Morgan's family will never be made whole. Morgan's dead, reanimated wife returns on occasion, possibly out of a distant, loyal memory of her family, but neither Morgan nor his son can love her again. The audience feels these relationships on a deep level and feels the need for community as a means to survive.

When I was a kid, we had three television networks, four if one counts PBS. At school we could talk excitedly about the stories we'd watched the night before, from *Battlestar Galactica* to *The Dukes of Hazzard*. We had a shared experience. Today the Internet and TV stream thousands of shows at any given moment. As we watch relationships develop on *The Walking Dead* while each episode first airs, it brings millions of us together that night in a way even the comic book series, which thousands read at scattered times, does not. The show allows us to share our thoughts and experiences. Together, we watch the pain of Rick being innocently betrayed by his wife and the despair of Andrea losing her sister. Together, we see Rick and Shane, brothers in arms who have risked their lives for one another, tear apart to the point of murder.

Experiencing *The Walking Dead* allows us a deeper social connection not only because we see our heroes' pain but also because 17 million of us are watching their pain together. Although *Breaking Bad* also created a powerful shared experience for its fans and became a phenomenon in its own right, *The Walking Dead*'s audience experiences a wholly different subject reinforced by the formula of gore and powerful relationships stripped of technology.

A colleague of mine said, "It is very notable that people seem to want to feel a sense of deep loss." In top-rated episodes, we lose Sophia, Lori, Hershel, Mika, Lizzie, and more. Viewers feel deeply, potentially "feeling" in a way that they do not feel in the real world. A part of us misses such deep connections and loyalties. *The Walking Dead* is not just about loss but also about excitement, betrayal, revenge, love, and loyalty. Psychological literature largely supports the role of social support as a significant ameliorating factor in the face of stressful life events.[7] Our societal stress is high, and we are losing the face-to-face connections that protect us. These characters are allowed to have those communities back in their lives, and through our identification with and love for them, we get a little piece of the connection back as well.

During the snowstorm of 1996, the lesson of social support was powerful. The bonds of stress-enhanced social connectedness created a lasting memory, one that resonates with me when I watch *The Walking Dead*. We are social animals surrounded by everything that makes real connections increasingly less and less possible. Just as in *The Walking Dead*, without true social community we are all as good as food.

Alone Together author Sherry Turkle believes that in some

meaningful ways we are becoming more alone.[8] Despite and because of social networks, an argument can be made that we are losing relationship depth as well as the skills needed to connect in a meaningful way. Social media can let us expose our best sides to the world and hide the worst. We don't usually take selfies of ourselves crying in despair. We escalate the war of "look how happy and connected I am!" The more we promote such false versions of ourselves, the more we lose who we and others truly are. Turkle describes the experience of a teenager going to a party. Those first parties can be exceptionally stressful but developmentally useful in creating strong social skills. Before the smartphone, teens had to figure it out on their own and navigate the shark-filled waters of social experience. With the smartphone, a teen can go to the party, but when the social stress and anxiety hits, she can turn on that smartphone and leave the party without physically exiting. Avoiding the social stress will not help her build her skills or gain confidence in her relationships. Society may be becoming increasingly isolated and superficial. As a result, we could be losing the value of deep, loyal, and ongoing relationships.

The Walking Dead's viewer is unable to escape from deep feeling. Relationships are among the gravitational forces that draw us in week after week. Their world has no social media, no book deadlines, and few boring routines other than maybe collecting firewood. It may be a stretch to say we actually want a zombie apocalypse, but the experience of a more simplified life is a draw. When Rick says, "Atlanta is not what we thought," he obviously is telling Morgan about the presence of walkers, but we can take a deeper symbolic message from this statement. Technology would not save them or restore their families. The tank was useless, the government failed, and all the impressive structures of humanity designed to keep us safe and comfortable collapsed. A rescuing force would not come. Audiences connect with their stories in part because we too long for these connections in our own lives. Relationships are our characters' salvation.

Survival

My first stress-built community was realized through a blizzard as I was trapped with strangers inside the concrete bunker of an apartment building. During the storm, neighbors opened doors. We were looking for information. Our technology was gone, cutting us off from the world. Through the stress of the storm, we became closer. No longer did we just say, "Hi." Now we went further by asking real questions: "How is your family?" "Are you still stressed at work?" "How about a nice game of chess?" Food, laughs, and real stories were shared by candlelight. Our community came together, and we became better for it. With superficial niceties apocalyptically stripped away, we became real.

The Walking Dead strips away the nothing to reveal the everything that matters to us all. The formula includes violence and gore, for sure. But within the why-we-watch equation are deep, powerful relationships and characters with whom we can identify and for whom we can cheer. Seeing a world in which the stressors of modern society and superficiality are stripped away leaves us longing. We watch to be excited by who we are now, to feel deeply, and to ponder who we would like to become.

George Romero was right as well. My wife and I moved into that small apartment knowing no one. All the store names were unfamiliar, and the roads were confusing. Scared and feeling alone, we longed for a connection to anything that would feel familiar. We were able to find such a connection on the second day of our adventure. We went exactly where George Romero would have expected us to go. We went to the mall.

References

Charuvastra, C., & Cloitre, M. (2008). Social bonds and posttraumatic stress disorder. *Annual Review of Psychology, 59*, 301–328.

Cohen, S., & Wills, T. (1985). Stress, social support, and the buffering hypothesis. *Psychological Bulletin, 98*, 310–357.

Edinger, E. R. (1999). *Archetype of the apocalypse: Divine vengeance, terrorism, and the end of the world.* Chicago: Open Court.

Paffenroth, A. (2006). *Gospel of the living dead: George Romero's visions of hell on earth.* Waco, TX: Baylor University Press.

St. John, A. (2014, October 13). *"The Walking Dead" season 5 premiere breaks ratings record as the most watched cable show of all time.* http://www.forbes.com/sites/allenstjohn/2014/10/13/ the-walking-dead-season-5-premiere-breaks-ratings-record-as-the-most-watched-cable-show-of-all-time/.

Stossel, S. (2014). *A brief history of anxiety: The invention of a modern malaise.* http://www. psychotherapynetworker.org/.

Turkle, S. (2012). *Alone together: Why we expect more from technology and less from each other.* New York, NY: Basic.

Williams, J. C., & Boushey, H. (2015, January 25). *The three faces of work-family conflict: The poor, the professionals, and the missing middle.* https://www.americanprogress.org/press/ release/2010/01/25/14506/new-report-the-three-faces-of-work-family-conflict/.

Notes

1. Issue 1 (2003).
2. Edinger (1999), p. 3.
3. Paffenroth (2006), p. 21.
4. Episode 1–1, "Days Gone Bye" (October 31, 2010).
5. Episode 1–5, "Wildfire" (November 28, 2010).
6. Stossel (2014).
7. Cohen & Wills (1985).
8. Turkle (2012).

The Seductive Nostalgia of
The Walking Dead

STEVEN C. SCHLOZMAN

"Nostalgia, it's like a drug."
—Shane Walsh[1]

*"Contemporary nostalgia is not so much about
the past as about vanishing the present."*
—scholar Svetlana Boym[2]

he Walking Dead manages to conjure an impressive array
of complicated feelings. Fans are prone to bouts of intense
anger, blinding avarice, uncomfortable laughter, mild to
severe nausea, and of course an abiding and sometimes paradoxically surprising love for the bleak and somehow beautiful apocalyptic landscape. Perhaps the most surprising reaction to *The
Walking Dead*'s narrative is the strangely soothing melancholy

engendered by the walker-laden world. What could possibly be so attractive about a storyline in which easily recognizable and pleasing scenarios are regularly destroyed or simply rotting? How can we love a tale that mirrors familiar ideas and settings with broken and perverted images? Why do the trials and tribulations of the humans in *The Walking Dead* allow fans to celebrate with impressive gusto the music and words of a world that is bent and irreversibly crooked? In other words, why do we feel the seductive pangs of nostalgic recollections when we read or watch this unfolding zombie apocalypse?

The answer, of course, is that the story is not *only* about a zombie apocalypse. More important, it certainly isn't a story *only* about zombies. A story about zombies would be like a story about snails. Snails in the woods don't do much (apologies to the experts on invertebrates reading this chapter). Snails basically walk into one another or over one another or around one another. Snails eat most of the time, and they excrete or evacuate with little predictability or control. A sleeping snail and an inactive walker look pretty much the same.

But remind a busy construction worker of the first time he went camping and saw a snail clinging impossibly to the underside of a maple leaf. Help a businesswoman who is rushing from one job to the next recall the way the snail in her childhood aquarium kept the glass meticulously and beautifully clean. You might very well get tears from your construction worker and businesswoman. They won't be crying about snails. They'll be crying about *memories*. They'll be engaging in the uniquely human freefall of nostalgic recollections. This is why the word *nostalgia* parses to *nostos*, Greek for "homecoming," and *algos*, Greek for "pain." Nostalgia literally means the pain of imagined homecomings, and homecomings are meant to include most potently the fond memories of familiar and pleasing scenarios.

Although nostalgia once was thought to be a primarily negative emotion,[3] more modern interpretations in psychology, cognitive neuroscience, and even neuroimaging suggest that the pangs of nostalgia play an important and potentially positive role in our emotional homeostasis.[4] For this chapter's purposes, we will utilize these mixed and sometimes competing definitions to explain the intense love that fans have shown for the forlorn humans in *The Walking Dead*'s legendarium.

You don't have to look very hard to find nostalgic moments in *The Walking Dead*. In the opening television episode, Rick indulges in flashbacks of his simple friendship with Shane as he tries to make sense of the surrounding ruined landscape. In fact, again and again readers and viewers are led down the path of seeing things as they once were. Morgan Jones must reckon with the memory of his wife before the plague while he confronts what is left of her lingering outside his front door. Lori must recall the gentler and less complicated years of experiences between herself and Rick, the husband she thinks died in a hospital, if she is to survive the thought that he is no longer with her. One could argue that she uses these memories to justify and make peace with her ongoing relationship with Shane.

Indeed, even the image of Rick riding his horse through the broken streets of Atlanta conjures a kind of mass nostalgia for viewers and readers. If the rugged cowboy is back, if the nineteenth-century icon of American wilderness survival lives, surely we stand a chance in the fictional twenty-first-century walker-induced wasteland. In other words, nostalgia, in all circumstances, brings pain and hope to the fans and characters of *The Walking Dead*. We can even make the case that nostalgia itself is a necessary ingredient for the otherwise dour narrative to remain buoyant and optimistic. Without this buoyancy, there would little to compel us to care much about what happens to the surviving humans.

Naming Nostalgia

The concept of nostalgia has shifted in modern psychology and neuroscience. By deconstructing key scenes from *The Walking Dead*, we can understand how nostalgia fosters emotional strength and perseverance in the face of what appears to be the direst and most deadly circumstances.

Nostalgia is in fact a diagnosis that had its birth in the field of medicine and has since that time been co-opted by the literary world. As we've noted, it translates roughly to "the pain of coming home."[5] It has several suggested derivations, but it is most often believed to have been coined by the medical student Johannes Hofer at the University of Basel in 1668 to describe the intense psychological and what he deemed often fatal suffering of Swiss soldiers fighting far from home. It is worth noting, therefore, that although nostalgia is a Greek term, its origins are neither Greek nor literary. The original conceptualization of nostalgia was unambiguous. The diagnosis was considered universally negative.

Importantly, it would be naive to suggest that the concept of painful and intense memories was first considered in the seventeenth century. Homer's Odysseus grieves for his lost love and home, just as Michonne grieves for her lost boyfriend. She sadly tells Rick that she "used to talk to [her] dead boyfriend."[6] In Homer's *Odyssey*, Odysseus tells us that "what I want and all my days I pine for is to go back to my house and see my day of homecoming."[7] In both cases, we are meant to infer that the process of recollection in the setting of current circumstances is largely negative. Michonne feels she is losing her mind; Odysseus feels he will never be happy. Even more profound are the Governor's relentless recollections of his prewalker daughter while denying the full weight of her current walker status. Here the Governor suffers from a kind of irrationality that is not at all different from the early conceptualizations of nostalgia in Hofer's original thesis.

Nevertheless, in more recent scholarly inquiries nostalgia has been viewed in an increasingly positive light. Oprah, certainly among the most widely read commentators on pop psychology, has seen fit to celebrate the benefits of nostalgia on her show and her website.[8] Her website quotes the British psychologist Tim Wildschut as praising the ability of nostalgia to give us all a powerful psychological boost. If we turn to Dr. Wildschut's many publications, we see that through a series of ingenious experiments, he has implicated nostalgia as leading to a decreased desire for money, a means by which international conflict might be averted, and an overall increase in self worth and self-esteem.[9]

Farmer Hershel Greene's ability to invoke nostalgic recollections of what his deceased wife would have wanted provides a powerful example of the benefits of nostalgic musing. Because of this exercise, Hershel is able to persevere through his own personal demons of alcoholism and isolationism and become a wise and optimistic leader throughout the current desperate circumstances of his newfound apocalyptic world.

Other researchers have suggested that nostalgia can activate regions of the brain associated with wonder and transcendence, especially through the experience of musical recollections.[10] When Hershel's daughter Beth sings Tom Waits's haunting song "Hold On"[11] while facing the likelihood that the Governor will soon attack the prison, viewers and characters alike can appreciate the nostalgic power of music from a simpler time. It is as if the pain of the song itself is paradoxically empowering, allowing Beth and her friends to rise above their current desperation.

Nostalgia has even been found to stave off dementia and depression.[12] Indeed, the tendency in *The Walking Dead* for characters who have been bitten to remind themselves of their lives before the plague is particularly worth noting. This can be seen as an intuitive attempt to stave off the dementing process that accompanies the sadly inevitable transformation.

It is not enough, however, simply to note that nostalgia can activate happy feelings and optimistic perseverance. To make sense of nostalgia as it relates to *The Walking Dead*, we also must ask ourselves how nostalgia manages to wield its unique power. This brings us to the brink of cutting-edge cognitive neuroscience. There exists an increasingly popular theory that nostalgia engenders happiness by resculpting memories into pleasant false narratives.[13] In other words, we distort past events into happy historical accounts with little or no sense that what we recall is being carefully edited. Even difficult memories are fondly recollected, and through this emotionally protective process we are able to tolerate what otherwise would be unbearable sadness.

This theory by itself could stand as the overall explanation for the strength of *The Walking Dead*'s narrative, or for that of any apocalyptic story for that matter. Survivors of the cataclysm recall the world before its fall through quintessentially rose-colored glasses. In this way, they can continue to pursue the life they once knew. If they dwell too much on how the previous world was dysfunctional, they quickly lose sight of their quest to restore order from chaos. Why bother, for example, to set the table for a meal? *The Walking Dead*'s characters do this simple act over and over. Setting the table won't in any way bring back the more civilized world that they miss, but the act itself allows them to long for a better life. Readers of this chapter will recognize that the majority of American families rarely consistently enjoy a similar level of goodwill at dinnertime.[14] Modern life, in other words, is associated only rarely with a happy and relaxing feast. Still, whenever possible, our protagonists engage in this festive ritual as a means of keeping alive the world from which they came.

Slash Hacks: Ways to Fool a Walker

Zombies are REALLY stupid. You might even say *brain-dead*. It's not that hard to fool them if you have enough time and creativity and aren't averse to getting your hands dirty.

Bang Pots and Pans. You're trying to go somewhere, so of course a hundred zombies flock to that exact place. How do you get through? Have someone bang on some pots and pans like a two-year-old hopped up on Pixy Stix! In *The Walking Dead*, Rick's Rebels do this at the prison when someone needs to get through the gate, and it seems to do the trick. Walkers get so riled up by the racket, they'll try to eat you just to put a stop to it.

Drive a Nice-Ass Car Down the Street with the Alarm Blaring. It's a mobile version of banging pots and pans. Not only do you get to joyride in a nice-ass car, you get to live out *Grand Theft Auto* fantasy by breaking into said nice-ass car and driving like a crazy person. Glenn sure seems to love it.

Dazzle the Zoms with a Light Show. Did you remember that zombies are really stupid? Well, they're *so* stupid—and their vision's getting so bad—that bright or flashing lights will draw their attention. Glenn and Tara manage to draw the zombies to one side of a tunnel so that they can then slip around the other side unnoticed, using just a couple of flashlights. Safe, effective, and hygienic! Flinging flaming magazines works, too, but risks creating a fire hazard.

Make Friends with a Zombie or Two. This requires a little more effort and is both yuckier and more dangerous than the previous methods, but Michonne and Andrea both prove it can be a very effective method. First catch a zombie or two, then do the equivalent of castrating them: Cut off their arms and jaws, knock out the rest of the teeth, and voilà! They pose no threat. Next, don't forget to put it on a leash—the world may have ended, but

This is where the lessons of *The Walking Dead* become particularly poignant. The strength of the show and the graphic novels involves a kind of cat-and-mouse game with fans. We are led continually to believe that the heroes of the stories have come upon a better life. The Governor's world looks like Mayberry from *The Andy Griffith Show*. Terminus resembles a utopian co-op. Rick raises pigs. Carl pretends he's a cowboy. But for each of these bursts of normalcy, the bubble of happiness is profoundly burst. The Governor is a crazed dictator who stages gladiatorial battles. Terminus is filled with cannibals. Rick's pigs bring disease. Carl must learn to use his guns for real. It is as if you can still keep some of your humanity by following leash laws. After that, feel free to go on as long of a walk as you want with your new zombie pet and the rest of the undead will completely ignore you. Any friend of a zom is a friend to them all.

Bathe in Blood and Bowels. For the really tight situations, you might have to pull out all the stops and just jump in feet first by taking a bath in zombie bowels and blood. This method's definitely not the most hygienic, but you can't argue with the results. When Rick and Glenn need to camouflage themselves, they do so courtesy of Wayne Dunlap of Georgia's zombified guts. They chop walker Wayne to pieces, smearing his gory insides all over their outsides so they can survive a zombie-filled trek down the street. Michonne and Carol later jump on the bloodbath bandwagon as well. Gross but effective—as long as it doesn't start raining.

Pro Tip: Live Bait. Don't try dangling canned ham in front of a zombie's face. It might interest him for a second but won't keep him occupied for long. Rick's Rebels figure this out with the well zombie at Hershel's farm. Walkers want their food raw and wriggling. Dangle Glenn. That works. Who knows how long that canned ham has been sitting on the Greenes' shelf. Maybe the zombie just doesn't want to get food poisoning.

Optional: Texas Chain Saw Massacre It Up. For the really sick and twisted (or desperate) or for hobbyists with time on their hands and a yearning for post-apocalyptic pastimes to replace knitting sweaters, make a new face for yourself out of walker skin. If you go this route, you might want to invest in some built-in air fresheners because it can't *possibly* smell good inside a zombie skin suit.

— Katrina Hill

the narrative of *The Walking Dead* progresses as a function of crushing the characters' recollections of simpler and safer times. Happiness, we learn, will not come through blind re-creations of the prewalker world. Even the failure of the CDC to have a viable cure[15] represents this warning. When Carol and Tyreese choose to kill Lizzie[16] (or when Carl kills Lizzie's comic book counterpart Ben[17]), they are leaving the old world behind in a particularly gruesome way. If we believe in the power of nostalgia, we can anticipate as well that in time there will be nostalgic recollections of Lizzie that celebrate her many strengths and leave out her deadly and deranged character flaws.[18]

The survivors of *The Walking Dead* must develop new memories for a new time. They must generate nostalgia for the here and now. The world simply cannot go back to what it once was. New stories will be told in the world of the walkers.

Solastalgia: Nostalgia's Evil Doppelgänger

But is this really possible? Can people surrounded by wreckage remember with fondness the prewreckage world? We don't need the landscape of *The Walking Dead* to explore this question. Our current world is sadly filled with its share of destruction and misery. Wars leave once recognizable citadels ruined. Disease ravages nations and turns villages in Africa and Asia into ghost towns. Native peoples see foreign buildings where their towns once stood.

In an effort to capture the despondency that these experiences can create, the Australian philosopher Glenn Albrecht coined the term *solastalgia*[19] for a kind of existential suffering. Taken literally, solastalgia is something that erupts when the existing landscape mirrors in a warped way the remembered world. Climate change, environmental disasters, and rampant disease all have the capacity to ignite solastalgic suffering. In this way, solastalgia exists as an evil doppelgänger to nostalgia. In fact, solastalgia frequently switches roles with the nostalgic indulgences of readers, viewers, and characters of *The Walking Dead*.

When our heroes reach Terminus, we see that they finally relax as AC Newman's soothing rendition of Bill Fay's "Be Not So Fearful" plays in the background. The show could end here. People have finally come together. There will be food and shelter for all. Life will soon get back to something closer to normal.

But there is something undeniably haunting about this scene as well. It simply doesn't add up to the careful observer who is not swayed by the spell of nostalgic fantasy. Where is the livestock for the clearly ample meat? *Where are the people?* This is the energy on which the story thrives and pushes forward. Nostalgia soon surrenders its seat to the reality of solastalgic comprehension. The world *has* changed. Terminus is far worse than a world of walkers. When Rick speaks in the dark of the cattle car, he rallies his friends by assuring them that the denizens of Terminus are "screwing with the wrong people."[20] Solastalgia, in other words, yields its seat to the rugged survivalist, the one we recognized in the nostalgic depiction of Rick as the lone horseman at the beginning of the series. Now we have Rick's behavior in the new and more brutal world to bolster our optimism. New legends, new memories, and newly formed nostalgic tales will continue to carry our heroes forward. And for these reasons, we will continue to turn the pages of this ongoing and epic saga.

References

Albrecht, G. (2005). Solastalgia, a new concept in human health and identity. *Philosophy Activism Nature, 3*, 41–44.

Albrecht, G., Sartore, G. M., Connor, L., Higginbotham, N., Freeman, S., Kelly, B., Stain, H., Tonna, A., & Pollard, G. (2007). Solastalgia: The distress caused by environmental change. *Australasian Psychiatry 15*(1), 595–S98.

Batcho, K. I. (2007). Nostalgia and the emotional tone and content of song lyrics. *American Journal of Psychology, 120*(3), 361–381.

Boym, S. (2001). *The future of nostalgia.* New York, NY: Basic.

Fritz, G. K. (2006, February). The importance of the family dinner. *Brown University Child and Adolescent Behavior Letter, 22*(2), 8.

Fuentenebro de Diego, F., & Ots, C. V. (2014). Nostalgia: A conceptual history. *History of Psychiatry, 25*(4), 404–411.

Leboe, J. P., & Ansons, T. L. (2006). On misattributing good remembering to a happy past: An investigation into the cognitive roots of nostalgia. *Emotion, 6*(4), 595–610.

Liberman, V., Boehm, J. K., Lyubomirsky, S., & Ross, L. D. (2009). Happiness and memory: Affective significance of endowment and contrast. *Emotion, 9*(5), 666–680.

Speer, M. E., Bhanji, J. P., & Delgado, M. R. (2014). Savoring the past: Positive memories evoke value representations in the striatum. *Neuron 84*(4), 847–856.

Stevens-Ratchford, R. D. (1993). The effect of life review reminiscence activities on depression and self-esteem in older adults. *American Journal of Occupational Therapy, 47*, 413–420.

Trost, W., Ethofer, T., Zentner, M., & Vuilleumier, P. (2012). Mapping aesthetic musical emotions in the brain. *Cerebral Cortex, 22*(12), 2769–2783.

Vatner, J. (2005, May). *The power of nostalgia.* http://www.oprah.com/health/Mood-Booster-The-Positive-Aspects-of-Nostalgia.

Vess, M., Arndt, J., Routledge, C., Sedikides, C., & Wildschut, T. (2012). Nostalgia as a resource for the self. *Self and Identity, 11*(3), 273–284.

Wildschut, T., Bruder, M., Robertson, S., Van Tilburg, A. P. W., & Sedikides, C. (2014). Collective nostalgia: A group-level emotion that confers unique benefits on the group. *Journal of Personality and Social Psychology, 107,* 844–863. http://psycnet.apa.org/journals/psp/107/5/844/.

Wildschut, C., Sedikides, C., & Cordaro, F. (2011). Self-regulatory interplay between negative and positive emotions: The case of loneliness and nostalgia. In I. Nyklicek, J. M. Vingerhoets, & M. Zeelenberg (Eds.), *Emotion Regulation and Well-Being* (pp. 67–83). New York, NY: Springer.

Yamagami, T., Takayama, Y., Maki, Y., & Yamaguchi, H. (2012). A randomized controlled trial of brain-activating rehabilitation for elderly participants with dementia in residential care homes. *Dementia and Geriatric Cognitive Disorders Extra, 2*(1), 372–380.

Notes

1. Episode 2–5, "Chupacabra" (November 13, 2014).
2. Boym (2001), p. 351.
3. Fuentenebro and Otis (2014).
4. Vess et al. (2012); Speer et al. (2014).
5. Fuentenebro and Otis (2014).
6. Episode 3–12, "Clear" (March 3, 2012).
7. Chapter 5, verse 219.
8. Vatner (2005).
9. Wildschut et al. (2011, 2014).
10. Batcho (2007); Trost et al. (2012).
11. Episode 3–11, "I Ain't a Judas" (February 24, 2013).
12. Stevens-Ratchford (1993); Yamagami et al. (2012).
13. Leboe & Ansons (2006); Liberman et al. (2009).
14. Fritz (2006), p. 8.
15. Episode 1–6, "TS-19" (December 5, 2010).
16. Episode 4–14, "The Grove" (March 16, 2014).
17. Issue 61 (2009).
18. Episode 4–14, "The Grove" (March 16, 2014)
19. Albrecht (2005); Albrecht et al. (2007).
20. Episode 4–16, "A" (March 30, 2014)

· 3 ·

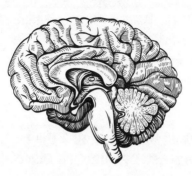

Inside the Head of the Walking Dead: The Neurobiology of Walker Dysfunction Disorder

E. Paul Zehr and Stephanie Norman

"Somewhere in all that organic wiring, all those ripples of light,
is you, the thing that makes you unique. And human . . ."
—Dr. Edwin Jenner, Centers for
Disease Control and Prevention[1]

"Sitting on your shoulders is the most
complicated object in the known universe."
—futurist Michio Kaku[2]

F ans often ponder the physical reality of walkers in *The Walking Dead*. What could produce the features of movement that all walkers share? Clinical neuroscience offers some answers regarding the motor system in the human brain and spinal cord that could—if there really were a zombie virus—cause the changes in movement control that walkers show.

Consider objectively how the walkers in the post-apocalyptic landscape of *The Walking Dead* move around. You can put together a differential diagnosis for *walker dysfunction disorder* (in their world, not ours) that is based on what we see walkers do and what we know about the neural control of movement.

The Dead Differential: A Diagnosis for Walker Dysfunction Disorder

Imagine yourself as a member of the biomedical science team in the Office of Infectious Diseases at the Centers for Disease Control and Prevention (CDC) in Atlanta, Georgia, while the emergence of walkers sweeps across the continent. Now imagine seeing someone slowly shuffle into view around the corner of the hall leading to your basement laboratory. You can't yet see her face, but you must decide quickly—is she a walker or a human ally? A *differential diagnosis* helps resolve this question. In addition to helping you solve the biological puzzle of the walker dysfunction disorder and what, if anything, you can do about it, this diagnosis helps you quickly determine whether you should lend a helping hand or reach for your weapon.

The walkers are like us, but not. Walkers show no pain reactions, shuffle or amble slowly around, react slowly, lack integration in balance and posture, and have difficulty with coordination. In contrast to these weaknesses, they have almost superhuman grip strength. These observations are your first bits of information used to create a symptoms list. Extensive debriefing with Rick and the others, including asking about all the walkers they've encountered, would provide a huge amount of information and data on the range of things walkers have been observed doing.

Symptoms	Neural Structures	Possible Causes
Reduced postural and balance reactions	Frontal cortex, cerebellum, basal ganglia, brainstem, spinal cord	Cerebellar disorders, Parkinson's disease, multiple sclerosis, concussion
Reduced connection between head and eye movement (vestibulo-occular reflex)	Cerebellum, frontal cortex, brainstem	Cerebellar disorders, concussion
Slowed movement speed	Basal ganglia, spinal cord, neuro-muscular junction	Parkinson's disease, myasthenia gravis
Exaggerated deficits on one side of the body	Basal ganglia, cortical and sub-cortical regions, spinal cord	Stroke, spinal cord injury, Parkinson's disease
Slowed walking speed	Motor cortex, basal ganglia, brainstem, spinal cord	Stroke, spinal cord injury, Parkinson's disease, concussion
Decreased pain reactions	Spinal cord, somatosensory cortex	Congenital insensitivity to pain
Resistance to movement (rigidity)	Basal ganglia, spinal cord	Parkinson's disease, multiple sclerosis
Sustained muscle contractions	Spinal cord	Tetanus infection, strychnine poisoning
Speech production	Frontal cortex (Broca's area)	Stroke, traumatic brain injury

Table 1. Differential Diagnosis for Walker Dysfunction Disorder (for more on neuro-anatomy and neurophysiology, see *Principles of Neural Science*[3])

With your team at the CDC, you'd create a parallel list of the possible causes of these symptoms.

If you worked in a flu pandemic scenario instead of a zombie apocalypse, your next step would be to list possible causes, sorting them from most to least urgent and health–threatening. Of course, this isn't so relevant to you. Despite what Dr. Hershel Greene may have thought about the "family" he kept "alive" in his barn, your "patients" are walkers who are already dead. You aren't worried about their overall health anymore.

Instead, you're using the differential diagnosis to (1) make sure that woman shuffling into your office is in fact a walker before raising your weapon and (2) figure out which parts of her brain are affected so that you can create a cure. Excluding and ruling out the items on the possible causes list by using

tests, observations, and available information brings you to the
solution and results in something that would look like Table 1.

The nervous system is a pretty complex place. You've got
about 100 billion nerve cells (*neurons*) in your brain and another
7 billion in your spinal cord. Each of those neurons has thousands of connections (*synapses*) from other neurons on it. That
network of over 100 trillion connections produces a lot of overlap between possible causes of symptoms and the related neural
structures in Table 1. Regardless, you'd work through the symptoms in the table, assess the likelihood of each nervous structure involved, and determine which walkerlike deficits could be
produced by alterations to these areas.

Evaluating the Dead Differential

Pain in the limbs. Pain starts at the skin with receptors that
detect imminent tissue damage (*nociception*). Problems with the
perception of pain can be due to lack of receptors in the skin,
very high levels of neurotransmitters (e.g., serotonin and norepinephrine) that block transmission in the spinal cord, and a
failure of the nervous system to integrate signals from the receptors. This happens in a condition so rare that fewer than a hundred cases have been reported in the medical literature: *congenital
insensitivity to pain*. People with this condition are unable to sense
warning signals of impending tissue damage.

The neurons that should bring information about tissue
damage to the spinal cord and up to the brain are working, but
the processing of those signals and interpretation as pain isn't
happening. It's a very dangerous thing because pain guides our
behaviors in avoiding certain things. When Michonne goes all
Miyamoto Musashi while lopping limbs off walkers with her
katana sword, the walkers don't even respond to what should be

Zombiform rhabdoviridae

What causes the symptoms present in the walkers? The most likely options are an auto-immune reaction or a virus. Let's say it's a virus, *Zombiform rhabdoviridae* if you will—a good working name if only because the infection has similarities with rabies. The virus would have two separate but parallel modes of infection—latent and bite:

- Latent: activated after death of the host and expression of the walker characteristics, occurring in a variable time line.
- Bite: activated upon biting. Rapid immune system activation accelerates onset and severity of symptoms.

Dale (in the comic book) or Bob (on TV) reveals to cannibals eating his leg that he has been infected by bite and is "Tainted meat!"[4] In his body, *Zombiform rhabdoviridae* hijacks the "fast" form of cellular transport and moves steadily up sensory axons from the site of the bite into the spinal cord at a rate of four centimeters a day. (You would almost guess that Glenn and Rick knew about this rapid pace when they amputated Hershel's leg after a walker bit his calf.[5]) Dale/Bob's symptoms appear faster than this, so there must be additional factors such as bacterial infection or complications from his wound.

The *Zombiform rhabdoviridae* virus continues to invade the nervous system, jumping from the motor neurons in the spinal cord to the descending connections from the brain that normally activate them. In another 24 to 48 hours the virus should arrive at the primary motor cortex—the main motor output center in the brain—and then spread to other areas of the brain. The infected "bite" side experiences more cell death on the same side of the brain. Because Dale/Bob was bitten on his right shoulder, the right side of his brain will experience more damage. We are spared seeing him suffer fully these effects of walker dysfunction disorder by the merciful actions of a distraught friend.[6]

hugely painful cuts. They just keep coming to meet their doom or, more truly, their merciful release. It remains unclear whether this problem walkers have with sensing pain is due to deficits in detection (by receptors in the skin), transmission (via spinal cord), or perception (in the cerebral cortex).

Muscle contraction. Walkers seem to have great grabbing strength. This indicates that the walkers' *central nervous system* (CNS: the brain and spinal cord) has trouble getting the muscles to contract gradually and relax properly.

Spinal cord. Your spinal cord's *motor neurons* (nerve cells that signal muscles to move) turn themselves off as fast as they are

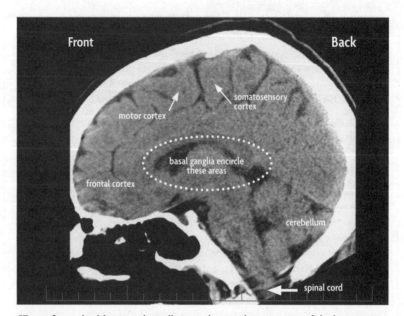

CT scan from a healthy, neurologically intact human showing some of the brain regions addressed in your differential diagnosis. This scan is courtesy of one of the authors (EPZ), who is probably not a walker.

turned on. When these motor neurons activate to contract a muscle, they simultaneously turn on other neurons that loop back directly to them and shut them down. This might seem odd but is in fact the reason Michonne can carefully reach, draw, and cut with her katana. Without it, she'd move like a walker with uncontrolled and sustained muscle contractions and an inability to strike with precision.

The walkers' "tetanic contractions" are hallmarks of botulinum toxin poisoning leading to the medical condition *tetanus*. The tetanus vaccination you get—and that one hopes Rick and the other survivors have access to—helps protect you against *Clostridium tetani,* a type of bacteria found in soil that typically enters the body through a wound such as a cut or a bite. The bacterium reproduces rapidly in the body and makes its way to the connection between motor neurons and muscle fibers. Once attached to the end of a motor neuron in a muscle, *C. tetani* climbs up into the spinal cord and blocks the effects of a neuro-transmitter that helps regulate the command for muscle contraction in the spinal cord. In clinical tetanus, sustained and powerful involuntary muscle contractions occur (the poison strychnine does something similar). Since muscles can't keep contracting forever with no relaxation, respiratory muscle failure eventually leads to death in about 40 percent of tetanus cases.

Spinal cord injury and multiple sclerosis are also clinical conditions that could produce some of the deficits seen in walkers. *Incomplete spinal cord injuries,* those with some sensory and motor commands preserved and relayed from the spinal cord to the brain, can produce the one-sided weakness that many walkers have but also often produce spastic muscle spasms during movement. Although one side often appears more affected in walkers, they don't seem to have spastic muscles.

The autoimmune disorder *multiple sclerosis* (MS) involves weakening of the insulation around nerves change. This degrades their ability to transmit information. The rapid onset of the changes seen in walkers, though, is too fast for the weeks-to-months cyclical changes often seen in multiple sclerosis.

The major human behavior retained in walkers is, well, walking. As with other mammals, human brains and spinal cords coordinate our arms with our legs when we walk. Evolutionary conservation in these connections and in the basic circuits in the brain and spinal cord (called *central pattern generators*) that regulate walking are found in almost all species, spanning the swimming lamprey, the crustaceans, the cat, the nonhuman primates, all the way to our species, *Homo sapiens*.

The walkers, just like the barnyard "chicken running around with its head cut off," can move around, using their spinal cord mechanisms to do it.

Cerebral cortex. Your cerebral cortex regulates almost all aspects of your movements. It's main role is controlling *voluntary* movement, that is, making your body do what you want it to do.

When you make a decision to move, a relayed command arrives at the main motor output center of your brain, the *primary motor cortex*, signaling the spinal cord motor neurons to produce the commands to contract muscle. Damage to the primary motor cortex produces weakness in the muscles normally activated by the damaged areas. Weakness is not an obvious deficit for walkers, and so the walkers' primary motor cortex—the direct motor output pathway from the brain—probably is not damaged extensively.

Although limb strength and movement remain relatively intact in walkers, coordination of the arms and legs is affected. Damaging the *supplementary motor area* (SMA), the major brain area that helps coordinate the brain's left and right hemispheres, reduces coordination between the arms and legs, and movements therefore become compromised.

Walkers make primitive speechlike sounds that can be pretty loud. This suggests they have partial ability to activate the brain's speech centers but that those centers are not functioning normally. You'd suspect damage in a particular part of the frontal cortex called *Broca's area*, which often occurs after stroke and results in the ability to make sounds but not form thoughts into words. Unlike after a stroke, it's unlikely that walkers have any thoughts they may be trying to express despite the Governor's best efforts to converse with his zombified daughter Penny during feeding times.[7]

Walkers lose the smooth, effortless control found in human locomotion. Instead, they show similarities in the motor control deficits seen after cerebrovascular accidents and incomplete spinal cord injuries. It seems that some parts of the connections that coordinate the arms and legs remain active in walkers but are quite rudimentary. Many walkers have an obvious deficit in which one side of the body is more affected than the other; this is a common outcome in stroke, in which damage to the brain's neurons is usually more concentrated on one side, producing larger deficits on the opposite side of the body.

Cerebellum. The *cerebellum* is tucked up at the back of the brain, just underneath the cerebral cortex. If the cerebral cortex is Veronica, the cerebellum is Betty. The cerebellum is less flashy and a bit hidden but is home to a staggering 50 percent of the brain's neurons—more than the cerebral cortex itself. As with other brain regions, neurons in the cerebellum are organized in very specific patterns. The cerebellum regulates movement indirectly by adjusting the output of the descending motor systems of the brain. This brain region is also critically important for learning and performing skilled movements.

The cerebellum has three functional regions with distinct inputs and outputs related to balance: (1) regulation and integration of eye and head movements, (2) control of limb movement, and (3) movement planning.

The critical piece here in your assessment of walker dysfunction disorder (while working under great pressure at a rapidly deteriorating biocontainment lab in the CDC) is that injury to different areas of the cerebellum produces different symptoms. The terrible balance, staggered walking, impaired coordination, and overly tense muscles that walkers display could all be attributed to changes in the cerebellum, making it a major candidate for a region affected in walker dysfunction disorder.

Basal Ganglia. The *basal ganglia* are a collection of neurons important for coordinating movement. As with the cerebellum, most of the initial information about what the basal ganglia do was deduced by researchers who correlated clinical observations in life to postmortem anatomical measurements of brains in conditions such as Parkinson's disease.

The basal ganglia help start movement and balance the ability to produce movement against expression of unwanted movement.

In the neurodegenerative disorder known as Parkinson's disease (after James Parkinson, 1755–1824), "shaking palsy" or tremor occurs at rest and is related to slowness of movement, lack of facial expression, lack of balance reactions, shuffling gait, and generalized stiffness or rigidity of limb muscles. As the disease progresses, movement becomes more and more difficult.

In contrast, degeneration in other sections of the basal ganglia can lead to excessive and involuntary movement of the limbs. In early-stage Huntington's disease, uncontrolled limb movements, *dystonia* (excess muscle activity occurs), cognitive decline, and dementia are found. Taken together, disorders of the basal ganglia have huge impacts on movement control but are also dominant diseases of cognition and thought.

Walkers show some aspects of basal ganglia disorders specifically related to rigidity, lack of facial expressions, and lack of balance. Walkers also exhibit involuntary limb movements superimposed on their other deficits. An example is when they lined up at the prison fence line and snarled at everyone while shuffling around and waving their limbs. The basal ganglia are probably an important candidate location for dysfunction in walkers.

Wrapping Up Walker Dysfunction Disorder

Whatever virus or other factor might be causing the deficits in walkers, it has effects from the muscle level all the way up to all the motor control regions in the brain. This suggests a widespread and systemically diffuse underlying cause leading to the presentation of "walkerlike" characteristics.

Our final conclusion is that as with many neurological conditions, symptoms in walkers cannot be uniquely assigned to one region or specific neurological deficit. Instead, in walker dysfunction disorder, the major constellation of effects that walkers express comes from something affecting all the motor control regions of the brain very diffusely. It should not be surprising, then, that the only sure way to stop the threat of walkers is to damage the brain itself.

The extensive brain alterations (cortex, basal ganglia, and cerebellum) and problems with controlling muscle contraction and relaxation explain why walkers can only walk and not run. The transition from walking to running is a more conscious decision that depends on the intact function of the human nervous system, which has been changed dramatically in walkers.

These alterations also explain why walkers are unable to perform complex sequences of movements. You don't see walkers performing skilled actions and limb movements such as those found in dance, parkour, or karate even if the walkers were experts at performing them before reanimation. This is probably a good thing. There is already enough thrills, tension, and drama watching *The Walking Dead* unfold on the small screen or reading the black-and-white pages of the graphic novel without adding reanimated black-belt-base-jumping-NASCAR-driving-ninja-walkers to the mix.

References

Kandel, E. R., Schwartz, J., Jessell, T., et al. (2012) *Principles of neural science* (5th ed.). New York, NY: McGraw Hill.

Lopate, L. (2014, February 25). *Behold the most complicated object in the known universe*. http://www.wnyc.org/story/michio-kaku-explores-human-brain/.

Notes

1. Episode 1–6, "TS-19" (December 5, 2010).
2. Lopate (2014).
3. Kandel et al. (2012).
4. Issue 64 (2009); episode 5–3, "Four Walls and a Roof" (October 26, 2014).
5. Episode 3–1, "Seed" (October 14, 2012).
6. Issue 66 (2009); episode 5–3, "Four Walls and a Roof" (October 26, 2014).
7. Issues 29–42 (2006–2007); season 3 (2012–2013).

Masculinity Narratives in the Post-Apocalypse

ALAN KISTLER AND BILLY SAN JUAN

"We'll be okay, because this is how we survive."
—Rick Grimes[1]

We each have a story inside us. This story is the culmination of values and worldviews we've encountered since birth. As we grow, we absorb ideals that narrate the very existence we live. For males, a large part of the narrative deals with masculinity. Fathers pass on these narratives unknowingly, often through actions and decisions rather than as a didactic lesson. Men are taught to be tough. Men are taught to be strong. Men are taught to be providers and defenders. The narrative constantly bombards boys to create an operating system.

Transmission of the Male Narrative

Men impart the masculine narrative through several methods, including a series of punishments and rewards provided by several sources, including parents, friends, and media.[2] The *reinforcement* (rewards) for "man" behaviors range from external to internal, singular to continued, physical to social. The reinforcements that transmit the male narrative may be glaringly overt. For example, a most valuable player award on a sports team celebrates the masculine traits of physical fitness, leadership, and perseverance. The transmission also occurs on a subtle level, such as a kind word from a father figure, which implies love and belonging. Either way, the narrative is passed from one male to another at all ages.

These narrative transmissions are apparent in *The Walking Dead*. Carl Grimes resists his mother's attempts to care for him in simple ways, such as giving him a haircut.[3] Shane Walsh, assuming a fatherlike role with Carl, tells the boy that going along with his mother's wishes not only will prove his character but will result in a reward: "You just get through this with some manly dignity, and tomorrow I'll teach you something special."[4] In this moment, Carl receives reinforcement of masculine behavior. His budding narrative now includes the idea that a stoic attitude (manly dignity) during an uncomfortable time (haircut) provides a reward (something special).

When Carl later wants to stay on the Greene farm,[5] Shane explains that helping with chores will increase his chances of earning respect and help from Hershel Greene's family, who might allow them to stay. Thus we have another reinforcement of masculine behavior: Carl learns, from a man, that physical labor leads to a home and safety.

Carl later begins to exhibit bouts of rebellion. The rebellion is a sign that he is eager to act on the narratives he has learned despite lacking the maturity to do so. His strong desire to help the group even jeopardizes his safety (such as searching for Sophia and taking weapons off a dead body that could be a walker). Despite his transgressions, Carl's biological father, Rick Grimes, understands that the boy is motivated to protect and is trying to apply the lessons he's learning from his mentors. They begin shooting lessons,[6] and the boy's maturing behavior, along with the progress he shows in learning how to survive, earns him the privilege of joining the adults on their supply runs and raids on walker-inhabited houses.[7] Carl's adolescence, though occurring in a post-apocalyptic dystopia, becomes a testament to the lasting nature of the narrative through generations.

The way a male narrative morphs when passed intergenerationally depends on several factors. Shane gave Carl pragmatic reasons and rewards for good behavior. Rick attempts to pass on wisdom to his son by pointing out that being a "man" means not only displaying strength but also using restraint, specifically, considering the feelings of others before voicing an opinion that may cause them distress.[8] Rick explains that such behavior has moral value because it is right to care about others. He later speaks to Carl about how his own father taught him "profound" things about the world and how to live in it but regrets that simply repeating such lessons isn't good enough in a post-apocalyptic earth. Rick admits he must adjust his own teachings: "No more kid stuff. I wish you could have the childhood I had, but that's not going to happen."[9] The narrative shifts. A value adaptive for civilization is abandoned because of its vestigial quality in the current world.

Normative Male Alexithymia

A fascinating aspect of the masculine narrative is the tendency toward a phenomenon known as *alexithymia,*[10] the inability to identify or describe emotion. Adult males are not *immune* to emotion. Just the opposite: They feel emotions as strongly as anyone else, whatever age or gender. Unfortunately, in traditional patriarchal societies, they are not often allowed or encouraged to develop the language or capacity to express it. Expression of emotions other than anger and a select few others is seen as weakness that merits punishment.

Playgrounds, school yards, and households set the scene for this narrative. Male culture teaches young boys that the expression of emotions is a direct contradiction of manliness with phrases such as "boys don't cry," "man up," "don't be a sissy," and "grow a pair." Boys are labeled as "crybabies" if they show sadness or frustration. Meanwhile, it is accepted that girls cry. This sexist dichotomy inhibits healthy emotional development through the expectations of the male gender.

Alexithymia is much like lye: Ignoring emotions can be useful in certain situations, dangerous in others. In the context of masculinity, alexithymia is highly adaptive in the social role men have traditionally taken. When Sophia goes missing, Carl is determined to find her even though others have concluded that she must be dead. Eventually Sophia is revealed as a walker. Carl cries in his mother's arms as the innocence of his youth betrays him. He then watches as his father shoots Sophia down, effectively shooting the hope Carl had hung onto. In this scene, we notice a dichotomy. The young Carl, whose masculine ideals are still fresh, has not yet fully succumbed to a numbness of feeling. Meanwhile, his older, masculine father suppresses his emotion while taking pragmatic action.

Carl later assures himself, affirming his father's actions by stating that he would have done the same thing. At this point, Lori worries about the boy's disconnect from emotion. This episode shows the progression of alexithymia in a dramatic fashion, but it provides an example of the process by which it occurs. When

Lori is on the verge of becoming a walker, Carl dons the mantle of masculinity and kills her. He arrives at the decision rationally, with emotion playing little part in it. His father cries upon the discovery of Lori's death, yet Carl simply bows his head with little more than a frown. He has embraced the masculine narrative. Or rather, the masculine narrative has embraced him.

These examples show that "shutting down" emotional pathways in specific situations is adaptive in areas related to masculinity. However, failing to explore and process the numbed emotions may cause adverse effects. Rick's inability to grieve properly for his dead wife leads to psychotic episodes, yet he keeps the hallucinations secret and adheres to the value of stoicism in men. He forces the illusion of mental stability, conforming to the idea that the alpha male's mind is sound. This same strict adherence to masculine norms causes men to turn to maladaptive forms of emotional coping such as drugs, alcohol, and thrill-seeking behaviors.

Men as Protectors

Knights. Princes. Kings. Traditional gender roles dictate a man's pride in providing for his family.[11] A rudimentary examination of media shows heroic males as protagonists, providers, and protectors. Father, brother, and husband characters act as de facto guardians. Countless B-movie reels flaunt men brandishing weapons, pitchforks, and torches while the women and children cower behind them. These observations reflect a core narrative that men pass down to their children: The family relies on you.

The Walking Dead perpetuates examples of the "family-guardian" narrative. During Rick's coma, Shane Walsh puts himself in the position of proxy protector of his friend's family. It is later revealed

The Faces of Rick

Over the course of *The Walking Dead*, Rick Grimes goes through the ringer and back, changing as the situation requires it and usually coming out each time a little more haggard and a little more bearded.

Sheriff Rick: Rick Grimes starts off as a man of the law through and through. He asks for things such as gas and supplies. He's fair and noble and believes every life is worth trying to save.

Ricktator: If Sheriff Rick can't survive this world, he'll become the Ricktator. He's in charge, making the tough decisions, and no one is allowed to question that. "This isn't a democracy anymore."

Red Rick: Losing Lori pushes Ricktator off the diving board, belly flopping into a pool of molten rage. He only sees red as he storms the tombs of the prison, killing dozens of walkers by himself, and as he repeatedly stabs the walker who ate Lori. Jack Torrance (*The Shining*) would be so proud.

Crazy Rick: Rick crashes straight into cray-cray town, imagining phone calls from his dead pals and hallucinating angry Shane and judgmental Lori. (No, *crazy* is not an appropriate psychological term, but that's how the characters come to see him.) This is Rick at his most broken: No matter what he does, it just doesn't seem to be enough to keep the people he cares about alive.

Farmer Rick: With some steady guidance from good ol' Hershel, Crazy Rick transitions from the depths of insanity into a more serene state. Farmer Rick no longer carries a gun. He eschews the stressors of leadership and buries his hands in soil instead. He won't even kill any of the walkers gathered at the fence; he's all about peace, love, and crops.

Survivor Rick: The Governor's final attack on the prison forces Survivor Rick to emerge. When the Claimers are about to rape Carl and murder Rick, Michonne, and Daryl, Claimer leader Joe asks Rick, "What the hell are you going to do now, sport?" Rick responds not with words but by biting a chunk out of the dude's throat! Nothing good lasts in a world of zombies. Survivor Rick will hack, shoot, or maul anyone to protect the people he calls family.

Citizen Rick: Rick's family reaches Alexandria. Soon there's a new sheriff in town—after he shaves.

—Katrina Hill

that after Rick enters surgery for the injuries that lead to his coma, Shane assures Lori that she wasn't alone.[12] Shane then guards the family, mentoring Carl and loving Lori. His relief at Rick's return gets overshadowed by resentment over having Lori and Carl taken from him. Shane and Rick come to inevitable conflict concerning Rick's duties as husband and father. Shane concludes that Rick's moral values are antiquated for the modern, walker-infested world. He declares, "Rick, you can't just be the good guy and expect to live. Okay? Not anymore."[13] These disagreements with Rick culminate in Shane's attempt to kill his best friend.[14] Shane's justification for murder stems from the belief that he is the better husband and father and thus is entitled to resume those roles with Lori and Carl.

A by-product of this narrative is the trope "male hero gets the girl." The recurring theme in hero stories of a male protagonist enduring hardship in order to save a damsel plays into the masculine narrative. The damsel eventually falls in love with the man for his valiant actions and self-sacrifice, which serve as emotional and sexual reinforcement. The narrative permeates countless fairy tales and movies and is reinforced by everyday language. Phrases such as "He won me over" and "He swept me off my feet" imply an active male role and a passive feminine role. The woman becomes a prize to obtain, the man's due, a ball that he must retrieve from an obstacle or opponent who guards it. As was mentioned before, a prime example of this value occurs in the story arc/love triangle of Shane, Rick, and Lori. Cognitive dissonance abounds between Shane's actions as hero and his inability to claim Lori as his own. The dissonance creates such negative feelings that he ultimately attempts to take the life of a person he once regarded as both his superior at work and his best friend.

Men as Action-Oriented

A review of masculinity-based theory and research found that a tenet of manhood is that masculinity requires "public proof."[15] A man must be *seen* being a man. This may explain the stereotype of a "handyman," a perceived natural state in which adult males are proficient at carpentry, yard work, and household repairs, whereas those who do not show such skill are considered strange or weak. Men are expected to be doers, fixers. Men don't wait to react; they take control and actively solve situations. A man who waits is seen as indecisive, but a man who takes charge and provides, especially in spite of difficult circumstances, is to be revered and admired.

At times, a man who embraces the narrative of action can attain almost godlike status. The Governor repeatedly stresses that considering all one's options cannot override the need for action. The town of Woodbury looks to him for guidance. They trust him and look to him for leadership. He solves internal conflict, acting as both hero and father figure to the entire population.

Other times, man becomes slave to this impulse. A prime example of the weakness caused by this narrative occurs when Rick, upon seeing Carl's prone and injured body, must be told several times to stay at his side. Rick knows that Carl needs his blood, but he cannot simply sit passively. He gets up several times, attempting to do something. It is in this moment that Rick's masculinity, normally adaptive, causes him great grief. He cannot bear to wait, watch, or worry. He must act.

The male behaviors exhibited in *The Walking Dead* show that traditional masculine narratives, for better or worse, thrive in a post-apocalyptic world. However, the fact that males are given these messages at such a young age does not mean they are condemned to follow them. It is possible to take charge of fate and, as Rick Grimes does, embrace both masculinity and over-all humanity. After all, a post-apocalyptic dystopian environment populated with zombies requires more than survival. It requires humanity to thrive.

References

Kilmartin, C. (2010). *The masculine self.* New York, NY: Sloan.

Levant, R. F. (1992). Toward the reconstruction of masculinity. *Journal of Family Psychology, 5,* 388–389.

Long, E., Fish, J., Scheffler, A., & Hanert, B. (2014). Memorable experiences between fathers and sons: Stories that shape a son's identity and perspective of his father. *Journal of Men's Studies, 22,* 123–124.

Vandello, J., & Bosson, J. (2013). Hard won and easily lost: A review and synthesis of theory and research on precarious manhood. *Psychology of Men and Masculinity, 14,* 103–104.

Notes

1. Episode 5–10, "Them" (February 15, 2015).
2. Kilmartin (2010), p. 80.
3. Episode 1–3, "Tell It to the Frogs" (November 14, 2010).
4. Episode 1–3, "Tell It to the Frogs" (November 14, 2010).
5. Episode 2–7, "Pretty Much Dead Already" (November 27, 2011).
6. Episode 2–6, "Secrets" (November 20, 2011).
7. Episode 3–1, "Seed" (October 14, 2012).
8. Episode 2–11, "Judge, Jury, Executioner" (March 3, 2012).
9. Episode 2–12, "Better Angels" (March 10, 2012).
10. Levant (1992).
11. Kilmartin (2010), p. 13.
12. Episode 2–2, "Bloodletting" (October 23, 2011).
13. Episode 2–10, "18 Miles Out" (February 26, 2012).
14. Episode 2–12, "Better Angels" (March 11, 2012).
15. Vandello & Bosson (2013).

Shane Walsh

Travis Langley

*"I hadn't read the comic. I read the script and I was
completely blown away. I said, 'Wow.' And then
actually getting the job—quadruple wow! And then
reading the comic, I'm like, 'Wait a second.'"*
—actor Jon Bernthal regarding his surprise upon
discovering Shane's comic book fate.[1]

After Shane Walsh becomes a father figure to Rick's son, a lover
for Rick's wife, and a leader among the survivors they join
outside Atlanta, Rick Grimes surprises them all by turning
up alive. Shane's mixed feelings about Rick's return degenerate
into resentment and anger as Rick not only reclaims his family
but emerges as the new leader. Embittered and feeling that Rick
has taken everything he had left in this dark, new world, Shane
tries to kill his lifelong friend.

Is Shane evil? Attempting murder because he covets his brother's wife is an evil deed, biblically so. An action is not a whole
person, though, and almost anyone is capable of doing wrong in
certain circumstances. Calling a person evil means talking about
enduring, inner qualities. In psychology, we tend to avoid the
word *evil* even as we struggle to study it and give it technical
names.

Diagnosing Evil: Dark Triad, Dark Tetrad

Some experts attempting to analyze evil view it in terms of the *dark triad*, a volatile combination of three overlapping sorts of selfishness: (1) psychopathy, (2) narcissism, and (3) Machiavellianism.[2] Because a person can coldly exploit others without delighting in cruelty, the dark triad falls short of meeting the full criteria for *malignant narcissism*, the cruel kind of grandiose selfishness that the psychologist Erich Fromm dubbed "the quintessence of evil,"[3] and so researchers began looking at *sadism* (delightedly hurting others) as a fourth component in a *dark tetrad*.[4]

Psychopathy

Psychopathy is a lifelong personality pattern high in fearlessness and insensitivity; low in empathy, inhibition, and remorse; and potentially dangerous to people in the psychopath's way. Chapter 11 in this book, "It's the Humans You Have to Worry About: Becoming a Sociopath," distinguishes psychopathy from sociopathy and details the two main sets of psychopathic qualities: *factor 1*, made up of the interpersonal and emotional traits (e.g., shallowness, remorselessness), and *factor 2*, meaning antisocial actions and lifestyle (e.g., impulsivity, lawbreaking).[5] Factor 1 fits psychopathy as classically described by the psychiatrist Hervey Cleckley,[6] and factor 2 resembles the *Diagnostic and Statistical Manual of Mental Disorders*[7] diagnosis of *antisocial personality disorder*.[8] Despite considerable callousness and insufficient empathy, Shane is not a psychopath. He cares about the well-being of others—albeit those he likes and in an infantile way—and guilt gnaws at him. He has a conscience. His impulsivity and adolescent attitudes in the midst of relentless stress and danger get in the way of his hearing that conscience.

He is arguably sociopathic, however, depending on which definition of *sociopathy* a diagnostician might apply. Even though he has not grown up as a psychopath, he resembles one many times. Apocalyptic circumstances have elicited evil he never showed before.

Narcissism

Shane is selfish. Even his affection for others is largely self-serving. He places his interests first, as when he tries to force himself on an objecting Lori, even if he does back off,[9] or when he later prioritizes his own yearnings over his best friend's life. *Narcissism* (vanity, overestimation of one's talents and importance, and excessive need for admiration) can combine dangerously with psychopathy or sociopathy, producing an individual who is supremely selfish and cocksure without emotional restraints to hold him or her back.

Machiavellianism

Named for the sixteenth-century diplomat Niccolò Machiavelli, Machiavellianism involves a calculating, manipulative attitude toward dealing with others, one that values cunning and deceit. Morality for cynical Machiavellians is pragmatic, based on instrumental, practical purposes. To them, ends justify means. After Shane deliberately wounds Otis and leaves the man for walkers to eat, distracting them so that he can escape with the medical equipment needed to save Carl's life, he lies about how Otis died.[10] Later, Shane constructs a ruse to lead Rick into the woods, meaning to murder his best friend. Shane shows a Machiavellian attitude but without great manipulative skill. He is a lousy liar. Inconsistencies in his stories keep exposing the truth, as does his own guilt.

Sadism

Shane can be mean or insulting, a form of self-assertion that seems to empower him. When he pummels Carol's abusive husband into submission, saying, "I'll beat you to death, Ed," he keeps punching even after he renders Ed bloody and unconscious.[11] He goes too far. He does not, however, continually seek opportunities to hurt others or light up with glee over doing so.

How Evil?

Even though Shane shows some features of every dimension of evil, he shows none consistently. His better qualities wane as ghastly circumstances bring out his worst, when goodness begins looking hazardously impractical, but he is neither an evil man before the apocalypse nor the worst of people in the post-apocalypse—as the rest of these case files will show. Compared with most of our featured foes, Shane's a teddy bear.

References

American Psychiatric Association (2013). *Diagnostic and statistical manual of mental disorders* (DSM-5) (5th ed.). Washington, DC: American Psychiatric Association.

Buckels, E. E., Jones, D. N., & Paulhus, D. L. (2013). Behavior confirmation of everyday sadism. *Psychological Science, 20*, 1–9.

Chabrol, H., Van Leeuwen, N., Rodgers, R., & Sejourne, N. (2009). Contributions of psychopathic, narcissistic, Machiavellian, and sadistic personality traits to juvenile delinquency. *Personality and Individual Differences, 47*, 734–739.

Cleckley, H. (1941). *The mask of sanity*. St. Louis, MO: Mosby.

Fromm, E. (1964). *The heart of man*. New York, NY: Harper & Row.

Hare, R. D. (1991). *The Hare psychopathy checklist—revised manual*. North Tonawanda, NY: Multi-Health Systems.

Hare, R. D., & Neumann, C. N. (2006). The PCL-R assessment of psychopathy: Development, structural properties, and new directions. In C. Patrick (Ed.), *Handbook of psychopathy* (pp. 58–88). New York, NY: Guilford.

Harpur, T. J., Hare, R. D., & Hakstian, A. R. (1989). Two-factor conceptualization of psychopathy: Construct validity and assessment implications. *Psychological Assessment, 1*, 6–17.

Jakobwitz, S., & Egan, V. (2006). The "dark triad" and normal personality traits. *Personality and Individual Differences, 40*, 331–339.

Paulhus, D. L., & Williams, J. M. (2002). The dark triad of personality: Narcissism, Machiavellianism, and psychopathy. *Journal of Research in Personality, 36*, 556–63.

Skeem, J. L., Polaschek, D. L. L., Patrick, C. J., & Lilienfeld, S. O. (2011). Psychopathic personality: Bridging the gap between scientific evidence and public policy. *Psychological Science in the Public Interest, 12*, 95–162.

TheRocketLlama (2010, October 8). *AMC's The Walking Dead: Andrew Lincoln, Jon Bernthal, Sarah Wayne Callies interview*. https://www.youtube.com/watch?v=n5SMLYhDaW0.

Notes

1. TheRocketLlama (2010).
2. Jakobwitz & Egan (2006); Paulhus & Williams (2002).
3. Fromm (1964), p. 37.
4. Buckels et al. (2013); Chabrol et al. (2009).
5. Hare (1991); Hare & Neumann (2006).
6. Cleckley (1941).
7. American Psychiatric Association (2013).
8. Harpur, Hare, & Hakstian (1989).
9. Episode 1–6, "TS-19" (December 5, 2010).
10. Episode 2–3, "Save the Last One" (October 30, 2011).
11. Episode 1–3, "Tell It to the Frogs" (November 14, 2010).

However we might imagine we'll act in an emergency, we really don't know until it happens. One person, having mentally rehearsed a disaster response, may react as he or she planned. One who has dreamed of saving the day might instead panic, whereas a cynic who scoffs at heroism, assuming that "I'll never risk my neck for any stranger," in the heat of the moment sometimes does exactly that. When no plan is possible or when a crisis seems too unlikely to be anticipated, posttraumatic reactions can be especially severe. In the world of *The Walking Dead*, where nobody has ever seen a Living Dead film, no one expects the zombie apocalypse.

· PART TWO ·
RESPONDING

Shock and Dread:
What Fear Does to Humans

DAVE VERHAAGEN

"In every calm and reasonable person there is a hidden second person scared witless about death."
—novelist Phillip Roth

"**O**nly one way to keep you alive," Rick says to the frightened, freshly bitten Hershel Greene. Rick lifts the ax and chops at Hershel's leg, blood splattering, until he hacks it completely off below the knee, not yet knowing if that will save Hershel from the effects of the walker's deadly bite.

No other series in comics or on television evokes powerful emotions of fear, disgust, and sadness—often at the same moment—as strongly as *The Walking Dead*. Never before have we seen such a magnificent case study in popular culture on what living in sustained, unrelenting fear and terror does to people. In *The Walking Dead*, we see how it affects decisions, relationships, and the integrity of the self.

> *"I've been starting to get afraid that*
> *it's easier just to be afraid."*
> —Beth Greene[1]

The Biology of Fear

Immediately after he has been bitten, we see Hershel's eyes: pure horror and panic. In that instant, his eyes—and ears and flesh and stimulated senses—send their information to his brain's *thalamus,* a mass of gray matter responsible for routing sensory information. Hershel reacts in milliseconds before he realizes what the threat actually is. That happens because his *amygdala,* a little almond-shaped mass of cells deep in the temporal lobe, processes sensory information and starts a behavioral response—*yell, pull away, seek safety*—before the information reaches his brain's awareness centers.

The thalamus sends information by two routes. The first route, directly telegraphed to the amygdala, is for lightning-fast reactions. The second route, relayed through the *cerebral cortex* (the outer, wrinkled brain layer responsible for higher functions), allows the information to be processed and assigned a meaning: *Does this pose a real threat?* If the answer is yes, the amygdala generates the proper fight-or-flight response. This longer route allows for a smarter reaction even if the amygdala already is calling for action.

Without the amygdala, we'd have been gobbled up by saber-toothed cats long ago. With it, we had a fighting chance long enough to develop a prefrontal cortex so that we could rule the earth. Sensory information floods in from the thalamus so that the amygdala, the command center for evaluating threats,[2] can scan it for danger. When the amygdala recognizes a potential threat in the environment, it triggers a series of cascading alarms that produce what we see as overt signs of fear and panic: racing heart, trembling, sweating, rapid breathing, blanching skin. These physical reactions serve the deep, essential purpose of preparing us to defend ourselves vigorously.

When it's lit up, the amygdala also jolts a portion of the cerebral cortex responsible for the conscious sensation of fear. At this point, the fear reaction isn't just a deeply visceral experience; it begins to take form in our consciousness. If the amygdala detects a potential threat but the frontal cortex analyzes the report and finds it lacking, it tells the amygdala to calm down.

In a world full of danger, the amygdala plays a vital role in keeping us safe, but an overactive amygdala kills our performance. We get tunnel vision, our hearing becomes too selective, and our fine motor control falls apart. With more and more stress comes worse and worse fine motor behavior—the kinds of basic skills we need to lock doors, make phone calls, or grab for a weapon—in other words, many of the very things we might need to keep us safe in those terrifying moments when the zombies are closing in.

Even worse than loss of fine motor skills, though, is the whammy high stress puts on decision making. Our ability to make good choices can fall apart under extremely stressful, frightening situations. Whereas moderate stress can compromise decision making, high stress can overwhelm us if our amygdalae hijack our brains.

One of the criticisms leveled at *The Walking Dead* is that the characters don't behave consistently. Their motivations and actions seem to shift. Tyreese, the man who becomes the main caretaker of the baby Lori delivered before dying, is a deeply compassionate man. Yet at one point he leaves baby Judith and two young girls to fend for themselves.

"That's not how normal people behave," laments one journalist in his criticism of the show, "especially people who go out of their way to protect others. It didn't make sense."[3]

Yet it did.

Although unreliable character motivations are fair game for criticism of other stories, the lack of character stability is actually a strength of The Walking Dead. To suggest that there are ways in which normal people behave in the zombie apocalypse is to minimize the weight of the catastrophic stress they are experiencing.

Thus, Rick is a rock and a pillar of strength, able to pick up the ax in a split second and cut off Hershel's leg in order to save him, but he hallucinates and makes shocking decisions at other times. Carol is meek and mild and trustworthy, but as we later learn, she is fully capable of murdering a child.

It's not just that tough times call for tough decisions. It's that high stress can fundamentally alter people's way of acting, reacting, and even perceiving the world around them. Over the course of many long months of surviving the zombie outbreak, the humans of The Walking Dead go from rational to irrational and back. This is no Downton Abbey with clear character motivations. It's the freaking zombie apocalypse, and even the best of these people are a mess.

To have any chance of survival in this nightmarish new world, their brains must maintain a delicate balance between the frontal cortex and the amygdale, with each part doing its share of the work, calming them when they need to be calmed and activating them when they need to be activated. Rick at times finds that balance and is able to make the right but gruesomely tough choice.

How is that possible? Because other processes are at work in his brain, too. When we become afraid, we sometimes have the ability to think more clearly about the situation. This is due partly to the effects of a neurotransmitter called *norepinephrine,* a natural stimulant in the brain that increases neural efficiency, animating us and charging us up. It also lights up the *hippocampus,* an area of the brain responsible for making memories that last. It's one reason we remember vivid details of alarming situations. Rick's brain, lit up by norepinephrine, is extremely efficient, thinking clearly and analyzing possibilities and options nearly at light speed.

If the infection spreads, he's worse than dead, Rick thinks, and scans for the ax. *That leg needs to come off.*

And so it does, thanks to a remarkable process that allows amazing decisions to be made in the blink of an eye.

> *"You walk outside, you risk your life. You take a drink*
> *of water, you risk your life. Nowadays you breathe and*
> *you risk your life. You don't have a choice. The only*
> *thing you can choose is what you're risking it for."*
> —Hershel Greene[4]

The Psychology of Fear

Humans experience a range of emotions, but there are four that are the primary building blocks of the others: happiness, sadness, anger, and fear. *The Walking Dead* allows fleeting moments of happiness—a baby found safe, a reunion, an unexpected kindness—but also offers plenty of the negative emotions—tremendous sadness and grief, righteous and unrighteous anger, and plentiful fear.

Sadness is usually the product of loss and is rooted in the past. After your dear father gets his head cut off by a sword-swinging Governor, you get sad. When a fat zombie eats your dead wife's body, you get angry. But fear occupies a special place in our psychology. We experience it when we perceive a threat in the future, sometimes the very imminent future. Something bad *may* happen. A zombie *may* bite us. Cannibals *may* eat us. These things have yet to occur, but the perceived likelihood of the threat moves fear along a continuum from anxiety to panic. We feel anxious at the thought of zombies in the woods near the farm; we feel panic when they overrun the property.

Even after a dreadful thing happens to us, such as getting bitten by a zombie in a prison corridor, we still feel fear. Why? Because we fear something worse might happen. Hershel would be afraid of having his calf muscle torn out by a hungry walker, but he would be more afraid of turning into a walker himself. The anxiety of searching through the dark hallway where something bad might happen gives way to the panic of knowing that something bad already has happened that may lead to an even worse thing happening. Over the course of the event, everyone's fear gets ratcheted up from anxiety and dread to full-blown panic.

Humans, like other mammals, have remarkably efficient biological systems that help keep us alive even in the face of serious threats. But very much unlike other mammals, humans also have a highly sophisticated *prefrontal cortex* that allows us to recognize what many of these threats mean for us in the long term. We realize that death is inevitable despite our best efforts to keep ourselves safe. Even before the outbreak, we live with this tension daily in which we have a biological imperative to stay alive coupled with the awareness that death will come to all of us.

Many characters on *The Walking Dead* wrestle with this deeper notion that death is around the corner while they also want to stay alive and hold onto reasons for living. This includes Maggie and Glenn, the young couple who found love in a hopeless place. Maybe it's that sense of love that makes them yearn for more than just survival, more than just freedom from fear.

What Would You Do if a Zombie Bit You?

Before *The Walking Dead* television series debuted, I interviewed its creators and cast members. I got to be the first interviewer to ask what each would do if bitten by a zombie.[5]

Steven Yeun (Glenn): Probably bite other people.

Norman Reedus (Daryl): Party like it's 1999. How hot was the zombie?

Laurie Holden (Andrea): A little baby bite or a big bite? . . . I could cut off part of my arm, I could be amputated, and I could still live. If I could save my life, I'd keep chopping.

Norman: I'd go see Peewee's show on Broadway.

Laurie: You don't have to be bitten by a zombie to see that.

Sarah Wayne Callies (Lori): Bullet. Bullet to the head.

Steven: You've thought about this.

Sarah: I wouldn't want to eat my kid.

Jon Bernthal (Shane): You kind of ruined my day with that question.

Andrew Lincoln (Rick): [Laughs.]

Sarah: You'd never get bitten by a zombie.

Jon: No, man. I'd bite that sucker dead.

Robert Kirkman (comic book writer): People often ask me how I would exist in this world, and I say, "Not very well." I would probably hang myself or jump off a building early on because I've written this comic and know how bad it would get. Bitten by a zombie, though? I don't know. In the movies, everyone always kills themselves immediately. "Oh, I don't want to turn into a zombie." I would wonder what that's like. Maybe it's great! Maybe when you're walking around as a dead guy, it's like everyone's a chocolate bar. So I'd get away from anyone I could hurt, and then I would go for it.

(Afterward, Jon assured me that I hadn't really ruined his day.)

— Katrina Hill

Katrina Hill onstage with Norman Reedus (Daryl Dixon).

> Maggie: I don't want to be afraid of being alive.
> Glenn: Being afraid is what has kept us alive.
> Maggie: No, it's how we kept breathing.[6]

Like us, they both have the biological drive to stay alive, yet they know they are going to die. Maggie doesn't just want to breathe. She wants to live fully and to have reasons to live even in the landscape of the zombie apocalypse.

To cope with the impossible dilemma of fighting to preserve a life we know will end one day, a psychological theory called *TMT* (*terror management theory*[7]) suggests that we turn to bigger and more permanent concepts and ideals such as identifying with a faith system, being a member of a specific country or community, or being an artist or scientist or anything else that suffuses meaning into our lives in a way that will outlast us. In turn, we commit deeply to these ideals and punish those who challenge them. We form groups that help us survive and that share our values and our outlook on the world.

We see this all the time in *The Walking Dead*. Fierce tribalism and closely knit communities evolve with "If you're not with us, you're against us" thinking, whether it is within the prison walls, the deceptively idyllic Woodbury, or Terminus, the trap at the end of the tracks. Each of these communities develops its own unique worldview, albeit bizarre and horrifying at times.

The Governor has created a seemingly safe haven in Woodbury that promises peace and protection, but his charismatic demeanor quickly comes unglued when he feels threatened by Rick and the others. Nothing will stand between him and his right to recline in front of a bunch of heads in jars.

Later, in Terminus, the once-good Gareth (presumably a version of Chris from the comic book series), having been terrorized by a gang of violent men, has concluded that you are either the hunter or the prey, and so he persuades his entire community to turn to cannibalism as a means of survival and domination. "Join us or feed us," he tells subsequent newcomers. Gareth and his people become so callous to the murder and consumption of their fellow humans that they talk casually about mundane things as they stand over victims they intend to slaughter by cracking their skulls with baseball bats and slitting their throats. Later, he cuts off, cooks, and eats Bob Stookey's leg in front of the man, the way Chris treats Dale in the comics.[8] He's beyond depraved but entirely congruent and accepted within his own community.

TMT suggests that although we don't always commit to ideals or worldviews that are morally good or lovely, we do hold strong views designed to outlast us. Whether Gareth, the Governor, and Rick realize it or not, these tribal worldviews emanate from their desires not only to stay alive but to be outlasted by something—a community, a set of ideals, an achievement, a legacy—that outlives them. They then set about to guard this precious something and punish all who would challenge it. It's a highly sophisticated way of dealing with their ultimate fear.

In a curious study that makes this point in a clever way, the psychologist Jeff Greenberg and his colleagues[9] asked district court judges to rule on a hypothetical prostitution case. The hypothesis was that the judges who were prompted ahead of time about their own mortality would punish the offenders more harshly than would those who were not because they were upholding the cultural beliefs they needed to outlast them. Sure enough, the judges who were reminded of their own mortality set bond at an average of $455 for the hookers, whereas those who hadn't been reminded that they would die one day set an average bond of $50.

When the fear of death seeps in just below our consciousness, we do things to forestall it, such as eating healthier or exercising. Sometimes we just distract ourselves with Netflix or alcohol or some other amusement, all designed to stuff the fear back down.

But when we are tapped on the shoulder about our unavoidable death, as occurs when we drive by a cemetery or hear of a celebrity's untimely demise or read about a car bomb going off, we start to focus less on our physical bodies and more on our symbolic value, such as our accomplishments or our legacy. And—here's where it gets weird but understandable—we also get more prejudiced and more aggressive toward those who are different from us, especially those who would dare to challenge our ideals or way of life.

The Walking Dead succeeds in large part because it depicts other humans as more terrifying than the walkers much of the time. Factions form out of necessity, and the groups—along with the worldviews within them—are zealously protected. It all serves as a way of coping with the looming death they all fear but know awaits them.

Individual Differences with Fear

Time and time again we see people like Rick react to the threats around them, whether from encroaching zombie packs or swarms of marauding humans, with fierce determination and decisive action, whereas others, such as Father Gabriel Stokes, freak out in the moment of crisis. Father Gabriel, the minster at St. Sarah's Episcopal Church, barricades himself inside the church, refusing to let anyone in, even members of his own congregation, out of fear for his own life.[10] By the time Rick's group meets him, he's wracked with guilt, believing he is damned to hell for this. (It probably didn't help his guilt that one of his parishioners scrawled, "You'll burn for this," on the side of his church.) We keep seeing the good reverend in flight, avoiding, running, trying to dodge conflict and hardship, and it keeps causing him trouble.

Why do some people react to terrifying situations with panic or avoidance whereas others seem to respond with a remarkable cool-headedness? Like most things in psychology, the answer is complex, although not so complicated as to be incomprehensible. Several personal characteristics may make an individual more likely to panic, such as a family history of anxiety disorders, past trauma, mental rigidity, social alienation, and a shy temperament.[11]

An even more intriguing answer to why some people panic while others remain calm in the zombie apocalypse lies in the notion of *anxiety sensitivity*, a relatively fixed, largely genetic personality trait that some people have in greater abundance than others. It's a tendency to fear the bodily sensations that often come with anxiety. The individual wrongly regards these sensations as being harmful or dangerous, which in turn makes him more fearful and anxious when he is experiencing them. This, of course, makes the symptoms worse. His accelerated heart rate and quickening breathing frighten him, and that only serves to make his heart beat faster and his breathing become quicker and shallower, which terrifies him and creates a cycle that quickly turns a little anxiety into a hot mess.

People who score high on the Anxiety Sensitivity Index are much more likely to develop panic disorder or posttraumatic stress disorder, and people with these disorders develop greater anxiety sensitivity. In other words, it's a vicious loop and a crappy hand they were genetically dealt. It's what makes the difference between being a Father Stokes and being a Sheriff Rick in the zombie apocalypse.

Fear is the most primal of all human emotions. It has kept us safe for millennia and gives us a fighting chance in the zombie apocalypse. It's an imperfect emotion, however. Even though fear can cause us to fight or take flight when it is necessary, it also can make us become irrational or turn into intolerant bigots. At the core of *The Walking Dead* is a question that also is at the core of all humankind: Will we keep our humanity when faced with our deepest fears?

References

Gardner, D. (2009). *The science of fear.* New York, NY: Plume.

Greenberg, J., Pyszczynski, T., & Solomon, S. (2002). A perilous leap from Becker's theorizing to empirical science: Terror management and research. In D. Liechty (Ed.), *Death and denial: Interdisciplinary perspectives on the legacy of Ernest Becker.* New York, NY: Praeger.

Hill, K. (2010, October 16). *AMC's The Walking Dead cast and creators: Bitten by a zombie?* https://www.youtube.com/watch?v=ypudSnw65cw.

Kain, J. (2014, February 19). *What "The Walking Dead" needs to do to survive.* http://www.forbes.com/sites/erikkain/2014/02/19/what-the-walking-dead-needs-to-do-to-survive/.

Roth, P. J. (2001). *The Dying Animal.* New York, NY: Vintage.

Sheikh, J. I. (2002). Lifetime trauma history and panic disorder: Findings from the National Comorbidity Survey. *Journal of Anxiety Disorders, 16*(6), 599–603.

Staal, M. A. (2004). *Stress, cognition, and human performance: A literature review and conceptual framework.* Moffett Field, CA: NASA Ames Research Center.

Taylor, S., Zvolensky, M., Cox, B., et al. (2007). Robust dimensions of anxiety sensitivity: Development and initial validation of the Anxiety Sensitivity Index-3. *Psychological Assessment, 19*, 176–188.

Wise, J. (2011). *Extreme fear: The science of your mind in danger.* New York, NY: Palgrave Macmillan.

Notes

1. Episode 4–10, "Inmates" (February 16, 2014).
2. Wise (2011).
3. Kain (2014).
4. Episode 4–3, "Isolation" (October 27, 2013).
5. Hill (2010).
6. Episode 4–1, "30 Days without an Accident" (October 13, 2013).
7. Greenberg et al. (2002).
8. Issue 64 (2009).
9. Greenberg et al. (2002)
10. Issue 63 (2009); episode 5–3, "Four Walls and a Roof" (October 26, 2014).
11. Staal (2004).

·6·

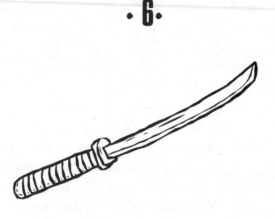

The Psychological Process and Cost of Killing in an Undead Wasteland

Colt J. Blunt

"He who fights with monsters should be careful lest he
thereby become a monster. And if thou gaze long into
an abyss, the abyss will also gaze into thee."
—philosopher Friedrich Nietzsche[1]

Many people see the possibility of a civilization–crippling zombie apocalypse as the perfect opportunity to become the ultimate badass. We all make ourselves out to be experts on tactics and strategies when an event has occurred in the past or is far removed from reality. Just listen to anyone discussing the previous evening's sportball match or the actions of a character in a Hollywood blockbuster. This form of armchair quarterbacking even extends to more serious topics; everyone can think of someone who claims to have the perfect plan for how he or she would have thwarted the most recent mass shooting, bank robbery, or attack on national security. The zombie apocalypse is no different.

When one takes a thoroughly unscientific poll of Internet forums, water cooler talk, and friend and family ramblings, it seems that everybody has a zombie plan these days. These plans all have a common theme: People plan to do what it takes to survive. However, anyone who has been in a real crisis situation will tell you the same thing: What you do when the chips are down is often not what you planned. Killing is not easy, and even if you bring yourself to do it, it comes with a cost.

If the zombie apocalypse were a *Choose Your Own Adventure* book and the question on the first page was "Do you decide to be a pacifist or are you willing to kill to survive?" the result of the first option undoubtedly would be your death. Sure, you might stick to a moral code and refuse to kill survivors or kill only in self-defense, but sooner or later you would have to defend yourself, whether from survivors or from walkers, or die. Hershel Greene begins the story as a peaceful individual who refuses to kill walkers. However, he eventually comes to realize that he needs to do whatever is necessary to protect those he cares about. Those actions ultimately require a decision and exact a cost.

The Decision to Kill

Our bodies are designed to make decisions for us efficiently when we are faced with dire situations. Think of your brain as being similar to the computer in a modern car. Even though you may have read what to do when you start to skid, your car often takes the first actions automatically, modulating the brakes and transferring power to whichever wheels still have grip. Beyond that, our bodies enter a heightened state of arousal in anticipation of such an event.

Imagine what it's like to be someone, anyone other than characters we've seen in *The Walking Dead*, struggling to survive in a world of constant conflict and danger:

> *Davin crawls through the broken storefront window of the abandoned grocery store, careful not to make a sound. His reconnaissance suggests that this part of the city is safer than most, but walkers might be anywhere. His eyes slowly adjust to the low light provided by the afternoon sun, casting the rows of shelves in deep shadows. His heart starts to beat a bit faster and his muscles tense up, forming a near death grip on the trusty M9 he pilfered from the corpse of a soldier back in Atlanta. He's been on edge since he evaded the cannibals that took the rest of his crew. Hypersensitive to his surroundings, he seemingly cues in on every creak, every shifting shadow, as if any one of them might be a potential threat. If it were just him, he might take his chances in the country, living off the land. But now he has Belinda to look after, and soon there'll be a baby. His eyes dilate, letting in as much light as possible, as he takes another cautious step into the store.*

With few exceptions, humans enter a "fight-or-flight" state when experiencing situations that require immediate action: We are programmed to either confront a threat or flee from it. Our bodies typically begin to move before rational thought even enters the picture.

> *CRASH! A pile of cans to Davin's right topples over. His heart kicks into overdrive. Davin feels blood pump to his arms and legs, preparing him to make a quick retreat or fight*

off an assailant. His vision narrows as he focuses on the origin of the sound. Unknown to him, many of his bodily functions grind to a halt, whereas other processes kick in, preparing to deal with conflict and injury. Shakily, Davin raises his Beretta toward the potential threat.

Glenn undertakes similar missions during the initial days of *The Walking Dead* and faces similar perils. Confronted with an immediate and close threat, he might lash out defensively, whereas a more distant threat might lead him to flee back through the entrance to the adjoining street.

A walker shambles out from behind a display of toppled cans of corn. Its name was Ashley, at least according to the badge on its chest. Davin's finger twitches on the trigger, but his legs take him back toward the window. Ungracefully, he dives through the window into the afternoon light.

Dave Grossman, a retired lieutenant colonel from the U.S. Army and a former professor of psychology at the United States Military Academy at West Point, has studied the subject of killing, which he has termed "killology," extensively.[2] Grossman concluded that the concept of fight or flight is overly simplistic and not representative of the full range of options available to individuals facing members of their own species. Rather, humans encountering other armed humans are wired to fight, flee, posture, or submit. Grossman suggests that the major decision made by a combatant in an intraspecies conflict is whether to flee or posture; that is, should he run away or intimidate the other party to flee or submit? In *The Walking Dead*, we typically see the main protagonist, Rick Grimes, Colt Python in hand, staring down a new potential adversary, hoping to end a confrontation without firing a shot. Conversely, we also see the survivors flee and ultimately submit in the face of an overwhelming adversary upon entering Terminus.

> *Davin rises to one knee, realizing he is not alone on the street. Another survivor stands mere feet from him, rifle pointing at his head. Davin raises his pistol, squaring off against this new foe. The man's rifle is shaking, and he seems as uneasy as Davin.*
>
> *"Back off. No one needs to get hurt!" Davin yells, hoping to avoid conflict.*

Humans do not like to kill other humans and usually will do whatever is necessary to avoid it. Even soldiers have had difficulty doing this throughout history. Military historians hypothesize that the majority of American soldiers did not fire at their enemies in combat situations until the Korean War, when fire rates reached approximately 55 percent. Based on an analysis of evidence[3] collected from the Battle of Gettysburg, the bloodiest battle of the American Civil War, as well as known information regarding the effectiveness of the weapons and tactics used at the time, Grossman concluded that a large proportion of soldiers in the battle did not fire at enemy soldiers and may have even pantomimed firing. Grossman concluded that a number of soldiers also elected to serve in support roles, such as providing aid and supplies to other soldiers, suggesting that the killing that did occur was done by a relative minority of the soldiers.

Why have fire rates increased throughout armed conflicts, and why have some people shown themselves to be better at killing than others? First of all, some people are better at emotionally divorcing themselves from the act of killing or, for lack of a better term, are simply psychopathic like the Governor or Negan. Beyond simply being wired to kill, training and programming play important roles in making the decision to kill. This is different

Ready, Aim . . .

Most people know of war as it is portrayed in movies and on television, often with individual soldiers serving as one-man armies, dispatching hordes of enemy combatants. However, historical data suggest that soldiers in combat situations often declined to fire their weapons. The data suggest that somewhere between 15 and 20 percent of American soldiers fired their weapons at enemies during World War II. Fire rates increased with new methods of training and conditioning, reaching approximately 55 percent during the Korean War and between 90 and 95 percent during the Vietnam War.

from simply drilling or practicing. Many people spend time at the gun range or practicing martial arts, but few actually will take a life when faced with a conflict situation.

The military has put significant resources into developing ways to make soldiers more effective at emotionally distancing themselves from the act of killing. Common advice dictates that hostages should make themselves appear more human, showing a complete picture to their captor rather than just nameless faces. Theoretically, doing so will make it harder for a captor to kill a hostage. Combat training can be seen as largely the opposite. Rather than killing another human—a person who might have a family, friends, hobbies, and a life outside of war—an effective combatant eliminates a threat. Unlike a firearms enthusiast who spends time shooting at stationary targets, a soldier trains in full gear in a setting that resembles the battlefield; targets are in motion and appear only intermittently. Thus, a trained combatant is rewarded for reacting quickly in selecting and engaging a target. Furthermore, the training received by effective soldiers combines psychological conditioning, both classical and operant in nature, to make the acts of combat second nature. These differences (above and beyond the "To Serve and Protect" motto of law enforcement) explain why Rick Grimes is typically more hesitant to fire on a new potential threat than is Abraham Ford, a trained soldier. Although both are obviously experienced with firearms and conflict, Abraham's training allows him to act more instinctively in threat situations.

The point is that if you think killing will be easy even when you are facing a life-or-death situation, you are probably wrong. Chances are, you lack the conditioning to easily take the life of another human being. Many of you would hesitate. The luckiest of you will face an opponent who is equally averse to killing. Given enough time, a minority will learn to kill, though a greater proportion probably will die or realize that their role is to support those who possess the necessary killer instinct.

> *"Ronnie says no one enters his realm and lives," the young survivor shakily proclaims.*
>
> *Davin notices the kid's finger tightening ever so slightly on the trigger of that old rifle. Everything drowns out around him as he squeezes the trigger of his Beretta, putting a neat hole in the forehead of the only person aside from Belinda he's seen in months. Davin begins to shake even more uncontrollably, dropping to both knees. He begins to sob.*

What about walkers? Should they not be easier to kill? By nature, they would seem to be already dehumanized, mere nameless hunks of rotting flesh with a singular desire to consume the flesh of the living. You might argue that killing a walker would be no different from defending against a hungry wolf. If only it were that easy. Imagine the nature of that hungry wolf but substitute its appearance with that of a five-year-old girl. Or your neighbor. Or your significant other. Can you honestly say you would not hesitate to pull the trigger then? A walker represents one of the most difficult adversaries imaginable as it can be humanized easily. Father Gabriel struggles to defend himself against walkers he knew in life. Even the otherwise bloodthirsty Governor has a soft spot for his daughter, keeping her around after she becomes a walker and defending her by any means necessary. Unless you are able to work past your attachment to the ways of old and divorce yourself from the emotional burden of having to slay those who once lived, you are destined to join the ranks of the undead. The survivors in *The Walking Dead* have shown themselves to be adept at killing walkers, even doing so nonchalantly at times. However, it would be ignorant to suggest that this comes without a cost.

The Cost of Killing

You did it. You managed to overcome human nature. Through training or sheer will to survive, you pulled the trigger, thrust the spear, or swung that really sweet rock attached to a rope you rigged up, but at what cost?

It may come as a surprise to some people, but research consistently identifies having to take a life as the most traumatic experience for law enforcement personnel.[4] Perhaps even more surprisingly, it ranks as more traumatic than having to witness another officer killed in the line of duty. Grossman suggests that the act of killing is the pinnacle of trauma for soldiers. If those best programmed and equipped still see killing as the most stressful experience imaginable, the average survivor is certainly not immune.

Trauma from such situations sometimes presents in the form of posttraumatic stress disorder. PTSD involves reexperiencing traumatic events, avoidance of similar situations, psychological distress when involved in analogous situations, hypervigilance, changes in behavior, and feeling detached from reality. PTSD also is associated with developing other psychological problems, including depression, substance use, psychosis, and suicide. Despite psychologists' best efforts, no one has developed an effective method of inoculation against PTSD. The most researched form of inoculation, *critical incident debriefing* (the immediate discussion and processing of a stressful situation), does not appear to prevent the onset of PTSD or other stress reactions and may even produce worse outcomes.[5] PTSD is pervasive among individuals returning from combat situations and is a likely result for many individuals who take lives in a zombie apocalypse. Indeed, research has shown that the act of killing significantly increases the likelihood of developing PTSD among soldiers.[6]

Trauma symptoms could play out in a number of ways for survivors of the zombie apocalypse. Survivors who killed other survivors might blame themselves and ruminate on ways they might have avoided killing; those who killed walkers who were family members, friends, or acquaintances might tell themselves they should have restrained the undead until they found a cure. Undoubtedly, survivors would become hypersensitive to their surroundings and jump at any noise that might resemble a potential threat with which they previously had to deal. Perhaps most prevalent would be feelings of sadness, loss, hopelessness, and regret, especially since the events of killing undoubtedly would play out in the survivors' minds repeatedly. Grossman additionally describes a correlation between the range of killing and the severity of the trauma, with individuals in control of long-range weapons such as intercontinental ballistic missiles (ICBMs) experiencing the least amount of trauma, individuals killing at firearm range experiencing more trauma, and those killing at intimate ranges, such as with knives or their bare hands, experiencing the most. Tyreese's experience outside the cabin,[7] where he kills multiple walkers with his bare hands, surely takes a significant psychological toll. In the world of *The Walking Dead*, most killing takes place with firearms, melee weapons, and hand-to-hand combat; thus, it is unlikely that anyone killing to survive could avoid significant trauma.

Symptoms of PTSD and its correlates are not difficult to spot among the characters of *The Walking Dead*. The Morgan Jones of the television series, once a loving father and husband, has to kill his reanimated wife after she bites their son, Duane. When the survivors next meet him, Morgan is a changed man who is (1) detached from reality, (2) hypervigilant against potential threats, and (3) seemingly incapable of positive emotion.[8] Even Michonne, the ultimate post-apocalyptic samurai, has been rendered seemingly incapable of forming emotional attachments with other survivors. Headstrong Rick is not immune from such effects either, becoming disconnected from reality and even swearing off violence for a time.

PTSD and its correlates are unlikely to abate on their own, especially in an environment where no one truly goes home and a respite from the horrors of the world is not an option. People experiencing PTSD often require years of therapy and even medication. It would be naive to believe there would be room in the world to develop a comprehensive system of mental health treatment after the turn. Even if some practitioners were still alive and did not have more pressing concerns (such as surviving), they would be few and far between. Additionally, one would assume that a much greater proportion of the population would be exposed to killing in the world of *The Walking Dead*, and thus PTSD would be much more prevalent. With limited access to treatment, survivors undoubtedly would be left to their own devices in dealing with the trauma resulting from their actions. Some would wallow in self-pity, becoming useless to society. Some would become increasingly paranoid, becoming reclusive. Some would resort to self-medication and, like Bob Stookey, a former military medic, rely on alcohol to numb their pain and help them sleep at night. The sad truth is that a number of survivors undoubtedly would take their own lives, unable to live with their actions. However, some simply would soldier on with a heavy psychological burden.

> *Davin sits on a stump, gripping his Beretta, alert to every cricket, owl, and bat piercing the silence of night. For the third night in a row, he contemplates turning the weapon on himself, hoping to finally be rid of the image of that young man and his scared look as he realized he was about to die. However, he realizes he could never do that to Belinda and their baby, so he quietly removes the bottle of Wild Turkey hidden at the bottom of his rucksack, hoping that another shot will still his nerves and quiet his mind.*

References

Grossman, D. (2014). *On killing: The psychological cost of learning to kill in war and society* (rev. ed.). New York, NY: Open Road Integrated Media.

MacNair, R. M. (2002). Perpetration-induced traumatic stress in combat veterans. *Peace and Conflict: Journal of Peace Psychology, 8,* 63–72.

Nietzsche, F. W. (1886/2014). *Beyond good and evil.* New York, NY: HarperCollins.

Roberts, N. P., Kitchiner, N. J., Kenardy, J., & Bisson, J. I. (2009). Multiple session early psychological interventions for the prevention of post-traumatic stress disorder. *Cochrane Library, 3,* 1–44.

Violanti, J. M., & Aron, F. (1994). Ranking police stressors. *Psychological Reports, 75,* 824–826.

Notes

1. Nietzsche (1886/2014).
2. Grossman (2014).
3. Military rifles at the time were muzzle loaders. One shot could be effectively loaded at a time, and the vast majority of the time would be necessarily spent reloading. However, of the 27,574 rifles recovered, nearly 90 percent were loaded. Half the loaded rifles had been loaded with 2 to 23 rounds.
4. Violanti & Aron (1994).
5. Roberts et al. (2009).
6. MacNair (2002).
7. Episode 5–1, "No Sanctuary" (October 12, 2014).
8. Episode 3–12, "Clear" (March 03, 2013).

Diversity and Strength in Zombie Apocalypse Atlanta

JOSUÉ CARDONA AND LARA TAYLOR

*"I'm the one black guy. You realize how
precarious that makes my situation?"*
—Theodore "T-Dog" Douglas[1]

When Rick Grimes gets shot on duty and falls into a coma, the population of Atlanta, Georgia, is 33 percent white,[2] meaning that the surrounding area has a majority of people of color. When Rick wakes up, the demographics have changed. The area is now majority . . . zombie.

Does that mean that race and culture have become irrelevant? Not at all. Although Rick and his group deal with issues that are almost never race-related, each member still has his or her cultural background, and most important, each audience member has a cultural identity and lives in a world where diversity remains relevant. The live-action series was not always known for how well it handled diversity, but it eventually became known for having one of the most diverse casts on television.[3] The comics introduced Tyreese as an equal to Rick very early on,[4] and Telltale Games' *The Walking Dead Season One* and *Season Two* video games star characters of color.

When people have fewer positive examples to look to in the media, their opinions of themselves (and their ethnic group) tend to be lower.[5] If the only depictions you see of people who look like you are of thugs, lowlifes, or cheats, you may think that it's all you'll ever be. Fortunately, every version of *The Walking Dead* seems to celebrate diversity by representing some of humanity's greatest strengths and virtues through its diverse cast, giving audiences relatable and positive characters of color.

The Good in the Bad

"What is it? The good that comes out of this bad?"
—Sasha[6]

Seeing anything positive in Robert Kirkman's zombie apocalypse might be difficult, but there is a branch of psychology that makes it simple. *Positive psychology* looks beyond the reckless behavior, poor judgment, and even symptoms of mental illness that Glenn, Michonne, or Tyreese may display and instead labels and categorizes the positive traits they and others have demonstrated. According to positive psychology, these strengths not only would help people survive this nightmare but in many cases would help them thrive (Table 1).

A testament to the diversity in *The Walking Dead* is the way so many of its minority characters exemplify the strengths and virtues of positive psychology throughout their journey.

Virtues	Strengths
Wisdom and knowledge	Creativity, curiosity, judgment, love of learning, perspective
Courage	Bravery, perseverance, honesty, zest
Humanity	Love, kindness, social intelligence
Justice	Teamwork, fairness, leadership
Temperance	Forgiveness, humility, prudence, self-regulation
Transcendence	Appreciation of beauty and excellence, gratitude, hope, humor, spirituality

Table 1. Positive Psychology's Character Strengths and Virtues[7]

Wisdom and Knowledge

The virtue of wisdom and knowledge consists of cognitive strengths that involve acquiring and using knowledge. These strengths are invaluable when the world changes because you have to adapt quickly. Interestingly, the use of these strengths also reduces stress.[8]

Glenn, a former pizza delivery guy, is his group's go-to person for supply runs. He seems to enjoy his role in this new world, demonstrating the strength called love of learning as he applies what he knows about getting around efficiently and expands those skills to help him get in and out of Atlanta safely. Enjoying his drive out of Atlanta in a red sports car,[9] theft alarm blaring, shows his strength of curiosity.

There may be no better example of creativity than Michonne's use of walkers as "pets" and deterrents.[10] She displays love of learning by developing fencing skills and wielding a katana.[11]

Lee Everett, the protagonist of The Walking Dead Season One game, demonstrates the clearest examples of judgment. Not only is he the narrative's central character, the player controls Lee's decisions when presented with possible courses of action. Lee displays use of perspective in his unexpected role as Clementine's

Let's Look on the Bright Side: An Introduction to Positive Psychology

The Walking Dead's protagonists do some "bad" things in order to survive, but it's the good or positive things they do every day that help them live and not just survive.

Positive psychology is the study of what people do correctly in life, not what they do wrong or which mental illness they have. Peterson and Seligman propose that emotional, psychological, and social well-being, when coupled with a person's degree of mental illness, paint a complete picture of mental health functioning that determines how a person is doing.[12]

Positive psychology is as concerned with building on the positive things in life as it is with reducing the negatives, and so its founders created a classification system for strengths and virtues in response to the American Psychiatric Association's *Diagnostic and Statistical Manual of Mental Disorders* (DSM-5), which addresses only what is "wrong" with people. Positive psychology's classification system (Table 1) allows mental health professionals to assess positive traits that can be built on to increase well-being and work toward not just living a life free of illness but living one that flourishes.

caretaker as he finds himself having to explain the world repeatedly to an orphaned eight-year-old.

Courage

Strengths in courage involve overcoming obstacles. When Lee and Clementine's group comes across a recently abandoned car, Clementine shows bravery when she speaks up to express her concern over taking someone else's property despite being the youngest person in the group.[13] Lee shows perseverance when, despite having been scratched by a walker, he stays committed to protecting Clementine until the infection takes over and he is about to die.[14]

The TV version of Tyreese stands out for displaying honesty in the form of incredible integrity even when confronting strong characters such as Carol, Rick, and the Governor.

Humanity

The strengths that fall under the virtue of humanity all concern relationships. Although people have spent centuries trying to identify what love is, positive psychology defines it as a strength related to the way a person values other people and relationships with them. Fans see strong romantic relationships between Glenn and Maggie, Sasha and Bob, Tyreese and Karen, and others throughout the show, along with other forms of positive relationships. Tyreese and Rick become best friends in the comics, Michonne and Carl share a special bond on the show, and Clementine sees Lee as a caretaker, friend, and mentor in the game.

Justice

Justice makes a healthy community life possible. It is clearly represented in teamwork, something essential to the characters' survival. Loyalty in turn fosters teamwork. Michonne repeatedly shows loyalty to Andrea as her friend and later to Rick as a friend and leader.

Temperance

Self-control would be an excellent synonym for the virtue of temperance, as it pertains to strengths that can help a person avoid getting into trouble. Tyreese is very much the poster child for temperance on the show when he demonstrates what forgiveness looks like by genuinely forgiving Carol for killing Karen. He shows self-regulation by not acting on his initial anger toward Carol[15] and later by sparing a resident of Terminus.[16]

Transcendence

Transcendence strengths, although the most abstract, help provide meaning to everything people see and do. Bob and Glenn do great jobs of exercising their appreciation of beauty and excellence, gratitude, and humor in a way that is often contagious. Bob exemplifies hope when he challenges a hopeless Rick to be more optimistic.[17] In the comic book, the strength of spirituality can be seen when Gabriel seemingly finds his purpose and therefore some comfort when he reaches a town with a chapel and no priest.[18]

Seeing Ourselves in Post-Apocalyptic Atlanta

> *You look around, we all see you hurting.*
> *We all know why, and we've all been there.*
> —Brianna, Hilltop Colony survivor[19]

The strengths and virtues of positive psychology are universal and evident across multiple cultures around the world[20] and so it is possible that a large part of the audience may relate to them, but why else do fans relate so strongly to these characters?

One of the great things about being a fan of fiction, regardless of format, is the ability to become fully immersed in the story and ignore the surrounding world for an hour or two at a time. Horror fans often imagine what kind of strategy they'd use against a zombie horde, whether going it alone as Michonne tries to do or creating strength in numbers. In Tyreese's shoes, would you forgive Carol for killing Karen?[21] Regardless of your answer, the ability to look at a character's situation and make connections to your own is part of the process of *identification*,[22] the ability of an individual to apply the behaviors, feelings, and characteristics of another individual to his or her own identity.[23] Characters fans identify with can also be seen as extensions of themselves. In this way, people can safely explore difficult emotions (grief) or frightening events (a lumbering walker horde) from a safe distance (their couches). Fans can then use favorite characters' experiences to learn how to behave or feel in particular situations. Although the average person will not land in rural Georgia during a zombie apocalypse, it is likely that he or she will lose a loved one at some point. When this happens, he or she might be able to relate to Sasha's difficulties after losing Bob or Morgan mourning the loss of his son.

Identification Phases

How do people decide which characters they love? Why are some of our favorite characters the ones who make horrible decisions? Why do fans forgive them even after the bad choices they make? There is a three-part process to explain how viewers go from watching Bob's struggle with alcoholism lead to dangerous situations for the group[24] to falling in love with his positivity and optimism. Each of the three phases of encoding, comparison, and response has its own factors that lead to possible identification with or dislike of the character.[25]

Encoding

In the *encoding phase*, the viewer/reader/player takes in all the information about a character and files it away for later use during the comparison phase. One important piece of information to be gathered about any character is *ethical orientation*: how that character approaches moral dilemmas in his or her world. *The Walking Dead* universe has no shortage of these moral dilemmas, which provide fans with multitudes of information to encode. Another factor that goes into encoding is aesthetics. As shallow as it may seem, human beings tend to like characters who are physically attractive or appealing. This is part of why fans like the survivors more than the zombies. How realistic a character seems is the last piece of information people encode during this phase. Characters who make choices with what viewers know about them and characters who appear realistic are more relatable. However, characters with a balance of realistic and unrealistic traits tend to be the most relatable, as they allow room for imagination, exploration, and comparison to oneself.

Comparison

After taking in all this information (which may seem like a lot, but this is all done subconsciously), the next step is comparing it to what the individual knows about himself or herself (*comparison phase*). A perceived similarity can be a powerful determining factor in relating to a character, whether it be a character strength, a moral belief, a shared background, or a shared experience such as losing a loved one. Humans feel safer and right in decisions when they know that another person agrees with them or would make the same decision. Fictional characters give people another way to explore their reactions to difficult situations and feel that they aren't alone. Fans of Telltale's game series may find the comparison stage easier because the player ultimately makes the decisions for Lee and Clementine.

Often the terms *sympathy*, *empathy*, and *identification* get confused and interchanged by the average person or professional to describe a sense of caring for another individual. *Sympathy* is simply acknowledging another person's feelings and showing compassion; *empathy* is an understanding of what someone else is feeling because of a similar experience or imagining being in that person's shoes; and *identification* makes the individual's feelings and features parallel the character. Table 2 shows some examples of each of the three in response to Tyreese's violent reaction to his girlfriend, Karen, being killed.

Sympathy	Empathy	Identification
"I felt sorry for Tyreese when Karen died. He must be devastated."	"Poor Tyreese. I know what he's going through. My wife was killed by a drunk driver a few years ago, and it changed me."	"Tyreese is right to want revenge. If someone killed my girlfriend, I'd snap too!"

Table 2. Tyreese's response example

Response

The *response phase* involves how an individual puts the information together from the encoding and comparison phases and decides to react to the character. Here, viewers decide whether they like or hate the character or neither. Having an abundance of good features may make a character seem fake or one-dimensional, which can push a fan away. Even the characters highlighted earlier have their flaws, such as Sasha's stubbornness and Bob's alcoholism. Their flaws make them real. A character's realness and moral values can outweigh a major failing if that is where the fan's priorities lie. If, shortly after finding Karen's body, Tyreese simply calmed down when Rick asked him to, he would seem unrealistic because simply telling someone to calm down rarely works. Morals, aesthetics, believability, and similarity all make up the way an individual sees a character, and so each individual's response to each character will be different.

Diversity and Strength

"I can live with potential. Potential has promise.
I can work with potential."
—Ezekiel, leader of The Kingdom[26]

When an adolescent African-American girl watching *The Walking Dead* sees Michonne protect herself by killing zombies and then bond with a boy who recently lost his mother, she can imagine herself doing the same things. A boy who sees a strong man like Tyreese also sees that it's all right to be nonviolent and try to solve problems peacefully. Through the lens of positive psychology, positive traits are more identifiable and easier to discuss.

When people who look like themselves are on our screens, in our comics, and in our books, audience members can more easily compare themselves to the characters. Similar appearance and experiences increase identification with characters, and that makes it easier to explore our feelings about the experiences those characters have. The same research that showed that poor media representation can cause lowered self and in-group opinions also showed that the portrayals of minority groups can have an influence on the way outsiders view a group.[27] If people see Asian men in television shows that depict them as weak and passive, more viewers will start to believe that all Asian men are like that. A viewer who instead watches Glenn's strength, resolve, and love of his wife may more readily notice those traits in real Asian men, too.

By exhibiting various strengths and virtues, the many characters of color in *The Walking Dead* create for the audience an expanded range of possibilities of what a person of color can be and do. This portrayal addresses the potential in everyone to have positive qualities. If Michonne and Glenn can use those strengths to get through a zombie apocalypse, maybe we can use them to overcome our own challenges.

References

Avey, J. B., Luthans, F., Hannah, S. T., Sweetman, D., & Peterson, C. (2012). Impact of employees' character strengths of wisdom on stress and creative performance. *Human Resource Management Journal, 22*(2), 165–181.

Compton, W., & Hoffman, E. (2012). *Positive psychology: The science of human flourishing* (2nd ed.). Belmont, CA: Wadsworth/Cengage.

Dahlsgaard, K., Peterson, C., & Seligman, M. E. P. (2005). Shared virtue: The convergence of valued human strengths across culture and history. *Review of General Psychology, 9*(3), 203–213.

Deggans, E. (2014, November 28). *Diversity on 'The Walking Dead' wasn't always handled well.* http://www.npr.org/2014/11/28/366655295/diversity-on-the-walking-dead-wasnt-always-handled-well.

Hoorn, J. F., & Konijn, E. A. (2003). Perceiving and experiencing fictional characters: An integrative account . *Japanese Psychological Research, 45*(4), 250–268.

Infoplease. (2007, January 12). *QuickFacts from the US Census Bureau: Atlanta, GA.* http://www.infoplease.com/us/census/data/georgia/atlanta/.

Keyes, C. L. M., & Lopez, S. J. (2002). Toward a science of mental health: Positive directions in diagnosis and interventions. In C. R. Synder & S. J. Lopez (Eds.), *Handbook of positive psychology* (pp. 45–49). London, UK: Oxford University Press.

Krause, R. (2010). An update on primary identification, introjection, and empathy. *International Forum on Psychoanalysis, 19*, 138–143.

Mok, T. A., & Driscoll, D. (1998). Getting the message: Media images and stereotypes and their effect on Asian Americans. *Cultural Diversity and Mental Health, 4*(3), 185–202.

Peterson, C., & Seligman, M. E. P. (2004). *Character strengths and virtues: A handbook and classification.* Washington, DC: American Psychological Association.

Schrier, H. (1953). The significance of identification in therapy. *American Journal of Orthopsychiatry, 23*(3), 585–604.

Seligman, M. E. P. (2002). *Authentic happiness.* New York, NY: Free Press.

Ward, L. M. (2004). Wading through the stereotypes: Positive and negative associations between media use and black adolescents' conceptions of self. *Developmental Psychology, 40*(2), 284–294.

Notes

1. Episode 2–2, "Bloodletting" (October 23, 2011).
2. Infoplease (2007).
3. Deggans (2014).
4. Issue 7, (2004).
5. Mok & Driscoll (1998); Ward (2004).
6. Episode 5–3, "Four Walls and a Roof" (October 26, 2014).
7. Peterson & Seligman (2004).
8. Avey et al. (2012).
9. Episode 1–3, "Tell It to the Frogs" (November 7, 2010).
10. Issue 19 (2005).
11. The Walking Dead Michonne special (2012).
12. Peterson & Seligman (2004).
13. *The Walking Dead: Season One* (2012 game), episode 2.
14. *The Walking Dead: Season One* (2012 game), episode 5.
15. Episode 4–14, "The Grove" (March 16, 2014).
16. Episode 5–1, "No Sanctuary" (October 12, 2014).
17. Episode 5–2, "Strangers" (October 19, 2014).
18. Issue 74 (2010).
19. Issue 109 (2013).
20. Dahlsgaard et al. (2005).
21. Episode 4–14, "The Grove" (March 16, 2014).
22. Krause (2010).
23. Schrier (1953).
24. Episode 4–1, "30 Days without an Accident" (October 13, 2013).
25. Hoorn & Konjin (2003).
26. Issue 115 (2013).
27. Mok & Driscoll (1998).

· 8 ·

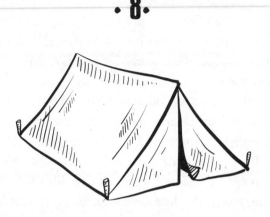

Who Needs an Untrustworthy Doctor? Maslow's Hierarchy of Needs

JENNIFER GOLBECK

*"Is that all you want to be? Wake up in the morning,
fight the undead pricks, forage for food, go to sleep at
night with two eyes open, rinse and repeat?"*
—Abraham Ford[1]

*"The study of crippled, stunted, immature, and unhealthy specimens
can yield only a cripple psychology and a cripple philosophy."*
—psychologist Abraham Maslow[2]

The pilot episode of AMC's *The Walking Dead*,[3] like the first issue of the comic book series on which it is based,[4] is practically an introduction to Abraham Maslow's *hierarchy of needs*, a psychological theory that lays out the levels of human motivation. Let's follow Rick through that first story.

Rick is a police officer. After being shot in a world free of zombies and falling into a coma, he wakes up alone in a hospital. Little does he know that he has awakened to a new world. Exiting the hospital, Rick works his way home in search of his family, Lori and Carl.

Later, Rick meets a few other survivors of the zombie disaster, Morgan and his son Duane, and together they take refuge from the flesh-eating monsters wandering the streets. After a brief recovery, Rick takes time to shower, shave, and dress himself in uniform before heading to Atlanta. As his final act in King County, he returns to a half woman he had seen crawling in the grass. He says, "I'm sorry this happened to you," and kills the zombie. With all these actions, Rick is reclaiming and reinforcing his sense of self and self-respect.

That brings us back to Maslow's hierarchy of needs.

What Is Maslow's Hierarchy of Needs?

Abraham Maslow proposed that a hierarchy (an arrangement of priorities from most to least) of psychological needs drives people. This often is represented as a pyramid (Figure 1), with the most basic needs on the bottom.[5]

Level 1: Physiological

The most fundamental needs are the physiological: food, water, air, and shelter from the elements. Without these, it can be impossible to focus on anything else. After all, if you can't breathe, it's not worth worrying about art or ethics.

Rick addresses this need as soon as he wakes from his coma, when he drinks water. Meeting these basic needs is a dominant theme in *The Walking Dead*; hunting and collecting supplies are

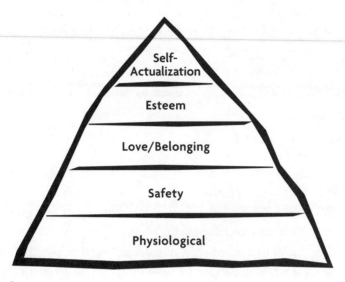

Figure 1.

common activities that appear in most episodes. At one point, when traveling the road after losing the shelter of the prison, Rick comments to Michonne, "Have you noticed? It's all we talk about anymore. Food."[6]

Level 2: Safety

Once physiological needs are met, the next level up on the pyramid is safety. This includes physical safety as well as law and order and freedom from fear.

Zombies really do a number on this level. Although zombies themselves do not seriously threaten our air, food, or water supplies, they completely destroy every aspect of safety on which society has come to rely. In addition to being dangerous in and of themselves, zombies (perhaps more insidiously) wipe out the foundations of civil society. Governments fall, law enforcement disappears, and people start acting without regard for the rules of society.

Indeed, whereas the zombies ("walkers") are a constant threat faced by everyone on *The Walking Dead*, the less predictable and often more terrifying threats come from other living humans. Whether it's marauding gangs, the Governor, or the "society" at Terminus, people pose a major threat to the safety of other survivors.

Level 3: Love and Belonging

If people feel relatively safe physically, they can move on to the next level in the hierarchy: love and belonging (a.k.a. *belongingness*). This is happiness that comes from being part of a group or family and from romantic relationships.

The manifestation of this is particularly interesting in *The Walking Dead*. Groups that form—Rick's group in particular—have close bonds among the members. They are familylike and Rick even says, "These people are my family,"[7] but we can't say the group is the same as a family. It is also there to help ensure everyone's safety and survival. In fact, there are many times when certain members put themselves at risk for the sake of others in the group.

Interestingly, the flourishing of love—both within families and within the group—comes at times when the people are safest. Lori and Shane become lovers in their relatively safe camp during the time leading up to the beginning of Rick's story. Glenn and Maggie's relationship develops in the safety of her family's farm. When the prison is at its safest, we see the group develop stronger personal bonds and friendships. Even doomed romances form in relative safety, such as the one between Andrea and the Governor in Woodbury.

Level 4: Esteem

When people have bonds of love and respect, they can work toward the fourth level of Maslow's hierarchy: esteem. These needs include self-esteem, self-worth, and dignity. We catch glimpses of esteem throughout *The Walking Dead,* but more often we see the characters struggling with it.

After the zombie apocalypse, people who had been safe, loved, and fulfilled were thrust into a world where all the base levels of Maslow's hierarchy disappeared overnight. They instantly had to shift their focus from esteem (or the more advanced need for self-actualization) to the lower levels. Often, this means they feel they have to sacrifice elements of esteem—what they probably considered the critical parts of their humanity—in order to survive.

Even when all the lower needs in the hierarchy are met, issues of esteem appear. Some are kind, such as Hershel giving Glenn his pocket watch. The act not only shows that Hershel accepts (and maybe even loves) Glenn but is a way for Hershel to reinforce his image of himself.

Others pursue esteem through power and abuse, such as the Governor in Woodbury. He's charming and seems to rule the town in a perfectly reasonable manner, at least on the surface. But when others cross him, they are ruthlessly punished. He sends Merle with orders to track down and kill Michonne after "allowing" her to leave Woodbury. He tortures Glenn and Maggie. He locks Andrea in a room to be killed by Milton once he dies and turns. The power wielded by the Governor feeds his narcissism, which in turn allows him to justify his abuse of anyone who threatens his standing.[8]

Level 5: Self-Actualization

Sadly, the peak of Maslow's hierarchy, self-actualization, does not really exist in the world of *The Walking Dead.* When people reach this level, they are working to live up to their fullest potential. People on this level seek out moments of intense joy, wonder,

Up the Pyramid

"We should be out looking for food, shelter," Sasha says, worried about the hierarchy's bottom levels (physiological, safety) while Maggie unrelentingly searches for husband, Glenn (love/belongingness). Bob, by this time, pursues growth higher up the pyramid (self-esteem, self-actualization).[9] Bob encourages Sasha, "Self-awareness is a beautiful thing. You should try it sometime."[10]

—T. L.

and happiness. They work to create art or solve problems larger than those of everyday life. They spend time reflecting.

In the post-apocalyptic world, the rest of the demands simply take up too much time and attention for the characters to devote themselves to being fully-realized human beings. This point is driven home when Beth finds herself in the hospital in Atlanta.[11] Her conversation with Dr. Steven Edwards turns to a Caravaggio painting that hangs in his office:

> Dr. Edwards: "It doesn't have a place anymore. Art isn't
>   about survival. It's about transcendence, being more
>   than animals. Rising above."
> Beth: "We can't do that anymore?"
> Dr. Edwards: "I don't know."
> Beth: "I sing. I still sing."

What Does It Mean for the Zombie Apocalypse?

The characters in *The Walking Dead* focus most of their energy on the safety level of Maslow's hierarchy. Although there are periods when safety is largely taken care of, such moments are the exception, not the rule.

The walkers' threat to safety is obvious, but the most interesting and challenging threats come from other people.

- Who should the characters trust?
- Who should they help?
- Who should they accept help from?
- Who should they bring into their group?

It's a fun party discussion to think about who to include in your zombie apocalypse survival group. A lot of times, such discussions turn to people's skills: "Do you bring along a doctor, some former marines, and a master gardener?"

Based on Maslow's hierarchy, skills may reasonably become a secondary consideration. Granted, safety improves when your group includes both a physician to tend wounds and a ready marksman to defend you. But what if that doctor goes on drunken rages in which he assaults group members? What if that rifle master considers herself superior to the rest of the group and steals food and supplies that everyone else needs?

The Walking Dead shows time and time again how important it is to surround oneself with the right people.

Case 1: The Woodbury Massacre

There is so much to say about Woodbury. Because it seems to be a place of relative safety and normality, its citizens pursue the happiness in many higher levels of Maslow's hierarchy. . . for a time.

Woodbury functions for a long time in large part because of the Governor's authoritarian rule. Its citizens have placed their trust in him, and that leads to their safety for a while. He does not deserve that trust. Many of the punishments and tortures in Woodbury hint at this, though the citizens seem to go along with it. But their misplaced trust will come back to haunt them.

When the Governor musters an army from Woodbury to attack the prison, the assault fails. The Woodbury survivors retreat. Enraged at the defeat, he insists that they return to finish the attack. When the citizens refuse, the Governor's true narcissism and irrationality are revealed when his rage boils over and he executes the entire group[12] (on television as opposed to in the comic book, in which one of them executes him[13]).

Placing trust in someone solely on the basis of his strong skills may ultimately be a bad decision in terms of safety.

Case 2: The Untrustworthy Doctor

Pete Anderson is a physician living in the Alexandria Safe-Zone. He is well respected for his skills and his role in the community. However, from their first meeting, Rick suspects him of being a violent man who beats his family.

As Rick and his group get to know Pete, they see signs of his domineering cruelty. His wife is submissive. His son, Ron, appears with a black eye. Ron even says to Carl, "Why's your dad get to be good but my daddy is bad?"[14] As Pete's violent tendencies become obvious, Rick argues to Alexandria's leader, Douglas (Deanna on TV), that Pete should be exiled. Douglas demurs, emphasizing Pete's value to the community as a doctor. It is an example of how much emphasis we can put on people's skills as we ignore the way they undermine the safety of the group.

After Pete brawls with Rick and is separated from his wife and son, Rick tells him, "You have a wife and son who are safe—and aren't living in fear."[15] In this comment, Rick emphasizes that Pete has been destroying the safety level of Maslow's hierarchy for his family.

Pete eventually cracks in response to what happened to him and becomes determined to kill Rick for ruining his life. In the altercation that follows, Pete kills another Alexandria resident. When Douglas sees that regardless of his skills, Pete is a true threat to the safety of the entire community, he agrees that he cannot remain. Rick shoots Pete dead with Douglas's permission.

Case 3: Lizzie Samuels

Lizzie and Mika are sisters in the TV series who come to the prison with their father, Ryan. They are parallel characters to brothers Ben and Billy in the comics, with Lizzie following much of Ben's original story. The stories of Ben and then Lizzie illustrate how the safety level of Maslow's hierarchy can be threatened by having untrustworthy people in the group—even children.

After a walker bite kills Lizzie and Mika's father, Carol assumes a parental role for the two girls. Throughout her time in the prison, Lizzie displays an unusual and unhealthy relationship with the walkers. She treats them very much as if they were still human, even giving them names at the prison fences.[16]

More problems with Lizzie emerge after the prison falls in the Governor's second attack. Led by Tyreese, Lizzie escapes with Mika and Rick's baby daughter, Judith. During one evening stop, Lizzie kills baby bunnies.[17]

Lizzie's antisocial actions become even more pronounced over time. When Tyreese leaves the children alone, Lizzie attempts to smother baby Judith. Though this begins as an act of protection—trying to keep her silent—Lizzie becomes hyperfocused on suffocating Judith before Carol interrupts her. This is the first real sign that Lizzie threatens the safety of others in the group.[18]

After Carol rejoins them, Lizzie shows more problems recognizing the walkers as dangerous. She plays tag with one, calling it her "friend." She loses the ability to perceive the distinction between walkers and living people. Eventually, she returns to a walker trapped in the railroad tracks that she passed earlier. She feeds the walker a mouse. When her sister Mika catches her,

A Personality Analysis of Two Leaders and a Follower

The "Big Five" personality factors are five facets of human personality, five sets of characteristics observed in people throughout the world, across cultures and generations.[19]

- **Openness:** A person who is willing to try new things, have new experiences, and consider new ideas is open.
- **Conscientiousness:** People who are organized, are attentive to deadlines, and work to meet or exceed others' expectations are strong on this trait.
- **Extraversion:** When you feel energized after spending time interacting with others, you are an extravert. Those who need time alone to reenergize are introverts.
- **Agreeableness:** Those who are kind, forgiving, and helpful and who promote social harmony score high on agreeableness. People who are argumentative or rude score low.
- **Neuroticism:** Emotional stability is the key to this personality trait. Angry, nervous people are strong neurotics. Laid-back, relaxed people are not.

Personality affects the way we interact with others, how we react to situations, and how we are personally fulfilled. In the extreme conditions of the zombie apocalypse, people's true personality traits are likely to shine through. That's the case both when the higher levels of Maslow's hierarchy are removed and people are fighting for food, water, and security and in times of relative safety when people focus on love, relationships, and esteem.

Using a standard 44-question Big Five test, we analyzed the personalities of three important characters from *The Walking Dead*: Rick, the Governor, and a walker.

Case 1: Rick

- **Openness:** Very low
- **Conscientiousness:** High
- **Extraversion:** Middle
- **Agreeableness:** Low-middle
- **Neuroticism:** High

Rick's openness score is low because he is down to earth and conservative in his choices. Circumstances force him into many new experiences, but he values stability. He is highly conscientious; he makes plans and works hard to carry them out effectively and efficiently. His agreeableness is low to medium. Because there is so much lawlessness in the post-apocalyptic world, Rick must engage in many conflicts. However, within his own group he is supportive and forgiving, and he tries to create peace.

The zombie apocalypse would make many people neurotic, and Rick is no exception. When the safety element of Maslow's hierarchy is missing, anxiety is a natural response to the nearly constant danger that people face.

Case 2: The Governor

- **Openness:** Middle
- **Conscientiousness:** Middle-high
- **Extraversion:** Very high
- **Agreeableness:** Low
- **Neuroticism:** Very high

Like Rick, the Governor has high neuroticism. He is full of anxiety, to the point of paranoia, though he tends to focus on threats to his power more than on threats to his life and well-being. He is a strong extravert yet scores very low on agreeableness. Although he wants to maintain a peaceful atmosphere in Woodbury, he will create conflict with others over the smallest perceived slight. His conscientious score is middle-high. He will carry out his plans to their completion, but he can also be distracted in the middle of them. His openness falls roughly in the middle of the scale. The Governor tends to run Woodbury conservatively, but he likes to experiment with new types of "entertainment" and "artistic" pursuits that reflect some openness.

Case 3: A Walker

- **Openness:** Very low
- **Conscientiousness:** Low
- **Extraversion:** Low-middle
- **Agreeableness:** Very, *very* low
- **Neuroticism:** Low

Walkers are single-minded. They're not interested in, say, trying a vegetarian diet for a week (openness). They do not make plans or care how others perceive them (conscientiousness) or try to promote social harmony (agreeableness). They aren't big talkers but are not especially shy or reserved either (extraversion). They don't worry about their success or failures. Although they may get worked up in the moment, their anxiety is low (neuroticism).

Lizzie tells her, "They just want me to change—to make me be like them," as she moves her hand toward the walker's mouth.

It takes a violent act before Carol and Tyreese see what they might do. After the two adults return from a walk, they find Lizzie holding a knife, covered in blood. She is standing in front of Mika's body. She insists that she didn't kill Mika, since she "didn't hurt her brain," and that she was just about to help baby Judith "change," too.

Tyreese learns that Lizzie had been feeding walkers at the prison and had mutilated a rat and nailed it to a board when they were there "just having fun." They both realize that she can't be trusted around other people. And since she cannot survive on her own because of her youth and her mental illness, they decide that she has to be killed. It is a heartbreaking event for Carol and Tyreese and one of the saddest moments in *The Walking Dead*.

Lizzie's story is based on the comic book account of Ben, who similarly kills his own brother, Billy, although it's another youngster, Carl, who then kills Ben even as Ben's adoptive father, Dale, argues against killing the killer child.[20] It is hard to recognize that a child can be a threat to the safety of a group. It is even harder to make the decision that the child must be removed from the group—one way or another—if everyone else is to remain safe.

The moment is shocking to us because we live in a world where any threats to our safety from a boy like Ben or a girl like Lizzie do not require such drastic and final measures. Maslow's hierarchy says we need safety, but we can protect ourselves from dangerous people in many ways. There are institutional checks on this behavior that probably would have detected it earlier. And there is support from medical professionals, mental health facilities, and even prisons.

With no safety protection available from anywhere else, the survivors on *The Walking Dead* have to protect themselves. It is the only way to preserve that level of Maslow's hierarchy. When their safety is threatened, as it truly is by Lizzie, they sometimes make hard and harsh decisions to keep people alive.

Critical Choices

Maslow's hierarchy of needs lays out the levels of human motivation, from basic physiological survival to self-actualization. The zombie apocalypse destroys the safety level that so many of us take for granted, not only because zombies roam the earth, bent on killing and eating any humans they encounter, but *also* because law enforcement, government, and other institutions that ensure safety have disappeared.

Consequently, it's other humans who pose the most complex and serious threat to one's safety. *The Walking Dead* is full of examples of this—from roving gangs that rape, assault, and kill others they find; to charismatic, violent, unstable leaders such as the Governor; to mentally ill, murderous children such as Lizzie.

Knowing who to trust with your safety is one of the most critical choices a survivor can make. If it's not the right decision, the consequences that follow—and the responses required—can be shocking and almost unbearable.

References

Maslow, A. (1943). A theory of human motivation. *Psychological Review, 50,* 370–396.
Maslow, A. (1954/1970). *Motivation and personality.* New York, NY: Harper.
Maslow, A. (1966). *The psychology of science: A reconnaissance.* New York, NY: Harper & Row.
McCrae, R. R., & Costa, P. T. (1987). Validation of the five-factor model of personality across instruments and observers. *Journal of Personality and Social Psychology, 52*(1), 81.

Notes

1. Episode 5–2, "Strangers" (October 19, 2014).
2. Maslow (1954/1970), p. 180.
3. Episode 1–1, "Days Gone Bye" (October 31, 2010).
4. Issue 1 (2003).
5. See also Maslow (1954; 1966).

6. Episode 4–16, "A" (March 30, 2014).

7. Episode 5–2, "Strangers" (October 19, 2014).

8. Season 3 (2012–2013).

9. Episode 4–10, "Inmates" (February 16, 2012).

10. Episode 4–13, "Alone" (March 9, 2014).

11. Episode 5–4, "Slabtown" (November 3, 2014).

12. Episode 4–8, "Too Far Gone" (December 1, 2013).

13. Issue 48 (2008).

14. Issue 80 (2011).

15. Issue 77 (2010).

16. Episode 4–1, "30 Day Without an Accident" (October 13, 2013).

17. Episode 4–10, "Inmates" (February 16, 2014).

18. Episode 4–14, "The Grove" (March 16, 2014).

19. McCrae & Costa (1987).

20. Issue 61 (2009).

Thomas Richards

Travis Langley

"Tax fraud—but it wasn't my fault!"
—Thomas Richards[1]

I n the barber shop at the prison where the survivors have taken shelter, someone beheads Hershel Greene's youngest daughters, Susie and Rachel. While Hershel, Rick, and others accuse some of the few remaining inmates, a different inmate—Thomas Richards, the self-proclaimed white-collar criminal who seems nerdy and oh so nice, beyond suspicion after having ingratiated himself by helping the women while they move into the otherwise vacant prison—finds Andrea in the laundry room and attempts to behead her. Andrea fights back. He chases her into the prison yard. There Rick beats him so hard and for so long that he mangles both the killer's face and his own hand. The incident scars Andrea's face, breaks Rick's hand beyond repair, and inspires a dictatorial attitude in Rick as he decides that they have to hang Richards. When one misguided survivor, Patricia, tries to free Richards, believing him to be "crazy, not evil," he attacks her too, and so the dead twins' older sister, Maggie, guns him down.[2]

Was Patricia right to assume he must be "crazy," needing help instead of a hanging? Some crimes are so monstrous that the average person assumes that their perpetrators must be mentally ill because no rational person could do such a thing. Many people

wonder how any jury could have looked at Jeffrey Dahmer—
who'd murdered, dismembered, and sometimes eaten 17 young
men and older boys—and found him sane. Dahmer knew what
he was doing, though. However bizarre his ideas, choices, and
actions might have been at times, he knew he was killing people
and knew it was wrong.[3]

Insanity is a legal term, not a psychiatric diagnosis, and its definition can vary from state to state and nation to nation, depending on how the relevant legal standards are worded. The most
common standard, the "right/wrong test," deems a defendant
insane only if, as a result of a mental disease or defect, the person
either didn't know what he or she was doing or didn't know it
was wrong.[4] When Thomas Richards attacks Andrea, he is not
trying to fight off some creature he has hallucinated; he know-
ingly tries to decapitate a living woman.

Richards appears to be a serial killer, although not even his
fellow inmates know the real reason for his incarceration. Had
he been arrested as a serial killer, they'd have heard. A police
officer's description at the start of *The Walking Dead: Season One*
video game indicates that he has been convicted for murdering and dismembering his own wife. Although Richard seems
accustomed to his role as beheader of young women, killing the
youngest girls first suggests that after months of confinement,
he is starting out small. He may be experimenting with decap-
itation to test the way the world now works, because an intact
brain means even a detached head can reanimate.

Tempting as it may be to throw together a profile of a typical serial beheader or any other serial killer, no one follows a
rule book when becoming a monster. There is no standard.[5]
Compared with other murderers, expressive beheaders are more
likely to kill relatives or engage in cannibalism or necrophilia,
although the majority do not. Compared with terrorists and
executioners, whose violence is more *instrumental* (with *extrinsic*

motivation, aimed serving an ulterior purpose), serial beheaders' violence is more expressive, *intrinsically* motivated: They kill for the way it makes them feel.

Thomas Richards meets every criterion for evil's dark tetrad: psychopathic in both personality and actions, dangerously self-centered, deceitfully manipulative, and sadistically cruel. Yes, sadistic. He leaves decapitated girls to reanimate just as Woodbury's Governor, the man who cuts off the hand that Rick ruined punching Richards, does with his own victims. Furthermore, if Richards simply wants to kill Andrea, he could slit her throat before she knows what's happening instead of flashing his knife and announcing what he plans to do. He toys with her until she escapes, and then his temper takes control. Insanity does not explain his actions because he is not insane. When he decides and prepares to kill, he realizes what he's doing. Subsequently losing control and recklessly running into the prison yard while shouting and wielding a knife does not change that.

References

Davidson, R. (2011, January 18). *Supervillains and the insanity defense.* Law and the Multiverse: http://lawandthemultiverse.com/2011/01/18/supervillains-and-the-insanity-defense/.

Nichols, D. S. (2006). Tell me a story: MMPI responses and personal biography in the case of a serial killer. *Journal of Personality Assessment, 86,* 242–262.

Ramsland, K. (2006). *Inside the minds of serial killers: Why they kill.* Santa Barbara, CA: Praeger.

Notes

1. Issue 13 (2004).
2. Issues 13–18 (2004–2005).
3. Nichols (2006).
4. Davidson (2011).
5. Ramsland (2006).

Life dies.

In an apocalypse, a world dies. A new age also begins, but very few of those who survive from the previous era welcome the reign of the dead.

The dead kill. The living kill. The elements kill. The world kills not only by ending physical life but by crushing the spirit. Buried beneath the rubble of grief, fatigue, stress, and far worse, what does it take to feel alive? What must a survivor do to keep humankind going and one's own humanity alive?

Don't open. Dead inside.

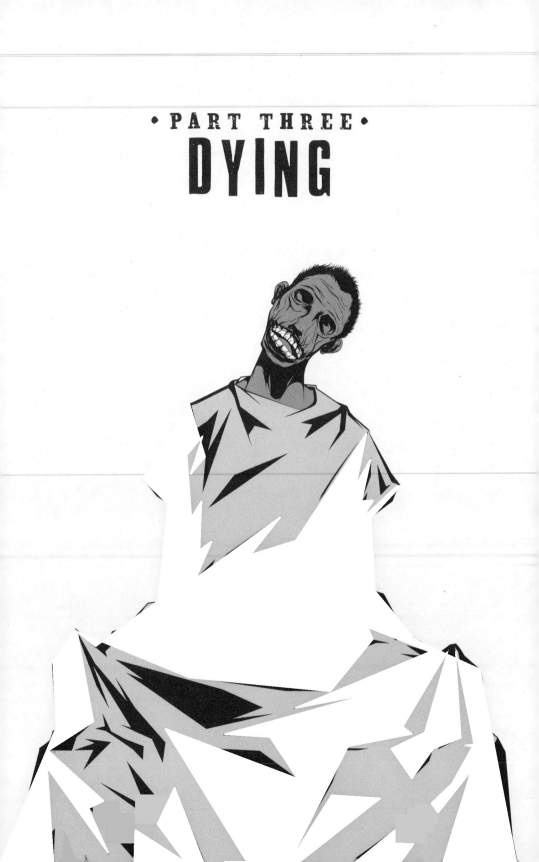

· 9 ·

Walker or Biter? Group Identity in a Grave New World

KATHERINE RAMSLAND

> **Rick Grimes:** We can all live together. There's enough room for all of us. . . . Now you put down your weapons, walk through those gates, you're one of us. We let go of all of it, and nobody dies. . . .
> **The Governor:** Kill 'em all.[1]

Group identity is a core component of *The Walking Dead*. Some groups welcome strangers, others shun them, and still others embrace them with evil intent. *The Walking Dead* provides a perfect forum for discussing the tenets of group behavior that psychologist Muzafer Sherif and his colleagues studied in 1954.[2] They designed a reality-based experiment to examine in-group identity in periods of conflict and periods of cooperation.

Parallels between their work and many of the situations depicted in *The Walking Dead* are so close, in fact, that the milieu itself could be framed as an experiment. What if protagonist Rick Grimes and his group discover that a researcher has placed them among flesh-eating creatures "for science"? With its extended conflicts and higher stakes, *The Walking Dead* builds on Sherif's discoveries but supports a less optimistic conclusion.

Rick understands the value of cooperation. Generally, he prefers to negotiate for a peaceful settlement, whether with a benign farmer such as Hershel Greene or with a tyrannical madman such as the Governor. By the time he leaves the prison encampment, though, Rick has learned that success comes only when the other party is willing to meet him halfway. The secret lies in two interacting factors: (1) having a "superordinate goal" that both groups want but cannot achieve without the other's help and (2) knowing that both groups possess, and will act on, this awareness. Sherif identified the first factor, but Rick learned the second one the hard way.

Groups

Groups are basic social units consisting of interdependent individuals with emotional ties and clear social status and roles in relation to other members.[3] Groups develop values and rules of behavior from which members absorb a sense of in-group identity that buffers them from out-group individuals. After the zombie outbreak (known among some as the Turn[4]), countless people have become mindless flesh eaters and the odds for survival favor groups over individuals. Overarching the franchise in every form (comics, TV, games) is the notion that only those who pool their strengths ultimately will find or create a safe place. After a group forms, it protects its own (the in-group) and tends to keep outsiders (the out-group) out. Part of this process is to identify threats.[5]

During the early days of post-outbreak awareness, individuals are in transition; it's like a game of musical chairs in which they're not quite certain which seat they'll get. Rick awakens from an unconscious state to a world transformed to chaos.[6] He must deal with the unfathomable fact that shambling people all around want to eat him. He seeks others like himself.

Groups form quickly in this grave new world. Sometimes they form among people already associated with one another, such as Hershel's family and the prison inmates. At other times, circumstance and location throw people together, as in the case of the roadside campers. Rick gets some of both.

He first meets Morgan Jones and his son, who orient him to what it takes to survive in the midst of these "walkers."[7] Rick learns that walkers are attracted to noise; their bite kills you, but then you come back as a walker; hunger drives them; and killing them requires destroying their brains. This helps, but he needs to find his wife, Lori, and son, Carl, and so he pushes on.

He crosses paths with Glenn and then, in the television version, Glenn's fellow campers Andrea, T-Dog, and Merle.[8] As they face off together against a walker herd, Rick proves his worth and gains in-group status. He travels with them to the campers' location and finds Lori and Carl, as well as his law enforcement partner, Shane.[9] The campers form *The Walking Dead*'s primary point-of-view group. They lose members but retain a core group.

It is evident that hierarchies and roles must develop for the group to function effectively in a world its members barely comprehend. Rick emerges as a leader. Tentative bonds form during the early days as weaker members look to stronger ones, and all cling to the hope that the nightmare will end. As they take risks, run missions (release Merle, rescue Glenn), and protect one

Information Conformity and Group Identity

Absorbing group norms can be a subtle process. The social psychologist Muzafer Sherif[12] ran an experiment to learn how people conform in unclear situations. Because every survivor in *The Walking Dead* experiences a loss of clarity, all are vulnerable to group pressure.

To study group influence on individual perception, Sherif projected a spot of light onto a wall in a dark room. From studies on perception, he knew that the *autokinetic effect*, a visual illusion, would make the stationary light appear to move. In the dark, people will estimate its movement in accordance with their mental norms.

He sent individual participants into the room. Their task was to estimate how far the light moved. Estimates varied from 8 to 31 inches. Each participant then entered a room with two others. Sherif composed each group of two individuals who had had similar estimates (say, 8 inches) and one whose estimate had diverged significantly (25 inches). As they watched the light together, they stated their movement estimates aloud. Over numerous trials, the estimates tended toward agreement. Without discussion, each group naturally found its own norm.

A week later, a more profound result occurred. When Sherif retested participants individually, he found that even if they once had diverged greatly from their group, they now replicated their group's estimates. Sherif believed that they had absorbed a group norm. Differing from conformity by pressure, this is known as *informational conformity*.

To demonstrate its effect on *The Walking Dead* characters, let's call Rick Grimes a low estimator and Shane Walsh a high estimator. The others in the initial group look to both as leaders until their differences put them at odds. The group absorbs Rick's reasoned approach rather than Shane's survival-of-the-fittest idea. With each new situation that requires a difficult choice, the group coheres around Rick's stance. In unclear situations, most people look to others for definitive information.

another, their associations strengthen. Nasty retorts fade as respect and appreciation grow. A group identity forms. No outsider can mess with any in-group member without consequences.

Each member brings to the group whatever he or she can. In the city, Jacqui provides knowledge as a city zoning officer when they hope to escape through the sewers.[10] In the woods, Daryl Dixon uses his skills as a tracker.[11] Some members will change—a lot—as they make choices for the group. Daryl is a prime example. After starting out as a redneck, ready to hurt anyone he doesn't like, he becomes a protector and even a leader. At first, its members view the group as temporary solace. Only as they realize that it might be all they will ever have do some adopt a new sense of themselves and their roles. Carol Peletier grows from a cowering, abused wife into a fierce and resourceful warrior.[13]

Dominant figures influence the group's core values. Rick's compassionate "family" seeks a safe haven,[14] the paranoid Governor makes preemptive strikes and creates strict rules for Woodbury,[15] the cannibal Gareth dictates the dehumanizing values of Terminus ("You're the butcher or you're the cattle"[16]), and the Monroes assign jobs in Alexandria. Personality issues recede in the face of collective effort and need. This is the first glimpse of how a goal that transcends differences—a *superordinate goal*—can inspire cooperation among adversaries.

Into the Robbers Cave

To learn about in-group versus out-group behavior, Sherif attempted to create controlled conditions in which relatively equal groups could compete for limited resources.[17] The research team set up those conditions in a Boy Scout camp at the 200-acre Robbers Cave State Park in Oklahoma. They sought to test the development of hierarchies and roles among strangers engaged in a series of choreographed tasks as well as to learn about the nature of in-group identity.[18] Over the course of three weeks, the experiment was to evolve through three stages:

1. *In-group formation*, involving activities that promoted group identification.
2. *Friction phase*, which would bring the groups into conflict.
3. *Integration phase*, which would encourage conflicting groups to cooperate.

Convening

In Phase 1, the team recruited twenty-two boys and randomly divided the volunteers into two groups while keeping the groups relatively balanced in skill and strength. All the participants were around eleven years old and had similar educational levels (above-average IQs). None had experienced unusual stress or frustration in their homes. None had been a failure academically or socially. None had known any of the other research participants before the study, and neither group initially knew about the other.[19]

A bus took each group separately to cabins in different areas of the park. Counselors (researchers acting as participant observers) encouraged them to bond through enjoyable activities done together, such as swimming, a treasure hunt, and sports. The researchers kept records of the speed with which group identity was established. Leaders soon emerged, along with low-status members and rules for behavior. One forbade swearing, for example, whereas the other allowed more vulgarity.

This is like Rick's group before Woodbury: Unaware of other groups, they work on doing what's necessary to survive. They meet and incorporate Hershel's family, lose a few members, and push on to find answers or at least a home. *The Walking Dead*'s in-group formation phase shows their bonding experiences, from entering dangerous terrain to talking quietly about their lives before the Turn. Andrea finds a necklace for her sister Amy in an abandoned store, and Rick, whom she previously had cursed out, mutes his law enforcement instincts and supports her impulse to take it.[20] The rules have changed, and their "secret" draws them into a friendship.

At Robbers Cave, each group chose a name: the Eagles and the Rattlers. Each name became a badge of in-group identity.

It helped establish to whom they were loyal. They even emblazoned flags with their group names.

In *The Walking Dead*, the groups normally don't identify themselves with labels, but the name they use for those who have turned reflects their in-group identity. Glenn calls them *geeks*,[21] but Rick, who heard the term *walker* from Morgan,[22] influences a change that sticks. Woodbury residents call them *biters*,[23] reflecting the Governor's more defensive and aggressive temperament, and the stagnant hospital group uses *rotters*.[24]

At Robbers Cave, still in Phase 1, the boys asked the staff to arrange competitions, as if they wanted to prepare themselves for possible future competition. This further cemented in-group identity and group status. Similarly, in *The Walking Dead*, group members with skills teach others. For example, Shane teaches Andrea how to shoot.[25] The Governor takes this further by creating dangerous contests with biters to keep his warriors primed.[26]

Conflict

In Phase 2 (the friction phase), the Eagles and the Rattlers became aware of each other. At first, they only caught glimpses. The Rattlers placed a flag on the baseball diamond to reinforce their claim to that territory. Each group asked the counselors to let them compete against the other to prove themselves.

The researchers set up tournaments, with prizes for different events. Only one group could claim the main trophy. The researchers also contrived certain situations, such as letting one group gain food items at the other's expense. As the competitions progressed, group identity became more cohesive, and this increased animosity toward the out-group. Threats and name-calling escalated to theft, raids, and property damage. Each group burned the other's flag. The Eagles won the trophy, but the Rattlers, claiming to have been cheated, stole the Eagles' lesser prizes. Reportedly, each group became so aggressive that the two groups had to be separated forcibly. Phase 2 ended early, yet the researchers considered it successful. They had produced conditions that inspired intergroup conflict.

The Eagles and the Rattlers are like Rick's prison group versus the Governor's group at Woodbury. When the Governor learns about Rick's group, he wants to lay claim to all it has.[27] In his mind, there are only winners and losers, and the winners should acquire the scarce resources. Insults fly back and forth, and both groups resort to violent forays. Each views the other as an enemy. There are no camp counselors in this world, but cooler heads in Rick's group prevail. After retrieving the group members they can save, the prison group hopes to coexist with Woodbury, but separately. The Governor, however, must have it all. He encroaches, prepared to take the prison and its resources by force. He will kill everyone there if necessary.[28]

After the Rattlers and Eagles cooled off, the counselors asked each participant to describe his group. To a man, each favored his own group and vilified the other. They demonstrated a form of *groupthink*, something the political scholar Irving Janis would define years later[29] as a maladaptive form of decision making in which the members of a group tend to overly idealize their own position while exaggerating the evilness of "bad" groups. The group leader implies that only *he* has the right solution. Anyone who questions or argues with the leader and his theory is ostracized. When groupthink dominates, there is little chance for a successful outcome. When *both* groups do it, the odds for a disaster are almost insurmountable.

The Governor and Rick both view themselves as morally right. Each faults the other leader and his group for any negative consequences. The more the other side has done, the more the "good" group feels justified in defending itself and launching assaults.

Cooperation

The final phase of the Robbers Cave experiment involved an attempt to integrate the two groups despite their sour feelings about each other. First, the researchers set up activities for the competing boys to get better acquainted, believing that mingling as equals would increase their tolerance. However, those activities had little effect. The boys refused to socialize. Mere contact proved insufficient to get them to like one another.

The researchers switched to plan B. They set up superordinate goals. In other words, they created situations in which both groups needed or wanted something but could get it only by working together.[30]

The counselors took both groups to a new location and told them about vandalism that had damaged the drinking water system. To get water, they would have to repair the damage, and neither group could manage it alone. The boys were thirsty. They figured out what they needed to do. The researchers watched them work together to achieve this goal. Once it was accomplished, though, they reverted to their in-group preferences.

The next task was to offer a movie, but the groups would have to pool their money to see it. Then they worked on a stalled food truck. With each new task, they softened toward each other. They started to mingle spontaneously. They ate dinner together for the first time. By the time the bus left the camp at the end of the three weeks, the groups had integrated, with self-selected seating arrangements that did not follow group lines. The Rattlers even used their prize money from earlier competitions to buy a treat for the Eagles.

As the Governor threatens an imminent assault, Rick offers a way to cohabit in the prison, with everyone working the gardens and fighting off walkers for the greater good.[31] Unfortunately, the Governor operates on Phase 2 thinking: Only one group can win, and *his* group is the most deserving. He cannot be persuaded. He gives Rick's group two options: leave or die. Nothing will compel him, a man who kills anyone outside his group without a second thought, to cooperate with Rick's inferior band. To the Governor's mind, they are nothing but a threat that must be eradicated.

Out of the Cave

Despite its insights, there were limitations to Sherif's experiment. The groups were small, the participants did not represent any general populations, and the time period was too brief to study such complex dynamics thoroughly. The science journalist Maria Konnikova says, "As the stakes rise, as the diversity increases, as the group identification becomes based on something more than a random division into cabins, so too does the difficulty of unraveling the enmity increase."[32]

Sherif found that when a number of individuals who have no previous relationships interact, roles and status hierarchies form. Leaders and followers emerge, and group identities form around a set of values and rules. If they compete for resources with another group, they will form unfavorable stereotypes about the out-group and keep them at a distance. However, differences can be overcome if conflicting groups see a benefit from working together toward a superordinate goal that neither can achieve alone.

Back to the opening question: What if Rick's group discovered that a researcher had placed them among flesh-eating creatures "for science"? Besides being upset, they could have told us much more than Sherif and his colleagues did.

Rick discovers similar principles with in-group versus

out-group conflicts. Mere tolerance exercises would fail, as would high-minded appeals. However, a superordinate goal, such as having to pull together against a herd of walkers, stands a better chance. Even so, not everyone in the Robbers Cave experiment could drop the animosity and get along. Sherif paid little attention to them, but the seeds of people like the Governor were among those boys who simply could not get along.

Rick could not afford to ignore this lesson. Having a super-ordinate goal is a good strategy, but it works only when *all* conflicting groups are willing to cooperate to achieve it. *The Walking Dead* effectively illustrates Sherif's results but also shows what's missing in his experiment.

References

Franzoi, S. L. (2003). *Social psychology* (3rd ed.). New York, NY: McGraw-Hill.

Janis, I. L. (1972). *Victims of groupthink: A psychological study of foreign-policy decisions and fiascoes.* Boston, MA: Houghton, Mifflin.

Kirkman, R., & Bonansinga, J. (2012). *The walking dead: Rise of the Governor.* New York, NY: Thomas Dunne Books/St. Martin's Press.

Konnikova, M. (2012, September 5). Revisiting Robbers Cave: The easy spontaneity of intergroup conflict. *Scientific American.* http://blogs.scientificamerican.com/literally-psyched/2012/09/05/.

Sherif, M. (1936). A study of some social factors in perception. *Archives of Psychology, 27*(187), 1–60.

Sherif, M., Harvey, O. J., White, B. J., Hood, W. R., & Sherif, C. (1954/1961). *Intergroup conflict and cooperation: The Robbers Cave experiment.* Norman, OK: Oklahoma Book Exchange.

Notes

1. Episode 4–8, "Too Far Gone" (December 1, 2013).
2. Sherif et al. (1954/1961).
3. Franzoi (2003), pp. 321–322.
4. Kirkman & Bonansinga (2012).
5. Janis (1972).
6. Episode 1–1, "Days Gone Bye" (October 31, 2010).
7. Episode 1–1, "Days Gone Bye" (October 31, 2010).
8. Issue 2 (2003); episode 1–2, "Guts" (November 7, 2010).
9. Episode 1–3, "Tell It to the Frogs" (November 14, 2010).
10. Episode 1–2, "Guts" (November 7, 2010).
11. Episode 2–1, "What Lies Ahead" (October 16, 2011).
12. Sherif (1936).
13. As Merle acknowledged in episode 3–15, "This Sorrowful Life" (March 24, 2013).

14. Episode 2–4, "Cherokee Rose" (November 6, 2011).
15. Episode 3–3, "Walk with Me" (October 28, 2012).
16. Episode 5–1, "No Sanctuary" (October 12, 2014).
17. Sherif et al. (1954/1961).
18. Franzoi (2003), pp. 243–245.
19. Sherif et al. (1954/1961); Franzoi (2003), pp. 243–245; Konnikova (2012).
20. Episode 1–4, "Vatos" (November 21, 2010).
21. Episode 1–2, "Guts" (November 7, 2010).
22. Episode 1–1, "Days Gone Bye" (October 21, 2010).
23. Episode 3–3, "Walk with Me" (October 18, 2012).
24. Episode 5–4, "Slabtown" (November 2, 2014).
25. Episode 2–6, "Secrets" (November 20, 2011).
26. Issue 31 (2006); episode 3–5, "Say the Word" (November 11, 2012).
27. Issue 28 (2006); episode 3–13, "Arrow on the Doorpost" (March 10, 2013).
28. Issue 42 (2007); episode 4–8, "Too Far Gone" (December 1, 2013).
29. Janis (1972).
30. Sherif et al (1954/1961).
31. Episode 4–8, "Too Far Gone" (December 1, 2013).
32. Konnikova (2012).

· 10 ·

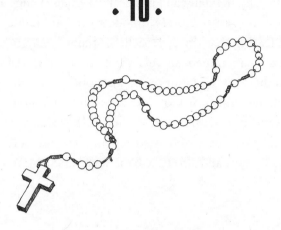

Apocalyptic Stress: Causes and Consequences of Stress at the End of the World

WILLIAM BLAKE ERICKSON AND JOHN BLANCHAR

"You don't know what it's like out there.
You may think you do, but you don't."
—Rick Grimes[1]

"It is not stress that kills us, it is our reaction to it."
—endocrinologist Hans Selye[2]

People like to complain about the stresses of everyday life. Homework, personal finances, and planning one's future are all normal stressors in day-to-day existence for most people. These stressors are puny, though, compared with those a zombie outbreak creates. In fact, psychological stress such as that experienced by survivors of the zombie apocalypse has transformative power socially, mentally, and physically: People change. Although some stressors are obviously unique to the zombie apocalypse, such as fearing that the approaching stranger may be dead and bitey, many are amped-up versions of those from daily experience. To those trying to survive in a chaotic world after a zombie outbreak, knowing what kinds of stressors they might encounter and how to deal with them is essential. *The Walking Dead* produces many examples of how struggling to survive affects people in the long term and also how basic social and cognitive abilities suffer.

Sources of Stress

Even a normal person facing the horrors of a zombie plague has limits: Enough environmental stress potentially can turn the most moral, empathetic person into a killer or transform the most brilliant strategist into a buffoon. Needless to say, the zombie apocalypse would be quite stressful for most people, but precisely what about it would be stressful compared with pre-outbreak life?

A Dangerous World

In a world in which the dead walk and devour the living, an individual's safety is paramount. People need to feel safe and secure, and they experience intense stress when this is jeopardized.[3] The ubiquity of walkers around every corner and within every structure and lodging keeps mortality at the forefront of the mind. The bottom line is that reminders of death and one's inescapable mortality are unpleasant.[4] Fear, anxiety, and stress follow the perception of a dangerous and unkind world.

Intergroup Competition

Perhaps more dangerous than zombies are other people. This becomes increasingly clear as *The Walking Dead* progresses. A long line of enemies pose significant threats to Rick and company. Limited resources (e.g., food, shelter, ammunition) create group competition and trigger "kill or be killed" survival instincts.

Social Isolation

The formation of small groups of survivors certainly results from a human need to affiliate with others; people want to belong because living in groups is mutually beneficial.[5] However, survivors of *The Walking Dead* outbreak continually find themselves separated from others—loved ones, friends, and community members—through death or when fleeing mortal danger. Social isolation takes a psychological toll on people; feeling alone increases anxiety and stress and hinders functioning.[6] The katana-wielding Michonne, having been alone for some time, tells Rick that she sometimes talks to her dead boyfriend.[7]

Instability and Control

Life is disordered and volatile for those struggling to survive in a dead-dominated world. Homes are lost, families are broken, and sustenance is hard to find. Repeated fluctuations between safety and danger, companionship and loneliness, and feast and famine put immense strain on people. Humans need stability and a sense of control to go about their daily lives with confidence.[8] Rick and his band of survivors take refuge at a secluded farm, a secure prison, and a (false) sanctuary at Terminus only to be run off. What follows is a sense of randomness, helplessness, and lack of personal control.

Internal Struggles and Moral Conflicts

Survival in this dark, chaotic, and dangerous world can require people to do bad things: betrayal, deception, greedy behavior, and even murder. Martin, a member of Terminus cannibals, verbalizes this to Tyreese before threatening Judith: "You're a good guy. That's why you're gonna die today."[9] However, the commission of sinful deeds conflicts with a basic need to see oneself as a good person[10] and therefore evokes an internal struggle.[11] This happens time and time again throughout the series as characters face moral dilemmas and confront shame. For example, the priest Gabriel Stokes is tormented by memories of locking his church and ignoring his congregation's pleas while hordes of the dead devour them.[12] Confronting internal demons associated with what one must do to survive invites psychological stress and discomfort.

Ambiguous Loss

Death in general is an obvious result of the zombie apocalypse. However, unlike other apocalypses, this is one in which the dead have taken over the world of the living, and death itself is an active agent against survivors. To individuals, the death of loved ones imposes a heavy cost on emotional well-being. From the very start, a survivor is faced with ambiguous loss[13] by not knowing if loved ones have survived or if they are alive but psychologically distant. The zombie apocalypse yields a unique variety of this type of ambiguous loss because the walkers are active and physically present but mentally gone. Some compelling emotional moments in the franchise, from Morgan's struggle with killing his own wife to Daryl's grief over the loss of Merle, arise because the people they loved are physical present but no longer alive.

Physical Needs

Trying to get along with other people is not the only thing that comes under strain when resources are scarce. After all, scarcity is a problem only because the things that are scarce are necessary. Food, clean water, weapons, fuel, and even sleep are now precious. Above all, scarcity arouses uncertainty, and the risk of uncertainty can make decision-making skills go off the rails.[14] For example, Andrea spends months surviving with Michonne. However, she decides to live what she believes will be a more familiar and comfortable life with the Governor in Woodbury despite warning signs. She thus abandons a high-survival-probability scenario in favor of a low-survival-probability scenario merely because the perceived risk in the latter is lower.

What Does Stress Do?

Deficits in Physical and Mental Health

Stress has profound effects on a person's physical and mental well-being.[15] For instance, heightened stress can trigger insomnia and restless sleep patterns, weaken the immune system, suppress or boost appetites, and cause headaches, tremors or shakes, shortness of breath, chest tightness, nausea, and fatigue. Psychological stress also can worsen existing conditions, referred to as psychosomatic diseases, such as stomach ulcers, eczema, plaque psoriasis, high blood pressure, and heart disease. Stress is a killer in waiting. Equally bad are the mental health consequences of stress. Some people are more vulnerable than others to the development of specific psychological disorders such as schizophrenia and depression. There is a genetic component and an environmental stress component, and their combination determines mental illness outcomes; this is the central idea of the diathesis–stress model.[16] Throughout *The Walking Dead*, psychotic breaks and other symptoms of mental illness plague the characters after traumatic events. Rick experiences visual and auditory hallucinations in response to the death of his wife, Lori. Morgan falls into delusional madness after the death of his son and wife. Finally, Lizzie Samuels, a young orphaned girl at the prison, shows clear difficulty understanding reality. Unable to discern critical differences between walkers and living persons, she murders her younger sister with no remorse, yet she is inconsolable after Carol kills a walker. Because major stress is more common in this new world, so too are the rates of mental illness among survivors.

Disrupted Cognition

Another consequence of increasing the number of stressors is an increase in *cognitive load*,[17] which refers to the working memory capacity that a person has to devote to ongoing tasks. These tasks include many abilities most of us take for granted, such as learning, long-term memory retrieval, and communication. The greater the load on a person's working memory capacity, the greater the likelihood that she or he will make a mistake at an otherwise easy task. The result is almost always that performance suffers. Imagine a group of survivors now. Many have almost no survival skills or knowledge of how to live off the land. Learning how to do so can be its own challenge, but the added danger brought by the undead and other survivors makes learning and applying these skills prone to mistakes.

Arousal and Performance

Stress increases the level of arousal that a person feels. Normally, heightened arousal is necessary, getting people "in the zone" for a task. However, arousal has a curvilinear relationship with performance.[18] As arousal increases, so does performance quality. However, at a certain point that varies among and within individuals, performance begins to decline because there is only so much a person can take.

This effect manifests throughout the series, particularly after the group grows accustomed to the walker threat. A small group of walkers is easy enough to dispatch with knives and arrows. However, relentless waves become difficult to handle because the constant sustained high arousal eventually hurts performance. Even the best zombie killer will make rookie

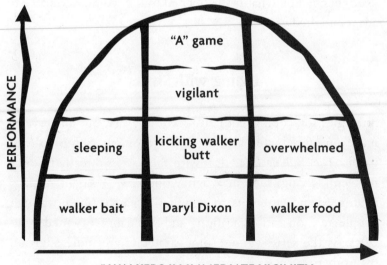

The ability to handle a group of walkers is directly related to the number of walkers one needs to handle.

Stress Creates Blind Spots

Have you ever been frustrated when a heroic character in a zombie movie seems unstoppable until, at an improbably inconvenient moment, a deader seems to sneak up on her seemingly without warning? You've just watched this character take on every challenge in her path only to be cut down by a zombie redshirt. There is a good reason for this that is rooted in the "cue utilization hypothesis."[19] Briefly, the hypothesis refers to the fact that there are many observable cues in an environment; however, under high stress, a person focuses only on cues related to surviving. The hero sees a few high-resolution patches of immediate danger in a sea of blurry, unimportant things. Most of the time, this works out well. However, the hero is now very easy to sneak up on. So the next time you want to scream at the screenwriters for cheaply killing off a character, remember that the hero can pay attention to only so much before being overwhelmed or worn down.

mistakes. Of course, the level of stress required to break varies from person to person and depends on experience and prior knowledge. Series favorite Daryl Dixon is a survivalist, and his pre-outbreak transient lifestyle makes him adaptable to life after the apocalypse. Andrea's sister Amy, a college student easily overwhelmed by what has happened to the world, is less able to adapt and died early.

Coping with Stress

Strategies for coping with stress widely vary, but all serve to make one feel better, at least in the moment. Some individuals in *The Walking Dead* deal with their stress directly through problem solving, such as when Woodbury's resident scientist Milton Mamet attempts to conduct research. Often, though, people rely on rationalizations and avoidance-oriented strategies. As the series shows, some strategies are more advisable than others.

Attentional Avoidance

Many characters adopt a strategy of *avoidance coping*, focusing their attention away from the major problems they face.[20] The best example may be the main characters' settlement of the prison. Settling the prison allows the survivors to recapture something of pre-outbreak life. Rick puts down his gun and begins farming, and the children who come from Woodbury take classes in the prison library. Woodbury itself is an example of avoidance coping on a massive scale: An idyllic little downtown is walled off and powered, giving its inhabitants a life similar to the one they once had with beer, electricity, community events, and sanitation. Although avoidance coping can help those suffering from stress, it also can produce undesirable by-products. The quaint, bucolic life at the prison softens Rick's resolve. The citizens of Woodbury turn a blind eye to the Governor's questionable ethics because their lives are easy. Eventually both Woodbury and the prison meet their downfall as a result of the survivors' avoidance of very real dangers.

Rationalization

When things look bleak, people often do their best to convince themselves that it isn't actually all that bad,[21] and survivors of the outbreak are no different. This is of course helpful for alleviating stress and discomfort. For instance, feeling helpless through a lack of control is unpleasant, but people irrationally perceive that they have more control over outcomes than is possible.[22] This may explain the sudden boost in Carl Grimes's arrogance after they leave the prison. Other times, people like Herschel cope by appealing to supernatural power to explain events in a way that maintains a sense of order and meaning.[23]

People also rely on explanations that cast the self in a positive light.[24] When people fail or do something immoral, they are likely to think it happened because that was the only option available, but when people succeed or do something honorable, they want it to be because of qualities inherent in them. Survivors of the walker outbreak at times have to do terrible things to endure, as when Carol murders and burns sick members of the prison community to halt the spread of disease. She tells Rick that she had to do it; the circumstances demanded it!

Learned Helplessness

Rather than rationalizing away or avoiding stressors, sometimes people succumb to the belief that they are powerless and lack control over their lives. In such cases, people fall into a potentially harmful coping strategy called *learned helplessness* in which they give up and stop trying to escape bad situations.[25] Right after the outbreak, the survivors strive to overcome a bleak situation, but this pattern breaks down later for some who display characteristics of learned helplessness. For instance, many scenes throughout the series show the suicides of people who feel trapped and powerless. Most characters don't succumb to learned helplessness, though, perhaps because they have a resilient personality,[26] an optimistic disposition,[27] or social support from close others.[28] Rick usually seems resilient, responding to most stressors as challenges; Hershel is optimistic, tending to see the glass as half full; Bob grows to see glass as all full; and Maggie and Glenn have a strong supportive bond to carry them through stressful events.

Stay Vigilant and Maintain Control

Traumatic, life-changing stress inevitably rears its head in a world where the dead walk among and feed upon the living. Many of the old outlets for meeting physical and psychological needs no longer exist, and survivors must acquire them by themselves. Worse yet, the post-outbreak world almost makes these things difficult to attain by design. In the face of overwhelming odds, though, the people who live in this dangerous, strange world may flourish as long as they can keep one eye around the next corner and the other down into their hearts.

References

Aspinwall, L. G., & Taylor, S. E. (1992). Modeling cognitive adaptation: A longitudinal investigation of the impact of individual differences and coping on college adjustment and performance. *Journal of Personality and Social Psychology, 63*(6), 989–1003.

Boss, P. (2009). *Ambiguous loss: Learning to live with unresolved grief.* Cambridge, MA: Harvard University Press.

Cozolino, L. (2010). *The neuroscience of psychotherapy: Healing the social brain.* New York, NY: Norton.

Easterbrook, J. A. (1959). The effect of emotion on cue utilization and the organization of behavior. *Psychological Review, 66*(3), 183–201.

Elster, J. (1983). *Sour grapes: Studies in the subversion of rationality.* Cambridge, UK: Cambridge University Press.

Festinger, L. (1957). *A theory of cognitive dissonance.* Stanford, CA: Stanford University Press.

Fiske, S. T. (2010). *Social beings: Core motives in social psychology* (2nd ed.). Hoboken, NJ: Wiley.

Greenberg, J., Pyszczynski, T., & Solomon, S. (1986). The causes and consequences of a need for self-esteem: A terror management theory. In R. F. Baumeister (Ed.), *Public self and private self* (pp. 189–212). New York, NY: Springer-Verlag.

House, J. S., Landis, K. R., & Umberson, D. (1988). Social relationships and health. *Science, 241,* 540–545.

Kahneman, D., & Tversky, A. (1988). Prospect theory: An analysis of decision under risk. In P. Gärdenfors & N. Sahlin (Eds.), *Decision, probability, and utility: Selected readings* (pp. 183–214). New York, NY: Cambridge University Press.

Kobasa, S. C. (1979). Stressful life events, personality, and health: An inquiry into hardiness. *Journal of Personality and Social Psychology, 37*(1), 1–11.

Langer, E. J. (1975). The illusion of control. *Journal of Personality and Social Psychology, 32*(2), 311–328.

Leary, M. R. (1990). Responses to social exclusion: Social anxiety, jealousy, loneliness, depression, and low self-esteem. *Journal of Social and Clinical Psychology, 9,* 221–229.

Levone, B., Cryan, J., & O'Leary, O. (2015). Role of adult hippocampal neurogenesis in stress resilience. *Neurobiology of Stress, 1,* 147–155.

Park, C. L. (2005). Religion as a meaning-making framework in coping with life stress. *Journal of Social Issues, 61,* 707–729.

Rosenthal, D. (1963). A suggested conceptual framework. In D. Rosenthal (Ed.), *The Genain quadruplets* (pp. 505–516). New York, NY: Basic.

Schachter, S. (1959). *The psychology of affiliation.* Stanford, CA: Stanford University Press.

Schneiderman, N., Ironson, G., & Siegel, S. D. (2005). Stress and health: Psychological, behavioral, and biological determinants. *Annual Review of Clinical Psychology, 1,* 607–628.

Seligman, M. E. P. (1975). *Helplessness: On depression, development, and death.* San Francisco: Freeman.

Shepperd, J., Malone, W., & Sweeny, K. (2008). Exploring causes of the self-serving bias. *Social and Personality Psychology Compass, 2,* 895–908.

Sweller, J. (1988). Cognitive load during problem solving: Effects on learning. *Cognitive Science, 12,* 257–285.

Yerkes, R., & Dodson, J. (1908). The relation of strength of stimulus to rapidity of habit formation. *Journal of Comparative Neurology and Psychology, 18,* 459–482.

Zeidner, M., & Endler, N. S. (1996). *Handbook of coping: Theory, research, applications.* Oxford, England: Wiley.

Notes

1. Episode 1–6, "TS-19" (December 5, 2010).
2. Selye (as cited in Levone et al., 2015).
3. Fiske (2010).
4. Greenberg, Pyszczynski, & Solomon (1986).
5. Schachter (1959).
6. Leary (1990).
7. Issue 53 (2008); episode 3–12, "Clear" (March 03, 2013).
8. Langer (1975).
9. Episode 5–1, "No Sanctuary" (October 12, 2014).
10. Fiske (2010).
11. Festinger (1957).
12. Issue 63 (2009); episode 5–3, "Four Walls and a Roof" (October 26, 2014).
13. Boss (2009).
14. Kahneman & Tversky (1988).
15. Schneiderman et al. (2005).
16. Rosenthal (1963).
17. Sweller (1988).
18. Yerkes & Dodson (1908).
19. Easterbrook (1959).
20. Zeidner & Endler (1996).
21. Elster (1983).
22. Langer (1975).
23. Park (2005).
24. Shepperd et al. (2008).
25. Seligman (1975).
26. Kobasa (1979).
27. Aspinwall & Taylor (1992).
28. House et al. (1988).

11

It's the Humans You Have to
Worry About: Becoming a Sociopath

MARTIN LLOYD

"You're the butcher or you're the cattle."
—both Gareth and Mary[1]

esidents of *The Walking Dead* universe find themselves beset by all manner of horrors. The most obvious are the reanimated rotting corpses constantly trying to tear human flesh from bone, turning each victim into a new walker. Despite the shocking presence of the hungry dead, the greatest tragedies visited upon Rick Grimes and the other heroes of *The Walking Dead* often come at the hands of their fellow humans. Whether it's the Governor publicly decapitating Hershel and driving everyone from the prison or subsequent cannibals nearly killing the entire group, the worst horrors come from living people.

What kind of person could so callously bring such suffering

to others? Who, for example, could lock a bound and unarmed Glenn in a room with a walker? Who could cut off a man's leg and then casually discuss its flavor with him? In psychology, the term for an individual who can easily do those things is a *psychopath*.

Psychopaths generally are defined in terms of a lack of empathy, meaning they lack awareness of or concern for the emotions of others. It might be easier to calmly butcher a line of prisoners for food if you genuinely did not care how they felt on any level. Psychopaths also tend to excel at manipulating people and often look at others as nothing more than a meal ticket or a means of getting something. They are often aggressive and may engage in a wide variety of criminal behaviors.

Professionals disagree about exactly what makes a psychopath a psychopath. Some have proposed that psychopaths are utterly lacking in any emotion, but this has not been well supported. Psychopaths seem to have no problem experiencing anger and are not insensitive to pleasure and feelings of contentment. There is, however, one emotion that genuine psychopaths do appear to lack: They seem to be without fear. They do not get anxious, and they do not experience the same physical reactions to crisis (e.g., sweating, shaking, racing heart, freezing up) as other people.

A person with these characteristics may be familiar to some readers by another name: *sociopath*. Sociopathy is among the most poorly defined terms in psychology, largely because the definition has changed a number of times. The most useful way to define it is probably to think of a sociopath as looking and acting exactly like a psychopath. The difference is that psychopaths seem to be essentially born that way; they never develop any empathy. Sociopaths, in contrast, develop psychopathic characteristics in response to the events in their lives.[2] Were various characters from *The Walking Dead* always without empathy and remorse (i.e., psychopaths), or did they develop those traits in response to their circumstances (i.e., sociopaths)? The primary

The Psychopathy Checklist

Most mental disorders are diagnosed by using the criteria set forth in the *Diagnostic and Statistical Manual of Mental Disorders* (DSM), but to assess psychopathy clinicians use the *Psychopathy Checklist—Revised, Second Edition* (PCL-R).[3] This test consists of twenty items, with each one referencing a specific behavioral pattern or mental state one expects to see in a psychopath. Each item is scored on a three-point scale in accordance with how well it describes an examinee: 0—not at all, 1—somewhat, 2—very well. Clinicians base their scores on interviews with the examinee and any other available information, usually medical and criminal records. In most settings, examinees who receive 30 or more of the possible 40 points are designated as psychopaths.

PCL-R items fit into two major categories called factors. Factor 1 items deal with the emotional aspects of psychopathy and the ways in which psychopaths tend to interact with others. Factor 2 items concern criminal behaviors and a psychopath's expected lifestyle.

Factor 1 Items

- Glibness/Superficial Charm
- Grandiose Sense of Self-Worth
- Pathological Lying
- Conning/Manipulative
- Lack of Remorse/Guilt
- Callous/Lack of Empathy
- Emotionally Shallow
- Failure to Accept Responsibility for One's Own Actions

Factor 2 Items

- Poor Behavioral Controls
- Impulsivity
- Irresponsibility
- Need for Stimulation/ Proneness to Boredom
- Criminal Versatility
- Lack of Long-Term Goals
- Early Behavioral Problems
- Revocation of Conditional Release
- Juvenile Delinquency
- Parasitic Lifestyle

Additional PCL-R Items

- Many Short-Term Marital Relationships• Promiscuous Sexual Behavior

No single item needs to be present for someone to be considered a psychopath—not even lack of empathy, which most experts would say is the cornerstone of the very idea of psychopathy. This means that someone who shows plenty of empathy and therefore receives a score of zero on the item *Callous/Lack of Empathy* can be labeled a psychopath if his or her scores on the remaining items total at least 30.

question, however, is whether the various characters meet the diagnostic criteria for psychopathy.

How Psychopathic Are They?

Many characters in *The Walking Dead* have done horrible things. Violence and atrocity are so commonplace that while residing at the prison, Rick and his people begin asking all prospective group members, "How many people have you killed?"[4] Answers greater than zero are not automatic disqualifications, and so Rick's people follow each newcomer's answer with another question: "Why?" Does having done horrible things automatically make one a psychopath? In truth, people hurt others for a variety of reasons, and many individuals who harm others are not psychopaths.

In clinical practice, one should never make assumptions about a subject's background in assigning that person a score. Only verifiable information is fair game. In assessing fictional characters, however, because of the lack of background information, certain assumptions may have to be made.

The Governor

Possibly no other character on *The Walking Dead* brings as much suffering to Rick and his group as the Governor. He is directly responsible for the deaths of Hershel and certain other characters, and it is he who ultimately forces Rick's group from their prison sanctuary. He can be cold and indifferent when carrying out these acts. But does *The Walking Dead*'s biggest villain actually meet the criteria for psychopathy?

The Governor definitely shows some psychopathic traits. Numerous characters respond to his considerable charisma, never

guessing, for example, that he is killing soldiers to obtain weapons.[5] As a result of this charisma, he easily receives full credit on
the item Glibness/Superficial Charm. Similarly, he is highly adept
at manipulation. He routinely convinces his followers that they
are in danger from Rick and his people solely to satisfy his taste
for revenge. In addition to their manipulations, psychopaths lie
for no reason. In the course of his travels both before[6] and after
Woodbury, he lies to strangers about more or less everything,
even assuming a new name.[7] He therefore receives scores of 2 on
both items concerned with honesty.

Among the other psychopathic traits shown by the Governor
is the one often thought to be most central to the concept
Callous/Lack of Empathy. Examples of the Governor acting
without regard for others' feelings are too numerous to list. The
Governor also seldom shows remorse for his actions, and he
constantly blames Rick for his own misdeeds and problems.
Thus, he receives full credit on three additional PCL-R items.

Although he has many psychopathic traits, the Governor
does not display all of them. It is difficult to say that he displays
Grandiose Sense of Self-Worth since he tends to occupy positions
of legitimate importance. The item Emotionally Shallow, which
connotes limited emotional experience, also does not seem to
apply to him. If anything, his emotions drive him. He has a
deep attachment to his daughter, even caring for her after she
becomes a zombie. Although this is pathological on many levels,
it is not psychopathic.

The factors discussed above are all part of the PCL-R's first
factor (i.e., the emotional and interpersonal aspects). On this
factor alone, the Governor would score a 12. To put this in
perspective, this score is higher than that of approximately 83
percent of male American criminal offenders.[8]

Although the Governor displays an excessive amount of the
first factor, his score on the second factor (i.e., his criminal life-

style) is much lower. His most notable traits from this factor are Irresponsibility and Poor Behavioral Controls. In the case of irresponsibility, although he often provides for the well-being of large groups of people, he also puts those under his command at unnecessary risk whether by letting them fight gladiatorial battles with walkers or by leading them into dangerous battles with his enemies. In terms of behavioral controls, the Governor allows his tendency to hold grudges overwhelm his reason. His death and those of many from his camp ultimately result from his inability to let go of his resentment.

In many respects, what little is known of the Governor's history is not consistent with the usual history of a psychopath. There is no indication he has any notable criminal history. Before the zombie apocalypse, he was a family man and an office worker and apparently not a particularly assertive one.[9] He also does not have a Parasitic Lifestyle, a pattern of using others to meet basic needs that is common to psychopaths. Whatever flaws he may have, he is a genuine contributor to the groups of which he is a member. Ultimately, his total score on the second factor is only about a 5, which is higher than that of only 13 percent of male American offenders.

The Governor's total score on the PCL-R (with an additional point for Promiscuous Sexual Behavior in light of indications that he may engage in impersonal sex[10]) ends up being only an 18, which is far below the 30 that normally would designate someone as a psychopath. Despite the presence of many classic psychopathic personality traits, his apparently benign history before the apocalypse results in only a moderate[11] degree of psychopathy.

Gareth of Terminus

Of all the adversity Rick and company have faced, perhaps nothing is quite so terrifying as being locked up and nearly eaten by the residents of the apparent sanctuary Terminus. The PCL-R is not intended to evaluate entire groups, but one individual can easily stand for the actions of the group, in this case its leader, Gareth.

Much like the Governor, Gareth displays high levels of the first psychopathy factor. He is able to put new arrivals at Terminus reasonably at ease, showing Glibness/Superficial Charm. The fact that he actively offers the hope of safety in order to lead people to Terminus and then use them for food is clear evidence of the Conning/Manipulative trait. There are few examples of him lying for reasons other than manipulation, but since he spends so much of his time lying, he receives at least one point for Pathological Lying. The fact that he is not only cannibalizing people but letting them sit with full knowledge of their impending death[12] warrants full credit for Callous/Lack of Empathy. Even if that somehow were insufficient, calmly discussing Bob's recently severed and eaten leg with him[13] clearly shows a lack of concern for others' emotions. Not only is he unconcerned with others, Gareth's own emotions seem rather shallow; he appears to order the consumption of his own deceased brother,[14] which would be beyond difficult for most people.

One item in the first factor that is difficult to assess is Grandiose Sense of Self-Worth. Gareth is not observed holding himself above others in his group, but the group's attitude that they deserve to prey on others is suggestive of the trait. Ultimately, Gareth's score on this factor is 15, higher than that of 98.6 percent of male American criminal offenders.

Little information is available about Gareth's life before the zombie apocalypse. Nonetheless, it is established that the Terminus group is initially much more altruistic in its mission. This makes any significant criminal history seem unlikely. As for Promiscuous Sexual Behavior or Many Short-Term Marital Relationships, there is simply no evidence.

Parasitic Lifestyle generally refers to financial exploitation in relationships. There is no evidence of this, as Gareth seems to contribute to his group. Being in a cannibalistic cult is something the developers of the PCL-R probably never considered, however, and using people as food certainly qualifies as parasitic behavior. Otherwise, Gareth shows almost no evidence of other Factor 2 traits. He does not exhibit Impulsivity or even Irresponsibility, as he keeps the Terminus group well organized to minimize risk to the group.

Much like the Governor, Gareth has an incredibly high level of the psychopath's characteristic emotional life but almost no evidence of the required criminal history. Without this history, his final score is the same as the Governor's—18—once again well below the standard cutoff for psychopathy.

Merle Dixon

Not a traditional villain like the others, Merle often helps Rick's group survive. Nonetheless, he also starts fights and often mistreats group members. He goes even further when working for the Governor, killing numerous people and locking a bound and unarmed Glenn in a room with a walker. In short, Merle demonstrates many traits that could be considered psychopathic.

One way Merle differs from Gareth or the Governor is that he shows more evidence of the criminal history that contributes to PCL-R Factor 2. Although both are plausible, there is no evidence of Many Short-Term Marital Relationships or Revocation of Conditional Release. He does, however, engage in criminal behavior before the apocalypse. He has been a known drug dealer[15] and later acknowledges[16] planning a robbery, suggesting Criminal Versatility. The criminal behavior seems to date back to childhood, indicating both Juvenile Delinquency and Early Behavioral Problems. In addition to selling drugs, Merle has been a user,[17] which often suggests Need for Stimulation/Proneness to Boredom. His brother, Daryl, states that they were basically drifters before the apocalypse,[18] indicating a Lack of Long-Term Goals, not to mention Irresponsibility. Perhaps the trait that most defines Merle is Poor Behavioral Controls in light of his tendency to react to most slights with physical violence. His criminal and aggressive behaviors ultimately give Merle a Factor 2 score higher than that of 91 percent of male American criminal offenders.[19]

Although not to the same extent as Gareth or the Governor, Merle shows some of the emotional coldness that makes up Factor 1. Although he is not charming per se, Merle's macho image is worth 1 point.[20] He does not seem to have a problem manipulating others, and Daryl's admission that he has spent his life doing whatever Merle tells him[21] certainly suggests the presence of Conning/Manipulative. He lies frequently, though it is unclear if he does so for reasons other than manipulation, and so he receives a score of 1. Likewise, he seems not to care about much of anything except, notably, his brother, and so he receives 1 point for Emotionally Shallow. There is plenty evidence for Callous/Lack of Empathy when he nearly robs a family freshly traumatized by a walker attack.[22] Seldom does he show a genuine indication of remorse.

Merle shows enough traits to score a 30 on the PCL-R, right at the standard cutoff for psychopathy and higher than the score of Gareth or the Governor. This score is higher than that of 84 percent of male American offenders.[23] Some fans may argue that Merle ultimately proves himself more caring and compassionate, but was his sparing of Michonne[24] an act of conscience or one last attempt at manipulation by someone who expected to survive? According to the actor Michael Rooker, who plays Merle, the character has a more shortsighted reason for releasing Michonne: "I think he just got tired of listening to her."[25]

How Did They Get This Way?

Despite his higher overall level of psychopathy, Merle seems to have less genuine emotional coldness than the Governor or Gareth. His relatively higher score is due mainly to the others lacking a psychopath's typical history. Merle, one gets the sense, has always been Merle. The others were changed by the events of their lives after the apocalypse, but could someone really be turned into a sociopath by such circumstances?

As opposed to the psychopath, who is temperamentally abnormal (i.e., "born that way"), a person becomes a sociopath as a result of a deficient environment. The factors that shape the sociopath usually occur throughout childhood.[26] The Governor and Gareth seem to have become sociopaths as adults. In the real world, this appears to be a rare phenomenon, but the apocalypse is an even rarer phenomenon. Trauma has been found to be associated with callous and unemotional traits in that some people show high levels of these traits along with significant trauma histories, but the trauma generally occurs in childhood.[27] Also, sociopaths with a history of trauma tend to be more impulsive than psychopaths, whereas Merle is the one who shows the most aggressive impulsivity.

Trauma generally produces not sociopaths but individuals with excessive anxiety. People may, however, react differently to repeated trauma from which they cannot escape than they do to discrete traumatic incidents. Some people who are exposed to continuous trauma (e.g., systematic abuse, high-crime neighborhoods, war zones) appear to develop callous traits and criminal, even violent behavior.[28] Could this explain the origins of *The Walking Dead*'s sociopaths? What is life in the zombie apocalypse but one long, unrelenting trauma?

References

Hare, R. D. (2003). *Hare psychopathy checklist—revised (PCL-R): 2nd edition technical manual.* North Tonawanda, NJ: MHS.

Kahn, R. E., Frick, P. J., Youngstrom, E. A., Youngstrom, J. K., Feeny, N. C., & Findling, R. L. (2013). Distinguishing primary and secondary variants of callous-unemotional traits among adolescents in a clinic-referred sample. *Psychological Assessment, 25,* 966–978.

Kirkman, R., & Bonansinga, J. (2012). *The walking dead: Rise of the Governor.* London, England: St. Martin's Griffin.

Lykken, D. T. (1995). *The antisocial personalities.* Hillsdale, NJ: Lawrence Erlbaum.

Roach, C. B. (2013). Shallow affect, no remorse: The shadow of trauma in the inner city. *Peace and Conflict: Journal of Peace Psychology, 19,* 150–163.

Notes

1. Episode 5–1, "No Sanctuary" (October 12, 2014).
2. Lykken (1995).
3. Hare (2003).
4. Episode 4–1, "30 Days without an Accident" (October 13, 2013).
5. Episode 3–3, "Walk with Me" (October 28, 2012).
6. Kirkman & Bonansinga (2012).
7. Episode 4–6, "Live Bait" (November 17, 2013).
8. Hare (2003), p. 164.
9. Episode 3–4, "Killer Within" (November 4, 2012).
10. Episode 3–3, "Walk with Me" (October 28, 2012).
11. Hare (2003), p. 31.
12. Episode 5–1, "No Sanctuary" (October 12, 2014).
13. Episode 5–3, "Four Walls and a Roof" (October 26, 2014).
14. Episode 5–1, "No Sanctuary" (October 12, 2014).
15. Episode 2–7, "Pretty Much Dead Already" (February 12, 2012).
16. Episode 3–10, "Home" (February 17, 2013).
17. Episode 3–15, "This Sorrowful Life" (March 24, 2013).
18. Episode 4–12, "Still" (March 2, 2014).
19. Hare (2003), p. 164.
20. Hare (2003), p. 35.
21. Episode 4–12, "Still" (March 2, 2014).
22. Episode 3–10, "Home" (February 17, 2013).
23. Hare (2003), p. 164.
24. Episode 3–15, "This Sorrowful Life" (March 24, 2013).
25. *Talking Dead* (March 24, 2013).
26. Lykken (1995).
27. Kahn et al. (2013).
28. Roach (2013).

12

Carl Grimes and Neglected Youth

Patrick O'Connor

"Someone is going to tell you to get used to this.
That feeling of being scared and sad.

They're going to say it'll be better when you learn to ignore it.
Don't listen to them.

Hold on to it, remember it. Don't let yourself forget it.
It's too easy to lose."
—Carl Grimes[1]

The *Walking Dead* may take place in a fictional universe that none of us will live to see, but a great deal of what happens to the central characters can be an all too realistic expression of the daily lives of many children and teenagers throughout the world. Problems such as abandonment, neglect, struggling for survival, and parentification that result from these issues rob many people of their childhood, just as they rob Carl Grimes of his. This can have a profound impact on a young person's development, as it ultimately affects the adult the child grows up to be. How did the zombie apocalypse affect Carl and his development? Through the lens of Erik Erikson's psychosocial theory of development[2] and my own experiences treating neglected youth, I will explore how elements of Carl's fictional story are lived every day by real youth.

Carl's Psychosocial Stages

Viewing Carl from a developmental perspective can help us understand how his environment is affecting his psychological growth, as these environmental factors substantially influence his personal identity.

Erik Erikson was a developmental psychologist, clinician, and professor who emphasized identity formation as the driving force behind human development. He described this as a "conscious sense of individual identity . . . an unconscious striving for a continuity of personal character . . . a maintenance of an inner solidarity with a group's ideals and identity."[3] Erikson proposed eight stages through which every person grows, with "Who am I?" being the question people seek to answer in each stage. According to Erikson, each stage blends together from one period to the next, with no stage completely disappearing from a person's unconscious mind. Thus, we can examine each stage through Carl's lived experience regardless of his chronological age in the storyline. Let's take a look at the earliest five of Erikson's eight stages through the eyes of Carl Grimes.

Basic Trust versus Basic Mistrust (Birth to One Year)

An infant works on developing trust toward self and others. As infants, we need to know that we can depend on our mothers to feed and care for us in a period in which we cannot care for ourselves. While working on strengthening trust with others, a person learns whether the world is a safe place or a dangerous place. If others cannot care for us or if we frequently find dangerous things to put in our mouths, the world will seem dangerous and we will develop a sense of mistrust. Shortly after the apocalypse, Lori notes that this stage has reappeared in Carl at age eight: "[Carl] can't sleep anymore unless he knows I'm right next to him. . . . None of us really sleep anymore. Soon as we hear one of the shots, we're up ready to defend this place."[4]

Autonomy versus Shame and Doubt (Two to Three Years)

Walking, talking, and toilet training symbolize a toddler's growing independence. By being able to move their bodies and speak their minds wherever and however they please, children make their personalities become apparent to others. The child separates from others and learns to become comfortable with autonomous action. It is in this stage that we first encounter rules and expectations as we discover limits within ourselves and those imposed by others. If these actions of independence are restricted by others, we become ashamed of our behaviors. Carl encounters these rules when he carries his own gun around the first camp shortly after Rick reunites with his family.[5] Being trusted with a responsibility typically reserved for an adult brings about its own set of rules and expectations, and Carl must take care to be aware of them when taking on such a responsibility.

Initiative versus Guilt (Four to Five Years)

This would be the last completed stage before Carl begins to experience a world changed by walkers. Here, creativity and bold ideas spark the imagination as the child takes the rules and expectations from the previous stage and asks, "What if things were different?" As children consider these creative ideas, they listen to the environment to see if they are rewarded or punished. A child whose creativity is hindered during this stage may develop a sense of guilt about having those bold thoughts in the first place. Several instances of initiation appear in Carl's actions throughout *The Walking Dead*; however, they often are suppressed by Rick in favor of more conservative action. Instead, we can focus on elements of role development, which is another hallmark of this stage. Children in this stage seek to imitate their parents, viewing them as all-knowing and all-powerful. This briefly appears in the comic book when Carl asks his father if he can tell if Carl is scared. When Rick says no, Carl replies, "Yeah . . . I'm going to be a good leader someday. Just like you."[6]

Industry versus Inferiority (Six Years to Puberty)

It is in this stage that we first meet Carl in the comic book at seven years of age. In the first episode of the television show, Carl is leaving this stage and entering the next at twelve years of age. Children in this stage focus on developing a sense of a work ethic as they learn how to use the tools on which they will rely as adults. These tools can be intellectual in nature, such as math or reading, or physical in nature, such as taking apart a toy with a screwdriver and putting it back together. An early clear example of this stage is when Carl learns to shoot a gun for the first time.[7] Things are a bit shaky at first, but he becomes comfortable with handling such a mature responsibility.

Identity Formation versus Identity Diffusion (Adolescence)

With the body rapidly changing, the previous stages reemerge in novel ways. The developing adolescent reassesses the world's security, wondering, "Can I trust myself to enter this world as an adult?" Autonomy also gains attention as teens ponder their independence. Initiation is important when a person considers forging her or his own path, whether by following those of their parents and siblings or by entering uncharted territory. As independence is gradually achieved, the work ethic becomes paramount to the adolescent's success. As these stages reappear and integrate, the person's identity either forms or becomes diffuse. In Carl's case, he repeatedly receives the messages that the world is not safe, people must be autonomous and master tools to survive, and initiation is largely suppressed in favor of more predictable, conventional approaches.

Erikson's psychosocial stages set the course for Carl's development when he is positioned among other people. That is, viewing a developing youth through a psychosocial lens allows us to examine how that person's internal growth and change are influenced by other people. It is not enough to view a child's psychology in isolation from others. Instead, we must consider how friends, family, strangers, and society at large affect a child's concept of self and where that self is positioned in this world. But what happens when youth are neglected? How do they, along with Carl, find themselves on a particular course of development because of the actions—and inactions—of others?

Neglected Youth

For three years, I worked as an in-home psychotherapist for kids in foster care. The next year, I worked with teens who had been

Carl's Future Development

Erikson also proposed three adult developmental stages, which Carl will face as he grows into adulthood.

Intimacy versus Isolation (Young Adulthood)

A fully integrated identity allows one to become intimate with another person. One must know who he or she is before figuring out the identity of an intimate partner. Being unable to form a deep, close bond with another person that is based on mutually complementary identities leads to cold, empty relationships.

Generativity versus Stagnation (Middle Adulthood)

A person seeks to guide the members of the next generation and prepare them for the future. This investment in the future stems from a belief in the human species and results in empathy for the struggles of inexperienced youth. Failure to do this results in stagnation, boredom, and self-absorption.

Integrity versus Despair (Late Adulthood)

At the end of life, a person accepts his or her limitations. People own their wisdom, sensing that they are part of a larger history. People who did not live with integrity for their identity feel despair, regret, and disgust.

removed from their homes to be placed in a six- to twelve-month program at a residential treatment facility. In both settings, I visited children and teens while they adjusted to living in someone else's home, eating someone else's food, and following someone else's rules. Some had it rough, although a certain baseline of "having it rough" already exists for the state to intervene and decide that your biological parents no longer can care for you. Sometimes the parents simply valued playing video games and smoking marijuana above encouraging their children's development. Other times, prostitution and familywide drug use (yes, children included) were the norm.

However, the one thing all these children had in common was their subjective experience. Although many children recognize the shortcomings of their parents, Mom and Dad are still that—Mom and Dad. No matter what atrocities I heard about in my sessions with these kids and teens, they would almost unfalteringly insist that their parents were good people at heart. Mom would ask my client how her day at school went, and my client would beam: "They want me to try out for the basketball team!" Later, Mom would be another face on the news, having been picked up for prostitution and drug possession. I heard stories similar to this over and over, yet the kids much more often than not communicated a strong desire to return home to their families. To these kids, their parents made some major mistakes but each were still good people who would never be just another face on the news. No matter how neglectful or abusive these parents may have been, it is still traumatic to have the state intervene and whisk you off to a stranger's house indefinitely.

We can see similarities in Carl's day-to-day life. Because of the threat of undead monsters, he has been whisked away by his family and thrust into a world that requires a faster rate of maturity than is typical for children his age. His home is deemed no longer safe, and he transitions from camps to homes to prisons as temporary living spaces while the grown-ups around him decide what to do. Despite watching his father make difficult decisions in regard to killing the dead and the living, he still views his father as a good man. Carl tells his father, "I love you because of what you do to keep me safe. I know why we do what we do. We do it to protect the weak. To survive."[8] This is a clear example of basic trust versus basic mistrust emerging once again to resolve itself further. He has learned quickly that his home, like the rest of the world, is no longer safe. Thus, the bonds he maintains with trusted family and friends become crucial to his hope for the future.

To further illustrate the parallels between Carl's story and those of neglected youth, I will explore the cases of two clients with whom I worked who were in different stages of development yet could identify a great deal with Carl's fictional struggles. Their identifying information, as well as other key details, have been changed or omitted to protect their identities.

Sarah and Nathan

While working with one particular pair of siblings, I found the theme of disconnection from the familiar, as mentioned previously, arising frequently. They lived in a home where a man and woman in their early thirties had two biological children of their own. Aside from those who were related biologically to one another, the children referred to each other as "cousins." At the point of my entering the treatment team, the children had lived in this home for a year. Yet they continued to struggle with the notion that these were not their real parents; this was not the life they had chosen for themselves.

The twelve-year-old girl, Sarah, had been *parentified* by having to look after her younger brother while living on the streets, meaning that she took on the role of parent and made the responsible decisions to the best of her ability when parents were not around to model appropriate, responsible adult behavior. Sarah's eight-year-old brother, Nathan, had been exposed to several controlled substances while still developing as a fetus and thus had unique needs. Their mother, Karen, hopped from boyfriend to boyfriend, trying to find a stable home environment for her children, and in between boyfriends lived on the street. In addition to prostituting herself, she sold and used narcotics and stimulants. Often, this meant she was away from her children for extended periods. Because of Karen's absences and Nathan's needs, Sarah became the de facto parent and essentially raised Nathan from an early age. At times, Karen might place her children in the care of a friend or boyfriend while she worked the streets, but because these faces would change frequently, Sarah was the most consistent loving person in Nathan's life.

Carl, as a son and older brother living as a nomad in the television series, struggles with many of the same issues, only in different circumstances. His homes are temporary, and many of the other survivors view Carl as a primary caretaker of his infant sister, Judith, when his father, Rick, is absent. The other survivors change from time to time, with Michonne, Tyreese, Carol, and many others trying to help Carl and Judith; however, as long as Carl and Judith are together, Carl is the most consistent loving person in her life.

Karen seemed aware that her children were not living in an ideal situation. During one session of family therapy, Karen indicated to me that she wanted to protect her children as well as she could by keeping them away from the life she was living but felt helpless in trying to provide them with a home. She knew the best option would be to find a family member to watch over them, but she said she could not stand the thought of losing her children. Karen struggled a great deal with cognitive dissonance in that she knew she was not providing the care Sarah and Nathan needed but also knew she did not want to relinquish her role as their mother.

The police later picked up Sarah and Nathan when they were discovered walking down a major street without a responsible adult. When they told the officer their mother was busy working and they did not have a home, the officer contacted the state-run family services department and began the process of bringing them into foster care. Reports indicated that the children resisted this move early on and frequently demanded contact with their mother. Little did they know that Karen had been arrested for prostitution and drug possession their first night living in a foster home.

After Carl's mother, Lori, passes away, Rick struggles with being a single father in a chaotic world. He seemingly feels helpless having to raise Carl and, in the television series, a new baby. Over the following weeks, Rick looks to other survivors to care temporarily for his children while he grapples with the sometimes opposing roles of confident group leader and loving father. A particularly poignant moment occurs in the prison as Rick begins to become delusional and his children are cared for by others.[9] Carl continues to view his father as a loving man despite his challenges.

The children were placed in the care of a family friend so that they could maintain contact with Karen and extended family members. Sarah sometimes struggled with her parentification, butting up against her foster parents' assigned duties as responsible adults. On the one hand, her parents would tell me she was "like a kid on autopilot." They knew that she could cook for herself and the other children, she could clean up after them, and she modeled mature behaviors. She helped Nathan with his homework, much of which consisted of practicing daily living skills, as well as her older foster brother, whose homework was similar as a result of his struggles as an adolescent living with the repercussions of a substance-induced birth defect. On the other hand, her foster parents knew this was a young adolescent girl who deserved to have a childhood of her own instead of always caring for other people. They struggled with this notion even further when she brought home straight A's and was consistently lauded for her athletic ability. When discussing their experiences with her, I frequently heard the question, "How do we help her when she seems capable of helping herself?" Even with her emotional and intellectual maturity, this was still a young person who had a lifetime of adult responsibility waiting for her well after she completed middle and high school. Doesn't every child deserve a childhood?

Time and time again, Carl demonstrates incredible maturity for his age, with even the foul-mouthed comic book villain Negan commenting, "It's easy to forget you're just a kid," as he attempts to engage Carl in banter after Carl has just killed six of Negan's men.[10] *Other children often seek Carl to ask for advice, and many members of their various camps treat Carl as an equal. Because of this, Carl spends a great deal of his time around other adults instead of around other children, probably because he is feeling that he has more in common with the adults. A child of eight years who is treated as an equal by adults moves rapidly toward adult developmental levels.*

Over the multiyear span I worked with this family, Karen made considerable progress in getting clean, finding a legal income, and living in stable housing. She relapsed twice in that period but maintained progress in all three of her goals for six consecutive months toward the end of our time together. Because of her legal and relapse history, the state-run family services department wanted her to demonstrate stable income and housing for a full year before granting her custody of her children.

With six months to go, Karen was diagnosed with a terminal illness. Social workers and advocates working at the agency volunteered to drive Sarah and Nathan from their foster home to Karen's home, about forty miles away, to see her more frequently. We stepped up the frequency of therapy in order to address end-of-life issues. Sarah seemed confused and in denial about the diagnosis and likely outcome; Nathan did not show much awareness of the seriousness of the events of he witnessed. We visited her at home, we visited her in the hospital, and shortly after being diagnosed, Karen passed away with her children at her side.

Childhood Lost

Carl's progression from doe-eyed boy to ruthless, hardened youth is the result of survival taking precedence over imagination and wonder. When a child no longer can get lost in make-believe because of the horrors of surviving in the real world, innocence

Carl loses his shoe, then eats pudding and reflects on this roof (Senoia, Georgia).[11]

is lost. Carl's fictional illustration of the difficulties of surviving a dangerous world as a youth gives readers a glimpse into the real experiences of Sarah, Nathan, and others like them. When parents are absent and adults put pressure on a child to develop, the child is socialized into adulthood at an alarming rate at the expense of his or her childhood.

References

Erikson, E. (1950). *Childhood and society*. New York, NY: Norton.

Erikson, E. (1959). Identity and the life cycle: Selected papers. *Psychological Issues, 1* (Monograph 1).

Erikson, E. (1968). *Identity: Youth and crisis*. New York, NY: Norton.

Erikson, E. H., & Erikson, J. M. (1998). *The life cycle completed* (extended version). New York, NY: Norton.

Notes

1. Issue 125 (2014).
2. Erikson (1950; 1959; 1968).
3. Erikson (1959), p. 109.
4. Issue 3 (2003); episode 1–1, "Days Gone Bye" (October 31, 2010).
5. Issue 5 (2004).
6. Issue 80 (2011).
7. Issue 5 (2004).
8. Issue 67 (2009).
9. Episode 3–6, "Hounded" (November 18, 2012).
10. Issue 105 (2012).
11. Episode 4–9, "After" (February 20, 2014).

The Governor

JONATHAN HETTERLY AND TRAVIS LANGLEY

*"He was a pure sociopath. . . . But he got things
done. I hate to admit it, but he seemed to most of
us—for a while, at least—a necessary evil."*
—Lilly Caul after the Governor's fall.[1]

Philip Blake, Brian Blake, Brian Heriot . . . by any name, the
man known best as the Governor may be the most Machiavellian of *The Walking Dead*'s monsters, especially in his TV
incarnation. He likes to do things with people's heads, in one
way while they live and in another way after they die. A "pretty
boy, charming, Jim Jones type"[2] according to Michonne, he
manipulates through cunning and deceit, which the sixteenth-
century diplomat Niccolò Machiavelli valued as important tools
in political intrigue. Past experience playing politicians shaped
David Morrissey's portrayal of the Governor.[3]

Welcome to Woodbury (Senoia, Georgia).

Social psychologists developed a twenty-item test, the MACH-IV,[4] to assess Machiavellianism, which later was seen as part of the dark triad or tetrad of human evil. Machiavellianism refers to the detached, calculating attitude toward such manipulativeness, not necessarily the manipulative skill itself. The following are a few of the specific examples of how the MACH-IV might measure the Governor.

Deception and Duplicity

Never tell anyone the real reason you did something unless it is useful to do so (MACH–IV #1)—**agree**.

Most people who get ahead in the world lead clean, moral lives (MACH–IV #11)—**disagree**.

The Governor conspires and double-crosses. Most of the Woodbury community seems oblivious to his devious and violent methods. Even those, such as Lilly Caul, who glimpse the true devil with whom they are dealing, cling to hope that "the Governor's Machiavellian methods will actually keep them safe. . . ."[5] Whether ambushing National Guard members to steal their supplies[6] or claiming that Rick's group attacked him as he tried to negotiate with them,[7] the Governor keeps his motives and actions to himself. His duplicity, double-dealing, and double-crossing come to a head when he gives Rick two days to turn over Michonne in exchange for peace while he secretly orders Martinez to kill all of Rick's group but spare Michonne for torture.[8]

Manipulation and Charm

It is wise to flatter important people (MACH–IV #15)—**agree**.

When you ask someone to do something for you, it is best to give the real reasons for wanting it rather than giving reasons which carry more weight (MACH–IV #10)—**disagree**.

Those who score high on the MACH–IV, meaning that they are impressive and charming in short-term encounters, are often persuasive and well liked.[9] The larger Woodbury community views the Governor as a king and a caring leader. Even Andrea succumbs to his charm and seduction, and that creates a wedge between her and Michonne. When Michonne sees through the Governor's glibness and superficial charm, he views her as a threat. After Woodbury falls on the television show, a woman and her daughter welcome "Brian" and want to rebuild a family life with him.[10]

Each time the Governor finds followers, his manipulation reinforces his power, position, and value in their eyes. He taps into all their fears to make them look to him for security and safety. Fear motivates them to follow his orders and hesitate to question his authority.

Power and Competition

All in all, it is better to be humble and honest than to be important and dishonest (MACH–IV #9) —**disagree**.

Whereas Rick surrounds himself with people who question his decisions, people with whom he can be open and honest, the Governor accepts no potential challenges to his control. Rather than welcome National Guardsmen, trained military personnel who could make Woodbury stronger and safer, he murders them all. Woodbury will not admit soldiers whose training and leadership might make them rivals for the Governor's power and authority. After losing Woodbury, the Governor and his newfound family cross paths with a group that includes his former lieutenant, Martinez, who knows too much about him. At the first opportunity, "Brian" murders his former ally to silence him and take power.[11]

His thirst for power takes him only so far. As one of the driving forces behind his desire to destroy Rick and take the prison, it leads to his demise.[12]

You can find more on the Governor throughout this book.

References

Bonansinga, J., & Kirkman, R. (2014a). *The walking dead: Fall of the Governor part one.* New York, NY: St. Martin's Griffin.

Bonansinga, J., & Kirkman, R. (2014b). *The walking dead: Descent.* New York, NY: Thomas Dunne.

Christie, R., & Geis, F. L. (1970). *Studies in Machiavellianism.* New York, NY: Academic Press.

Feinberg, D. (2012, October 28). *Interview: "Walking Dead" star David Morrissey discusses the Governor.* http://www.hitfix.com/the-fien-print/interview-walking-dead-star-david -morrissey-discusses-the-governor.

McHoskey, J. W., Worzel, W., & Szyarto, C. (1998). Machiavellianism and psychopathy. *Journal of Personality and Social Psychology, 74,* 192–210.

Notes

1. Bonansinga & Kirkman (2014b).
2. Episode 3–7, "When the Dead Come Walking" (November 25, 2012).
3. Feinberg (2012).
4. Christie & Geis (1970).
5. Bonansinga & Kirkman (2014a), p. 74.
6. Episode 3–3, "Walk With Me" (October 28, 2012).
7. Episode 3–11, "I Ain't a Judas" (February 24, 2013).
8. Episode 3–13, "Arrow on the Doorpost" (March 10, 2013).
9. McHoskey et al. (1998).
10. Episode 4–6, "Live Bait" (November 17, 2013).
11. Episode 4–7, "Dead Weight" (November 24, 2013).
12. Episode 4–8, "Too Far Gone" (December 1, 2013).

Gareth

Travis Langley

For insight into how evil Gareth—the television counterpart of comic book cannibal Chris—may have been, we turned to the actor who played him, the insightful Andrew J. West.

> **West:** I don't think that Gareth was a guy who was excited about living in a world like that or thought that it was going to give him some sort of special opportunity to live a life that he wasn't able to live before the apocalypse. I think it was something that he wished had never happened, but then he figured out a way to survive and was like, "You know what?

Actor Andrew J. West knows why apples await him at our Wizard World panel on *The Walking Dead Psychology*. "In case I get hungry?"

I'm good. I can do this." Of course, until he met Rick Grimes.

Langley: Was Gareth always a psychopath?

West: No, no, definitely not. I never looked at him that way. Of course I'm biased. I came to really like this guy a lot. But no, I looked at him as a very normal guy who probably had a severe case of PTSD after some things that went down. I think something mentally snapped for him, and it was a case of "I can't let anything like this happen again." I think his view toward humanity certainly changed, but not in a complete way. I think he still valued human life but only those humans with whom he was close to begin with—his family, certain people—but I think he also was introduced to an aspect of humanity, a really dark aspect . . . that he didn't know existed before. It broke something in him, and it changed him in a way that a stronger person like maybe Rick or Glenn probably wouldn't be changed. But I don't think that Gareth was a psychopath. I don't think that he was a sociopath to begin with, but it is an interesting study in how a traumatic event can alter someone. And their eating habits.

Langley: There's a whole lot of us-versus-them in *The Walking Dead*, and in crisis situations that's a common human response. For a lot of people, the normal thing is to dehumanize people on the other side. As Gareth, you're humanizing them, calling them by name, trying to be a person and have a conversation with Bob. Why are you having a conversation with your dinner?

West: It's a good question, and the answer is complex. A lot of that is strategy. Gareth and his little crew, they didn't want to kill Bob. That was never the plan. I don't even think it was about that particular meal. They got a little snack in the meantime, but what's really going on there is that they want to send a message to Rick and the rest. What they do is take his leg and they eat it. They send him back [to Rick's crew at the church] because they want to put a profound fright into the group and they want them to scatter, and they almost succeed. They get part of them to leave and they think that the group will be a little bit more vulnerable, that they can attack them in the church. So I think he has that long conversation with Bob because he wants Bob to go back and to share all of that and say, "Look, these guys are nuts. Look what they did to me. They're not playing around." Which is exactly what happens. Gareth's plan almost succeeds. So there's a lot going on there. But you have to have a detached viewpoint and you certainly have to dehumanize somebody to a certain extent to be able to talk to him that way. At the end of the day, the endgame is that they are going to get a huge meal out of the entire group. They're going to have a big roast, a big old party.

Langley: They left all the veggies they'd been growing back at Terminus. That's a protein-heavy meal.

West: I know. They were sick of veggies, I guess.

Langley: Could Gareth have redeemed himself? Could he have decided, "You know, I shouldn't have eaten those people," and turned himself around to try to help others?

West: I think so, yes.

> "We are the walking dead."
>
> —Rick Grimes[1]

People who are freezing, starving, or suffering other immediate biological deficits have trouble pursuing long-term goals. A loaf of bread can trump a philosophical discussion. A dangerous bed-claiming stranger's arrival can make a startled Rick abandon the book he fell asleep reading. Even when people are warm and fed, long-term survival requires the maintenance of supplies and shelter that can take priority over their emotional, intellectual, and other psychological needs. People desperate to survive can find it hard to *live*.

Like the dead, the survivors just keep walking.

Notes

1. Issue 24 (2005); episode 5–10, "Them" (February 15, 2015).

· PART FOUR ·
WALKING

13

"It Should Have Been Me": Survivors' Guilt in *The Walking Dead*

MARA WOOD

"Rick, it's not your fault when someone dies.
It's your fault when the rest of us live."
—Andrea[1]

obert Kirkman's storytelling in *The Walking Dead* comic book provides several in-depth examples of what happens to people after they lose someone in their lives. At any point in the story, fans brace themselves for the imminent tragedy that will befall the characters. Allen loses Donna.[2] Tyreese loses Julie.[3] Hershel loses several members of his family.[4] Rick and Carl lose Lori and Judith.[5] Each of these deaths comes at a time when hope and security seem to be within sight.

Those left alive are survivors, and their view of the world is warped in a way that affects their continuing survival. Survivors' guilt runs rampant through *The Walking Dead*. Guilt—the feeling that a real or imagined moral transgression has occurred[6]—is the key factor in many of the survivors. These moral transgressions often center on what could have or should have been done. Regardless of the situation, there is a degree of self-blame:

> *I should have been more alert.*
> *I should have been more careful.*
> *I should have seen this coming.*
> *It should have been me.*

Characters who are literally fighting for their lives each day can attribute the loss of a loved one to their own actions or failure to act rather than to the harsh world they live in now. Personalizing such loss is extremely detrimental to the survivors, especially in a new world that works to kill them each day.

Survivors' guilt (a term that first was used to explain the depressive symptoms that concentration camp survivors exhibited[7]) can arise after natural disasters, terrorist attacks, war, and sexual assault. We may experience a much less severe version of survivors' guilt when we pass a test and a friend fails. At its root, survivors' guilt deals with haves and have-nots, the guilt of being better off than someone else. Though psychiatrists no longer formally recognize survivors' guilt as a separate diagnosis, it is a possible symptom of posttraumatic stress disorder.[8]

There are several key markers of survivors' guilt. For starters, the survivor has undergone a traumatic experience: In *The Walking Dead*, every character has experienced some degree of trauma. The survivors lose people who are close to them. In some cases, that close person could be an individual who shares some common characteristics, such as religion or position. That loss must feel like the fault of the survivor. More often than not, though, the fault is imagined or overemphasized by the survivor.

The idea of the perceived cause of fault can be thought of through the concept of *locus of control*, which is a way to explain the cause of the bad and good things that happen in a person's life.[9] For example, an external locus of control statement would be "The teacher gave me a bad grade because she doesn't like me." Internal locus of control shifts the external blame to an internal reason: "I didn't study for the test, so I got a bad grade." Developing an internal locus is an important part of childhood development. Children with internal locus are able to take responsibility for their actions and develop some degree of control in their lives.[10] However, always deferring to an internal locus of control regardless of circumstances can be detrimental to a person's psychological well-being, as occurs when a surviving military combatant takes the blame for the death of a comrade or a battered wife such as Carol blames herself for her husband's abuse.

Survivors' guilt plays out differently in each character's journey. Some characters from *The Walking Dead* succumb to the sadness, whereas others rely on protective factors to pull them out. Regardless of their response, they all engage in high-risk behaviors, blame themselves for their losses, and see their survival as a moral crime. In the comic book series, Allen sees Donna's death as the beginning of the end of his life; he stops caring for himself and his two sons. Tyreese responds to Julie's death with a mixture of extreme aggression, high-risk behavior, and suppression with a hint of "I should have seen it coming." Hershel falls into depression marked by emotional numbness and distrust when he starts losing his children. Maggie reacts to losing her entire family by attempting suicide. Yes, each character experiences some degree of survivors' guilt in this new world, but no two characters suffer from it the same way Rick and Carl do.

The fall of the prison[11] presents a unique situation for exploring survivors' guilt. Rick, along with the rest of the crew, works

Hershel's Stages of Grief

The psychiatrist Elisabeth Kübler-Ross observed that many individuals undergo five *stages of grief*[12] in coping with death and other losses.[13] Farmer Hershel Greene manifests them all:

Stage 1: Denial. When Hershel's wife and neighbors become walkers, he refuses to believe they have died. However much denial may alleviate potentially crippling stress, it can blind people to genuine threats and raise the likelihood of their later developing PTSD.

Stage 2: Anger. After Rick's group destroys the barn walkers, an enraged Hershel orders them off his property. On television, his anger is brief. In the comic books, he stays mad enough to send them away.

Stage 3: Bargaining. A person may hope to undo or prevent the loss by means such as pleading to a higher power or seeking out different medical opinions. Hershel does this out of order. In conjunction with his denial, this devoutly religious man bargains to care for "those people" until a cure becomes available.

Stage 4: Depression. After the barn walkers' destruction in the comics, Hershel puts a gun to his head to take his own life until Rick stops him. On television, the recovered alcoholic Hershel goes drinking.[14]

Stage 5: Acceptance. Once Hershel moves past his depressive episode to face his new reality and learn to cope, he reveals himself to be a voice of wisdom.

Kübler-Ross's stages do not apply to all people, especially in a post-apocalypse in which the world itself can make anyone feel terminally ill. Grief follows no set pattern, obeys no rules.

—T. L.

tirelessly to make the prison secure for long-term living. In situations in which extreme loss has occurred, survivors may join together to create communities with an emphasis on helping.[15] This type of behavior is proactive; survivors want to ensure that the loss they experienced will never happen again.

Rick has an additional motivator: Lori, his wife, is pregnant. Although the circumstances of this pregnancy are met with mixed feelings, one thing is certain: The birth of this child represents the return to normality Rick and his fellow survivors need. They have spent too long surviving from day to day. A baby means there has to be some sort of future in store, a specific person for whom to rebuild the world. Their life at the prison is an attempt to return to normality, and Lori's baby plays a huge part in it.

Pinpointing how the prison falls is hard. A series of events lead to the Governor's decision to take the prison. There is the first encounter with the Governor which, in the comic book, results in Rick, Michonne, and Glenn being taken prisoner.[16] Rick loses a hand, Glenn is psychologically tortured, and Michonne is raped and tortured in ways that could not even be considered for viewing on the AMC television series. The Governor blatantly informs the trio that he wants their home. Their prison outfits indicate that they have been holing up in a prison facility nearby, an oversight for which Rick takes the blame. At that point, little can be done to prevent the Governor from searching for the prison. Additionally, the extensive revenge Michonne enacts on the Governor and the chaos they bring to Woodbury factor into the eventual fall of their own home.

Events at Woodbury offer the characters few, if any, options. Before they arrive, they have no way of knowing that they will be captured in their prison uniforms, they are not expecting to meet a highly militarized organization, and they certainly do not expect to be met with such hostility. Their actions to get back home are probably the only ones they can take and live to see their own people again.

When the Governor appears again later to attack the prison, Rick knows exactly how much trouble he has caused the Governor. After months of peaceful living, of false hope for their future, Rick and his family suddenly are faced with a life-or-death situation again. The assault kills many members of Rick's team. Hershel dies. Billy dies. Tyreese dies. The company is cut down significantly. No matter how much Rick cares for these people, two other deaths change him forever. Following Carl out of harm, Rick looks back just in time to see Lori and Judith die and collapse to the ground. With no time to mourn, he follows Carl and survives the attack on the prison.

Rick sees his wife and infant gunned down; Carl reaches safety only to discover that his mother and baby sister did not make it. The two experience survivors' guilt in different ways. Rick initially focuses on saving and protecting his last living family member, Carl, who cannot find the words to express his loss. As Carl quietly admits that he misses his mother, Rick falls into sickness. Carl, a temporary orphan for all intents and purposes while Rick remains unconscious, is briefly left to fend for himself.[17]

One of the hallmarks of survivors' guilt is high-risk behavior. For soldiers coming back from war, this could mean involvement in substance abuse or dangerous hobbies. In *The Walking Dead* comic book, the characters pursue high-risk behaviors a little differently. After Allen loses his wife, Donna, he goes out on a mission without being prepared. After Tyreese loses his daughter, Julie, he takes out a whole gym full of zombies single-handedly,[18] much the way Rick reacts after losing Lori on TV.[19] When Carl loses his mother and sister and his father appears to be on his deathbed, he goes out by himself.[20]

For Carl, this high-risk behavior has an underlying reason. He needs to find out if he can survive without his father. Though he lacks the proper caution for the test, Carl proves that he is capable of taking care of himself. For children, guilt itself can act as a protective factor, something that can spur adaptation.[21] Carl quickly learns that with some practice, this world may be something he can handle.

Rick experiences this loss much differently. Rather than engage in high-risk behaviors, he clings to the one thing he has left. Carl is the last surviving member of his family and possibly the only thing holding everything together in Rick's life. Rick becomes overprotective of Carl.

And has auditory hallucinations.

It all starts with a telephone call. The voice on the other end promises refuge but also expresses uncertainty as to whether Rick and Carl belong at the refuge. Rick becomes obsessed with getting more information about this possible haven. When Carl points out that there could be no haven, Rick brushes him off. The voice is so real, so comforting, that he cannot believe there is anything suspicious about it.

Things turn sour when Rick realizes that the voice he hears on the phone is Lori's and everything is in his head. The telephone is important to Rick. He feels he's still in touch with Lori even though she explicitly says it is not real. However, their exchange provides insight into Rick's guilt:

> **Lori:** Rick, listen to me, Rick. You blame yourself for what happened to me—to Judith. It wasn't your fault.
> **Rick:** I did everything wrong. Everything. I made all the wrong decisions, I should have known better— we should have left. . . .[22]

Grief overwhelms Rick. When he first wakes from the coma at the beginning of the series, the driving force in his life is finding his wife and son. From there, he works tirelessly to protect his family and friends. Traumatic events can affect a person's ability to adapt,[23] and Rick's judgment quickly deteriorates after the shock of losing half his family.

This imaginary connection to Lori persists even after Rick admits that it is all in his head. Rick's guilt is so deep that he must make amends to her well after she dies. Rick is not alone in this practice. After fans find out about Rick's auditory hallucinations, they learn who Michonne has been conversing with in secluded corners. Michonne's case is similar to Rick's. Not only did she see her boyfriend turn into a zombie, she mutilated his body and carried it around with her for much of the early part of the event. Even though she knows he is not really with her, she talks to him when others are not around. Intimately familiar with the pain of loss, she acts as a normalizing force in Rick's life.

One major challenge survivors often face involves the personal relationships they have after they experience trauma. Rick experiences depression and guilt over "letting" Lori die, and Carl expresses anger toward his father for not protecting his mother and new baby sister. Carl's anger is expected; children often express depression in terms of anger and acting out.[24] Children are in an especially vulnerable position when it comes to severe trauma. Without the more developed cognitive skills or the language to express emotions, Carl is left lashing out at Rick. Carl, like many children who undergo severe trauma, has a blunted affect and limited vocabulary to communicate his emotional needs.[25]

Carl's emotional response to the world becomes an important theme in *The Walking Dead*. Fans come to see Carl, the youngest of the main characters, as what the world will become. With his lack of appropriate emotional response, his black-and-white worldview, and his willingness to engage in high-risk behaviors, Carl looks to be one wrong decision away from death.

The feeling of helplessness that originates in deaths such as Lori and Judith's can be uncomfortable—especially for people like Rick, accustomed to being in charge of the welfare of others. Some survivors succumb to the helplessness; others convert that helplessness into excessive responsibility.[26] With that excessive responsibility, Rick faces existential guilt. Eventually, with time, Rick comes around to seeing his real role in the death of his wife and daughter.

The juxtaposition of feeling that something could have been

done to prevent the loss with the fact that the loss is irreversible results in cognitive dissonance that infiltrates multiple aspects of the survivor's life. The characters of *The Walking Dead* have little time to sit and reflect on their grief, and they lack access to the psychological care necessary to mitigate their maladaptive behaviors. Rick's phone calls with Lori may be the only relief he has in terms of his guilt.

Over time, Rick and Carl both move on from their loss. The phone calls become less and less important to Rick, and Carl regains some of his personality. The two continue living their life, building and rebuilding the world around them. They find the will to survive. With time and distance from the trauma, they truly start to see that Lori and Judith's deaths were no fault of their own. Rick sums it up best in a later conversation with Andrea:

> **Andrea:** Yeah. You can get caught up in dwelling on all the horrible things that have happened; it can slow you down, get you killed.
> **Rick:** Exactly. So I just don't do it. I rarely stop and reflect on anything that's happened. Doesn't mean I don't miss Lori. I do—I just can't think about her too much or it's . . .[27]

Rick has found a way to move on. Fast-forward a few dozen issues and we see Carl address Andrea as "Mom." There is hope for those left behind. The hard truth of survivors' guilt is that the death of the survivor would not have protected the loved ones. Rick finding some way to sacrifice his own life would not have saved Lori and Judith. Tyreese killing Chris early on would not necessarily have protected his daughter. There is certainly no way Allen could trade places with Donna and let her live and take care of their sons. Maggie is left powerless as each family member dies until she becomes the last of the Greenes. Despite this fact, the survivors live each day blaming themselves for living while another person is dead in the ground. The best step a survivor can take is to find a way to honor the memory of the fallen and continue surviving.

References

American Psychiatric Association. (2013). *Diagnostic and statistical manual of mental disorders* (5th ed.). Washington, DC: Author.

Blacher, R. S. (2000). "It isn't fair": Postoperative depression and other manifestations of survivor guilt. *General Hospital Psychiatry, 22*(1), 43–48.

Cohen, J. A., Mannarino, A. P., Kliethermes, M., & Murray, L. A. (2012). Trauma-focused CBT for youth with complex trauma. *Child Abuse and Neglect, 36*(6), 528–541.

Herman, J. L. (1997). *Trauma and recovery.* New York, NY: Basic.

Kübler-Ross, E. (1969). *On death and dying.* London, UK: Routledge.

Kübler-Ross, E. (2005). *On grief and grieving: Finding the meaning of grief through the five stages of loss.* New York, NY: Simon & Schuster.

Lindy, J. D. (1985). The trauma membrane and other clinical concepts derived from psycho-therapeutic work with survivors of natural disasters. *Psychiatric Annals, 15*(3), 153–160.

O'Connor, L. E., Berry, J. W., Weiss, J., Schweitzer, D., & Sevier, M. (2000). Survivor guilt, submissive behaviour, and evolutionary theory: The downside of winning in social comparison. *British Journal of Medical Psychiatry, 73*(4), 519–530.

Ross, C. A. (2013). Self-blame and suicidal ideation among combat veterans. *American Journal of Psychotherapy, 67*(4), 309–322.

Rotter, J. B. (1966). Generalized expectancies for internal versus external locus of control of reinforcement. *Psychological Monographs, 80* (whole no. 609).

Tilghman-Osborne, C., Cole, D. A., & Felton, J. W. (2010). Definition and measurement of guilt: Implications for clinical research and practice. *Clinical Psychology Review, 30*, 536–546.

Wayment, H. (2004). It could have been me: Vicarious victims and disaster-focused distress. *Personality and Social Psychology Bulletin, 30*(4), 515–528.

Notes

1. Issue 103 (2012).
2. Issue 9 (2004).
3. Issue 14 (2004).
4. Issues 11 (2004) and 15 (2005); episode 2–13, "Beside the Dying Fire" (March 18, 2012).
5. Issue 48 (2008); episode 3–4, "Killer Within" (November 4, 2012).
6. Tilghman-Osborne et al. (2010).
7. Blacher (2000); O'Connor et al. (2000).
8. American Psychiatric Association (2013).
9. Rotter (1966).
10. Ross (2013).

11. Issue 48 (2008); episode 4–8, "Too Far Gone" (December 1, 2013).
12. Kübler-Ross (1969).
13. Kübler-Ross (2005).
14. Episode 2–8, "Nebraska" (February 12, 2012).
15. Wayment (2004).
16. Issue 27 (2006).
17. Issues 49–50 (2008).
18. Issues 15–16 (2005).
19. Episode 3–5, "Say the Word" (November 11, 2012).
20. Issues 49–50 (2008).
21. Tilghman-Osborne et al. (2010).
22. Issue 51 (2008).
23. Herman (1991).
24. American Psychiatric Association (2013).
25. Cohen et al. (2012).
26. Lindy (1985).
27. Issue 86 (2011).

· 14 ·

The Walking Traumatized

JANINA SCARLET

Shane: "Jim, nobody is gonna hurt you, okay?"
Jim: "That's a lie. That's the biggest lie there is. I told
   that to my wife and my two boys. I said it 100
   times. It didn't matter. They came out of nowhere.
   There were dozens of them. Just pulled 'em out of
   my hands. You know, the only reason I got away was
   'cause the dead were too busy eating my family."[1]

The Walking Dead provides a window into emotional trauma. The protagonist, Rick Grimes, seems especially traumatized by the events that follow the apocalypse. After Rick has to kill his best friend, Shane, his personality changes drastically. Once calm, friendly, and level-headed, Rick becomes controlling, suspicious, and angry. He grows distant from his wife, Lori.

After she dies in childbirth, Rick has hallucinations, hearing the voices of people who have died since the outbreak and then seeing his deceased wife haunt the prison.

What's Wrong with Rick?

What does this mean for Rick? Does he have posttraumatic stress disorder? Does he have schizophrenia? Is his reaction normal? How does he get better?

Does Rick have PTSD?

Posttraumatic stress disorder (PTSD) is a mental health disorder that can occur among a substantial minority of those who experience life-threatening trauma.[2] The symptoms people with PTSD experience fall into these categories:

- **Intrusions:** flashbacks, nightmares, or constant thoughts about the traumatic event. Rick's flashbacks dealing with Shane's death are an example of intrusions.
- **Hyperarousal and change in mood:** being easily startled, overly vigilant, having trouble sleeping or relaxing, feeling angry and irritable, acting aggressively. When Rick first learns of Lori's death, he reacts by lashing out at the prison's walkers and anyone in his way, including Glenn.
- **Avoidance:** This is perhaps the biggest manifestation of PTSD.[3] Symptoms typically include avoiding anything related to the traumatic event, including thoughts and feelings about the trauma and reminders such as people, places, and conversations.

> After Lori dies, Rick stays away from his children
> and friends. Not until after he hallucinates a phone
> conversation with Lori, who reminds him of his
> duty to protect their children, does he hold his
> daughter for the first time.

To be diagnosed with PTSD, a person must experience symptoms from these categories for at least a month. Although Rick's symptoms become most severe immediately after Lori's death, he already experienced most of them after killing Shane. He continues to show most of the PTSD features long after he stops hallucinating. When one considers all these symptoms together, it does seem likely that Rick has PTSD.

Although hallucinations are not part of the PTSD diagnosis, research suggests that as many as 20 percent of people with PTSD are likely to develop some kind of psychosis,[4] especially if they experience hyperarousal, as Rick does. *Psychosis* refers to a loss of reality in which a person may create false beliefs (*delusions*) or see, hear, or smell things that are not there (*hallucinations*). Rick experiences visual and auditory hallucinations when he sees Lori and speaks to her on the telephone. On the television show, his auditory hallucinations stop after he realizes he is hallucinating and says farewell to Lori. In the comic books, the phone conversations continue for a longer time but eventually stop when his PTSD symptoms start to subside. This suggests that his hallucinations most likely were triggered by the traumatic loss rather than by another condition, such as schizophrenia.

Along with PTSD, a likely diagnosis for Rick might be *brief psychotic disorder*, which is characterized by the presence of one or more of the symptoms listed for schizophrenia but lasts less than one month. This disorder often results from a major stressor or trauma, and this fits with what we know about Rick.

PTSD Beliefs

Research[5] suggests that PTSD affects a number of different beliefs, especially those related to safety, trust, control, esteem, and intimacy.[6]

- **Safety beliefs** relate to our ability to protect others or ourselves. Rick confides to the CDC scientist Jenner that he feels he may not be able to protect his family.
- **Trust beliefs** have to do with people's ability to trust themselves and others. When Tyreese and his friends ask to live in the prison, Rick refuses, shouting at them to leave.
- **Control beliefs** have to do with needing to be in control. Rick, Shane, and the Governor push themselves to control situations and don't usually trust others to lead.
- **Esteem beliefs** relate to self-esteem as well as regard for other people. Rick blames himself for Lori's death and confides to Daryl that he has "screwed up too many times."[7]
- **Intimacy-related beliefs** have to do with our ability to get close to other people. Shane's death causes a rift in Rick and Lori's relationship and is undoubtedly traumatic for them in different ways. When Lori tries to talk to Rick, he pushes her away: "You want to talk? Talk to Hershel. I'm doing stuff, Lori. Things."[8]

What Causes PTSD?

Many people (approximately 60 percent)[9] are exposed to traumatic events during their lives. Nearly all who are exposed to trauma initially may have some symptoms similar to those seen in PTSD, but most people get better.[10] Approximately 4 to 10 percent of those exposed to trauma develop PTSD. Some of the most common reasons for developing PTSD have to do with how we feel, think, and act.

After a traumatic event, a person may learn to associate certain cues in the environment with danger.[11] For example, because Lori dies as an indirect result of the inmate Andrew's actions, Rick regards all strangers as dangerous to his group. He drives Tyreese's group away.[12] Because he remembers Andrew, his automatic response becomes that of mistrust and defensiveness toward anyone outside the immediate crew. Occasionally he is right, of course, but there are also times when he isn't.

Another *cognitive* (thinking-based) cause of PTSD has to do ·with the way a person interprets the trauma. Those who blame themselves for traumatic events are more likely to feel guilt and shame about them, and this makes PTSD more likely. For example, Morgan, the first person to tell Rick about walkers and the apocalypse,[13] later blames himself for his son's death.[14] Even though Morgan is not directly responsible, he could not bring himself to kill his walker-turned wife, who later kills their son. The blame that he places on himself prevents him from mourning his son adequately. Mourning is a natural process after losing a loved one. If it is interrupted, a person can develop a mental illness.[15] Morgan appears to be spiraling downward: He doesn't recognize Rick when he sees him again, mutters to himself, and writes strange notes no one can interpret.

When forced to act against their moral code, people with strong moral values such as Morgan and Rick are very likely to feel guilty, possibly affecting their self-esteem and identity; this change is called *moral injury*.[16]

Rick, a county sheriff, often feels responsible for protecting others and is overall a moral and compassionate person. Even when he exterminates a walker, a woman crawling around in a park, he bends down to tell her, "I'm sorry this happened to you." However, between his old life ending, his son Carl getting shot, and his wife getting pregnant, Rick's goals shift from saving the world to protecting his family. As he tells Shane, "I'm not a good guy anymore. To protect Carl, I would do anything!"[17]

Not until Rick kills Shane does he seem to experience the effects of moral injury. Specifically, Rick stops trusting his group, stating, "This isn't a democracy anymore."[18] Feeling defensive, guilty, and angry about killing Shane, he pushes away those closest to him, including Lori. All these symptoms are consistent with moral injury,[19] which can make a person more likely to be suspicious, distant, and prone to sabotaging his or her relationships with others.

Moral injury, insufficient social support, and continuous exposure to violent trauma not only make it more likely that a person will develop PTSD, they make it less likely that that person will recover from it.[20] Unlike the other characters, Rick awoke into the post-apocalyptic nightmare. Nearly dying from a gunshot wound can traumatize even the most resilient people. Subsequently waking from his coma alone in an abandoned hospital, starved and dehydrated, and then discovering dead people's remains (both inanimate and reanimated) might push anyone over the edge, and the stresses keep piling up. Learning that the outbreak affects the entire world, nearly losing his son to a gunshot wound, killing his best friend, repeatedly losing members of his group, and losing his wife all form a perfect combination of continuous mind-boggling traumas that finally knock Rick off his feet, causing a mental breakdown. After Lori dies, Rick goes on a rampage, slaying walkers throughout the prison. In the process, he becomes covered in blood and guts, looking a bit like a walker himself.[21]

After all his painful losses, Rick is not the same optimistic person he once was. He sometimes loses hope that things will ever improve again, and he is not the only one. Beth Greene (after the extermination of the walkers in her family's barn, including her mother) and Abraham (after losing his entire family) attempt suicide at different times. Others, including Jacqui and Jenner at the CDC, do take their own lives, believing that there is no hope left. Hopelessness is one of the biggest factors in why a person may commit suicide, especially when it relates to all three of the following aspects: *negative view about oneself*, having to do with the person's own negative judgments (for example, Abraham might have thought, "I'm a failure as a husband and father");

negative view about the world through evaluations of other people (e.g., when Father Gabriel says, "Nowadays people are just as dangerous as the dead"); and *negative view about the future* (e.g., Jenner saying, "There is no hope. There never was").

Because hopelessness is such a painful emotion, the sufferers often look for ways not to experience it. *Experiential avoidance* is the unwillingness to experience the painful thoughts, feelings, or other sensations that may occur when an individual is going through a hard time and is looking for a way to avoid experiencing these painful sensations.[22] Paradoxically, trying to avoid painful emotions actually can make people feel worse and may make them more likely to want to commit suicide. Bob's drinking and Merle's drug use are examples of experiential avoidance. In the short term, experiential avoidance can temporarily mask or reduce physical or emotional pain. In the long term, though, it can make the pain worse because avoidance supports the idea that the situation is hopeless. Avoiding problems instead of facing and working on them often can cause or worsen PTSD, depression, panic, obsessive-compulsive disorder, and other mental health disorders.[23]

What Does *The Walking Dead* Teach about Survival?

Rick, Abraham, and Beth, like other apocalypse survivors, have been through some of the most horrific traumas, and all attempt suicide at various points in their lives. Each finds a reason to live and changes drastically in order to stay alive. What do the three of them have in common? How do they manage to overcome their fears and hopelessness? What keeps them alive for as long as possible? They each find a purpose.

After walkers eat his family, Abraham is ready to commit suicide before Eugene runs toward him, asking for help. Abraham saves

Eugene's life, and then Eugene saves Abraham's by offering him a "secret mission." This gives Abraham a reason to live. He is a soldier. Being needed, being responsible for the lives of others, and having a specific goal are exactly what he needs to regain hope and fight to stay alive. For most service members, belief in the importance of their mission can reduce the likelihood of developing PTSD.[24]

Like Abraham, many people struggling with depression, overwhelming anxiety, or PTSD can recover faster if they stay true to their values.[25] *Values*—different categories of areas that are important to a specific person—can include family, friends, compassion, altruism, health, spirituality, and many others. When people stay true to their values and act in ways consistent with them, they are more likely to recover from mental illness.

Beth loses hope after Shane and others execute all of her walker family and friends who were kept in a barn. She concludes, "It's just so pointless!" Terrified that she will be gutted and unable to cope, she begs her older sister, Maggie, to die with her. Not until she actually attempts to kill herself does she realize that she wants to stay alive.[26] What arguably changes Beth's outlook on life the most occurs when Daryl later tells her that she will be responsible for taking care of Rick and Lori's newborn child.[27] She finds purpose and follows her value of taking care of others.

Another value that helps people recover from depression and trauma is *compassion*,[28] recognizing that another person is suffering, being able to empathize with that person (to "put yourself in their shoes"), and being able to offer kindness. Daryl Dixon provides a great example of how someone can heal through compassion. Daryl survives severe childhood abuse and neglect, which left him angry and mistrusting. He and his brother, Merle, are even planning to rob the rest of the crew before Rick arrives at the campsite. Over time, Daryl begins to connect with others, starting with Carol when her daughter, Sophia, goes missing.

Tirelessly looking for Sophia, Daryl performs the ultimate act of compassion when, recognizing that Carol is in great emotional pain, he brings her a Cherokee Rose, a Native American sign of strength and hope for the mothers of lost children.[29]

It is through compassion, social support, and staying true to his values that Daryl is able to heal the scars of his turbulent past and Rick, Beth, and Abraham are able to face their new experiences. Ultimately, opening up to painful experiences and being true to our core values and to ourselves seem to be the key ingredients in overcoming trauma.

References

American Psychiatric Association (2013). *Diagnostic and statistical manual of mental disorders* (DSM-5) (5th ed.). Washington, DC: American Psychiatric Association.

Beck, A. T., Rush, A. J., Shaw, B. F., & Emery, G. (1979). *Cognitive therapy of depression.* New York, NY: Guilford.

Boelen, P. A., & van den Bout, J. (2010). Anxious and depressive avoidance and symptoms of prolonged grief, depression, and posttraumatic stress disorder. *Psychologica Belgica, 50,* 49–67.

Cribb, G., Moulds, M. L., & Carter, S. (2006). Rumination and experiential avoidance in depression. *Behaviour Change, 23*(3), 165–176.

Ehlers, A., & Clark, D. M. (2000). A cognitive model of posttraumatic stress disorder. *Behaviour Research and Therapy, 38*(4), 319–345.

Farnsworth, J. K., Drescher, K. D., Nieuwsma, J. A., et al. (2014). The role of moral emotions in military trauma: Implications for the study and treatment of moral injury. *Review of General Psychology, 18,* 249–262.

Ferraj ão, P. C., & Oliveira, R. A. (2014). Self-awareness of mental states, self-integration of personal schemas, perceived social support, posttraumatic and depression levels, and moral injury: A mixed method study among Portuguese war veterans. *Traumatology, 20,* 277–285.

Foa, E. B., Zinbarg, R., & Rothbaum, B. O. (1992). Uncontrollability and unpredictability in post-traumatic stress disorder: An animal model. *Psychological Bulletin, 112*(2), 218–238.

Hayes, S. C., Strosahl, K., Wilson, K. G., et al. (2004). Measuring experiential avoidance: A preliminary test of a working model. *The Psychological Record, 54*(4), 553–578.

Kaštelan, A., Franciskovi T., Moro L., et al. (2007). Psychotic symptoms in combat-related post-traumatic stress disorder. *Military Medicine, 172,* 273–277.

Kearney, D. J., Malte, C. A., McManus, C., et al. (2013). Loving-kindness meditation for post-traumatic stress disorder: A pilot study. *Journal of Traumatic Stress, 26,* 426–434.

Litz, B. T., Stein, N., Delaney, E., et al. (2009). Moral injury and moral repair in war veterans: A preliminary model and intervention strategy. *Clinical Psychology Review, 29,* 695–706.

Loew, B., Carter, S., Allen, E., et al. (2014). Military beliefs and PTSD in active-duty U.S. Army soldiers. *Traumatology, 20*(3), 150–153.

National Center for PTSD (2014, November 10). *How common is PTSD?* U. S. Department of Veteran Affairs: http://www.ptsd.va.gov/public/PTSD-overview/basics/how-common-is-ptsd.asp.

Orsillo, S. M., & Batten, S.V. (2005). Acceptance and commitment therapy in the treatment of posttraumatic stress disorder. *Behavior Modification, 29*(1), 95–129.

Plumb, J. C., Orsillo, S. M., & Luterek, J. A. (2004). A preliminary test of the role of experiential avoidance in post-event functioning. *Journal of Behavior Therapy and Experimental Psychiatry, 35*(3), 245–257.

Resick, P.A., Monson, C. M., & Chard, K. M. (2008) *Cognitive processing therapy veteran/military version: Therapist's manual.* Washington, DC: Department of Veterans Affairs.

Resick, P.A., & Schnicke, M. K. (1992). Cognitive processing therapy for sexual assault victims. *Journal of Consulting and Clinical Psychology, 60*(5), 748–756.

Schnurr, P. P., Friedman, M. J., Engel, C. C., et al. (2012). Cognitive behavioral therapy for posttraumatic stress disorder in women. *JAMA, 297*(8), 820–830.

Notes

1. Episode 1–4, "Vatos" (November 21, 2010).
2. American Psychiatric Association (2013).
3. Plumb et al. (2004).
4. Kaštelan et al. (2007).
5. Resick & Schnicke (1992).
6. Resick et al. (2008); Schnurr et al. (2012).
7. Episode 4–2, "Infected" (October 20, 2013).
8. Episode 3–1, "Seed" (October 14, 2012).
9. National Center for PTSD (2014).
10. Ehlers & Clark (2000).
11. Foa et al. (1992).
12. Episode 3–9, "The Suicide King" (February 10, 2013).
13. Issue 1 (2003); episode 1–1, "Days Gone Bye" (October 31, 2010).
14. Issue (2009); episode 3–12, "Clear" (March 3, 2013).
15. Boelen & van den Bout (2010).
16. Litz et al. (2009).
17. Episode 2–10, "18 Miles Out" (February 26, 2012).
18. Episode 2–13, "Beside the Dying Fire" (March 18, 2012).
19. Farnsworth et al. (2014).
20. Ferrajao & Oliveira (2014).
21. Episode 3–5, "Say the Word" (November 11, 2012).
22. Hayes et al. (2004).
23. Cribb et al. (2006).
24. Loew et al. (2014).
25. Orsillo & Batten (2005).
26. Episode 2–10, "18 Miles Out" (February 26, 2012).
27. Episode 3–5, "Say the Word" (November 11, 2012).
28. Kearney et al. (2013).
29. Episode 2–4, "Cherokee Rose" (November 6, 2011).

· 15 ·

Eros, Thanatos, and an Armory of Defense Mechanisms: Sigmund Freud in the Land of the Dead

TRAVIS LANGLEY

". . . fear of the dead is so strong within us and always ready to come to the surface at any opportunity. Most likely our fear still contains the old belief that the deceased becomes the enemy of his survivor. . . ."
—Sigmund Freud[1]

Sigmund Freud (1856–1939) had plenty to say about sex and death, especially sex. This famous and infamous psychiatrist, who saw sex as life and therefore the greatest force driving our progress as people, described defenses we use to feel better about ourselves. He believed that these defenses help us persist throughout the journey between birth and death. Instinctively, inherently, Freud felt, we know in our bones that the end must come even though we do not completely believe it. To keep going, we find ways to cope even though that sometimes entails playing tricks on ourselves.

Instincts

Ashes to ashes, dust to dust. However much life and death may cycle back and forth at our beginning and end, both await inanimate states with life as the disturbance, the chaos in between. Life is fire between ashes and ashes. We fuel the flame. We burn to cope, to defend, to enjoy, to live better and longer, to fight death however we can. Because wildfire can spread beyond its burned-out source, we create and procreate as ways to blaze beyond our own life spans. When *The Walking Dead* characters Lori and Shane have sex, they feel alive. Coupling helps Maggie and Glenn, Abraham and Rosita, and others escape the horror of living in a world overrun by ravenous reanimated corpses. Actors Michael Cudlitz and Christian Serratos both said that their characters, Abraham and Rosita, realizing death can strike at any turn, would not be the only ones to seize the moment in their post-apocalyptic world and have sex often.[2] Others, though, may be wary of celebrating life even briefly, perhaps because getting close can make the pain of inevitable loss hurt even more; an example is Daryl Dixon, the rugged redneck hero who keeps hesitating in areas of intimacy.

A great proportion of Freud's *psychodynamic theory* considers how our need to keep ourselves and our species alive may motivate us—a need driven by the life instinct or instincts he sometimes collectively called *eros* after the Greek god of erotic love. Even though he had resisted Alfred Adler's suggestion that people also have an aggressive drive deriving from a death instinct, Freud later hypothesized the existence of the *death instinct* or instincts[3] his colleague Wilhelm Stekel would dub *thanatos*.[4] Whereas Adler meant it more like a drive to assert oneself, Freud speculated about its being more destructive. Because we know death is inevitable and life is the struggle against it, Freud felt, we sometimes give up the struggle and give in to death or destruction.

*"In the unconscious, every one of us is
convinced of our own immortality."*
—Sigmund Freud[5]

Along the way, how do we keep from giving up? According to Freud, our instincts drive us toward both life and death whereas our minds, both conscious and unconscious, resist accepting death. How does someone who gives up at one point, such as *The Walking Dead* character Beth who attempts suicide on TV or her sister, Maggie, who attempts it in the comics,[6] find renewed reasons to live? In our mental repertoire, fortunately, we have a whole armory of weapons and shields, the defenses with which we protect ourselves from internal conflicts and from our feelings about external reality.[7]

Ego Defense Mechanisms

Although the life and death instincts fall into that untestable area of Freudian theory that many criticize and reject as unscientific, the defense mechanisms take us into an area where Freud receives some of his highest praise. Even if we don't always do these things for the reasons he assumed, we do go to great lengths to cope with life's stresses. We all lie to ourselves sometimes. *Defense mechanisms* involve self-deception and other techniques for relieving stress and anxiety, reducing emotional conflicts, and protecting self-esteem, generally without our realizing that that is why we do these things.

His daughter Anna Freud cataloged the defense mechanisms he described. She named most of them and identified more.[8] The Freuds and neo-Freudians viewed these as unconscious safeguards against stressors. Later investigators identified additional defenses. The psychiatrist George Vaillant categorized them as *mature, neurotic, immature,* and *psychotic* in accordance with the way they correspond with healthy psychological development.[9] We all do some of these things whether we realize it or not.

> *"I don't know why I do the things I do.*
> *Never did. I'm a damn mystery to me."*
> —Merle Dixon[10]

Healthy, Mature Defenses

People need ways to manage stress and anxiety. In addition to conscious coping activities such as *thought suppression* (deliberately trying not to think about something unpleasant or distracting,[11] such as how badly your friend hurts while you need to aim at oncoming zombies), Freudians say that we cope in other ways unconsciously, without realizing it. Even when we know we're doing these things, we supposedly don't know we're doing them to protect our emotions and self-esteem.

The more mature defenses tend to be practical:

- *Anticipation* involves foreseeing difficulties and planning accordingly. Once the protagonist, Rick Grimes, and his group dispatch walkers in a prison yard, some characters want to rest but Rick prefers to plan ahead and prepare for potential problems in this new environment, to turn the prison into their own fortress.[12]

Thought Suppression

Fans have wondered why, after losing the prison, Maggie doesn't talk about her sister at a time when she doesn't know if Beth is alive or dead. Even though she does not believe her sister is alive,[13] Maggie does not have to think of Beth as dead either—and therefore herself as the last living Greene—if she simply does not think about Beth.

- *Affiliation*, forming relationships with others, offers safety in numbers and security as part of a group even when people must keep relocating.[14] "Surviving together is all that matters," Rick eventually decides.[15]
- Instead of acting on unacceptable impulses, a person may *sublimate* that mental energy, directing it into creativity[16] or any other activity. This occurs when Rick takes up farming on the prison grounds as an alternative to violence.[17]
- Humor helps us face life's worst without breaking down.[18] Many *TWD* characters have good senses of humor, even if laughing sometimes feels wrong. After chuckling at Morgan's remark, Rick turns his smile down. "After everything I've seen today, I feel guilty for laughing," he says, but Morgan reassures him, "You can't let it get to you. You just gotta keep going."[19] Daryl wisecracks, Merle mocks everyone, Father Gabriel amuses himself even though his jokes often rub others the wrong way,[20] Michonne says that toddlers find her funny,[21] and after hearing bad news about Eugene's mission to save the world, Tara starts making jokes instead of letting the sudden lack of a goal tear her down.[22]

Helping others through mercy, tolerance, acceptance, gratitude, or respect can emotionally fortify the person who helps:

- *Altruism*[23] involves helping others without
  expectation of reward. Abraham Ford offers canned
  food to Glenn and Tara when they are about to
  part ways even though at this point he expects
  never to see them again.[24]
- After weeks of wanting to kill his girlfriend's
  murderer only to discover that one of his own
  friends euthanized her, Tyreese shakes with anger,
  gripping a revolver, then abruptly stops and says, "I
  forgive you." *Forgiveness* has not made him forget
  what has happened, but granting mercy helps take
  a great weight off him.[25]

Even these healthier defenses can reach maladaptive extremes.
Using humor instead of sharing real feelings can keep a person
from achieving intimacy. Excessive anticipation, obsessively over-
thinking instead of straightforwardly planning, can create stress,
expend energy, and waste time. Granting mercy can come back
to haunt the granter if its recipient later harms others; cannibals
might not have eaten Bob's leg if Tyrese had killed one when he
had the chance.

Neurotic Defenses

Freud used the term *neurosis* for behavior that was mentally
unhealthy without broadly breaking from reality. He considered neuroses to be manifestations of unconscious processes that
involve using defense mechanisms either too little or too much.[26]
He felt that we are all neurotic to varying degrees. Neurosis is
not a modern diagnostic term partly because of controversy

regarding Freud's assumptions about unconscious causes,[27] yet the word *neurotic* remains popular with the general public. Regardless of the underlying mechanisms, people do these things.

Whereas the mature defenses involve finding ways to avoid acting on unhealthy impulses, several neurotic defenses involve creating ways to pursue them:

- Through *displacement*, a person acts out an impulse by directing it toward a target that seems safer (e.g., snapping at a coworker when you're really mad at your boss).[28] Upset over his girlfriend's murder, Tyreese punches Rick.[29] Hospital dictator Officer Dawn strikes Beth, scarring her face, over nothing Beth did.[30]
- Irrational as lying to yourself may seem, *rationalization* means making rational-feeling excuses so that you can do the things you want to do. Even though Dr. Steven Edwards rationalizes staying at Dawn's hospital by blaming the walkers on the first floor,[31] he does not leave when Rick offers him the chance.[32]
- Through *reaction formation*, a less healthy way to sublimate, a person follows the impulse in a paradoxical way. The person redirects energy into the opposite of what's desired, such as campaigning against pornography as a way of wrestling with a porn obsession. Afraid, reluctant to admit how desperately he needs his father, Carl shouts angrily that he doesn't need him at all, although soon enough the boy admits he's simply scared.[33]

Other neurotic defenses involve distracting oneself instead of handling things maturely:

- Facing possible slaughter by cannibals, Eugene gets matter-of-factly analytical about dismantling a lock (*intellectualization*) until he is told to shut up.[34]
- Characters repeatedly show examples of *isolation*, separating feelings from ideas and events. Teenager Beth Greene takes in the news of her boyfriend's death with no emotional display: "I don't cry anymore."[35]
- Rick, Daryl, Michonne, Beth, and more—one character after another grows distant, removing himself or herself from everyone else in a process of *withdrawal*.
- With *dissociation* (for dis-association), different parts of the mind function simultaneously but separately. A simple example is *highway hypnosis*, when part of you daydreams while another part drives, until you may realize you don't remember the last several miles. In a world of survival horror, many characters dissociate to shield their best parts from the dark sides they sometimes unleash.

Immature Defenses

A child, who has yet to learn so many of life's most basic lessons, manages stress in ways that may be normal for a child but inappropriate in adults. As part of the growing process, we adopt behaviors, values, and traits from others through *identification* with them. As a boy, Carl wears his father's deputy hat as a symbol of his identification with the heroic man his father was before the zombie apocalypse began. Emulating a specific admired figure to the point that doing so changes who you are is unusual in adults, whose personalities have grown more stable and complex.

Regression

Upset over the destruction of zombified family and neighbors he'd hoped could be cured, the recovered alcoholic Hershel goes binge drinking[36]—a case of *regression*, immaturely reverting to old habits during stress as if to carry the person back to more familiar times.[37]

Hershel's drinking hole (Sharpsburg, Georgia).

Other immature defenses involve finding ways to avoid reality rather than face it:

- Instead of confronting a tormentor directly, a person may express aggression indirectly or passively (*passive aggression*) through means such as procrastination. Rather than face the tyrannical Officer Dawn directly, hospital residents bolster their self-esteem by means that include withholding information from her.
- Although fantasy, escaping into daydreams and other imaginings but without mistaking them for reality, can help us dream up solutions or simply get away from problems for a while, *infantile fantasy* keeps a person from dealing with real issues. Michonne converses with people who are long dead because doing so helps her think. Not suffering from delusions, she knows they're gone and does not believe they are present and answering her no matter how vividly she imagines

them.[38] The comfort of fantasy, though, detaches Michonne from her living companions and hinders relationship growth.

- *Projection* involves perceiving one's own undesirable qualities in others, for example, when the inveterately deceitful Governor rejects Rick's peace offer by whispering, "Liar."[39] When Father Gabriel warns Alexandria's leader that Rick's people will betray others to protect themselves, the guilt-driven Gabriel is projecting his feelings about himself onto them.[40]

These behaviors, which are normal enough in children, can seem childish in adults. They lessen immediate distress but create problems, interfering with a person's ability to cope effectively with real life.

Pathological Defenses

Rearranging reality in one's head can take irrationality to a dangerous extreme:

- *Denial* involves refusing to acknowledge an unpleasant truth: "She's not dead!"
- *Splitting* simplifies life excessively by dichotomizing everything into all-or-nothing categories, for example, by seeing people as all good or all bad with no middle ground.[41] One minute the Claimers' leader, Joe, counts Daryl among his companions, but then Daryl stands up for Rick, whom Joe intends to kill. Joe instantly decides that the Claimers should beat Daryl to death.[42]

Freud's term for any condition involving seriously losing touch with reality, *psychosis*, remains a standard psychiatric term even among non-Freudians.[43] Though schizophrenias, dementias, and other long-lasting psychotic conditions often involve genetic, neurological, or other physical causes beyond their sufferers' control, some people with none of these disorders react to crisis, perhaps briefly, by "losing their minds" in a *psychotic episode*. After Lori Grimes dies,[44] her husband, Rick, starts having *hallucinations*, perceptual experiences not reflecting real input to the physical senses. He has phone conversations with a voice only he hears. After the voice identifies itself as Lori, he understands that it is not real, and so he does not linger in a state of *delusion* (a belief grossly out of touch with reality), yet he keeps hallucinating Lori. Hallucinations comfort him until he can, in time, move onward without them. When a wounded, weary, and addled Daryl Dixon hallucinates seeing his brother, Merle, in a forest, however, Daryl's injury-induced hallucination is more akin to a waking dream (*daytime parahypnagogia*[45]) than to an unconscious attempt to escape from reality. It may, in fact, save his life by making him wake up enough to fend off walkers and then keep moving through the woods.[46]

Feeling betrayed, rejected, and patronized by the living, the comic book version of Carol commits suicide by walker, letting one bite her.[47] Even though she talks to the walker, sounding delusional by saying that she hopes it likes her, a sane person can speak conversationally to a pet, plant, picture, or toy without misunderstanding what is going on. Carol comprehends well enough to tell Tyreese in her final moment, "Just let me die."[48] Her daughter, Sophia, in contrast, reacts to this loss by escaping another way: entering a *catatonic* state in which she sits staring blankly, unresponsive for days until the Governor attacks the prison.[49] The television character Beth Greene similarly falls into "some kind of catatonic shock," as Lori calls it, after witnessing her zombified mother's extermination.[50]

Life and Death: A Contrary Balance

We live, we die, and we know it. The characters in *The Walking Dead*, much like people who live in war zones, concentration camps, hostile climates, and the rest of the worst this world has to offer, stay more aware of the death and danger in order to stay alive and lessen the danger. For some, misapplying coping behaviors instead of facing cruel reality can prove deadly. For others, though, the reactions our distant ancestors developed during harsher parts of history can help them survive. Instead of causing problems such as anxiety disorders when activated and misapplied in a world that lacks the kinds of threats those ancestors faced, our defense mechanisms can help us fight the fear. They can keep us alive longer and keep our species going.

References

American Psychiatric Association (1980). *Diagnostic and statistical manual of mental disorders* (DSM-III) (3rd ed.). Washington, DC: American Psychiatric Association.

American Psychiatric Association (2013). *Diagnostic and statistical manual of mental disorders* (DSM-5) (5th ed.). Washington, DC: American Psychiatric Association.

Diamond, S. (2010, March 10). Normalcy, neurosis, and psychosis: What is a mental disorder? *Psychology Today*. http://www.psychologytoday.com/blog/evil-deeds/201003/normalcy-neurosis-and-psychosis-what-is-mental-disorder.

Duschinsky, R. (2011). Methodological issues of explanation: Evaluating "displacement" as an explanatory concept. *Journal for the Theory of Social Behaviour, 41*(1), 33–47.

Freud, A. (1936). *The ego and defense mechanisms*. London, UK: Imago.

Freud, S. (1915/1961). Thoughts for the time on war and death. In J. Strachey (Ed.), *The standard edition of the complete psychological works of Sigmund Freud* (Vol. 19, pp. 3–66). London, UK: Hogarth.

Freud, S. (1915/1963). Repression. In P. Rieff (Ed.), *General psychological theory* (pp. 104–115). New York, NY: Collier.

Freud, S. (1919/1963). The uncanny. In P. Rieff (Ed.), *Studies in parapsychology* (pp. 19–60). New York, NY: Collier.

Freud, S. (1920/1955). Beyond the pleasure principle. In J. Strachey (Ed.), *The standard edition of the complete psychological works of Sigmund Freud* (Vol. 18, pp. 7–64). London, UK: Hogarth.

Gantt, E. E., & Burton, J. (2013). Egoism, altruism, and the ethical foundations of person-hood. *Journal of Humanistic Psychology, 53*(4), 438–460.

Gurstelle, E. B., & Oliveira, J. L. (2004). Daytime parahypnagogia: A state of consciousness that occurs when we almost fall asleep. *Medical Hypotheses, 62,* 166–168.

Horwitz, A., & Wakefield, J. (2007). *The loss of sadness.* New York, NY: Oxford University Press.

Kim, E., Zeppenfeld, V., & Cohen, D. (2013). Sublimation, culture, and creativity. *Journal of Personality and Social Psychology, 105*(4), 639–666.

King, S. (1977). *The shining.* New York, NY: Doubleday.

Metzger, J. A. (2014). Adaptive defense mechanisms: Function and transcendence. *Journal of Clinical Psychology 70*(5), 478–488.

Savvopoulos, S., Manolopoulos, S., & Beratis, S. (2011). Repression and splitting in the psy-choanalytic process. *International Journal of Psychoanalysis 92*(1), 75–96.

Stekel, W. (1950). *Autobiography of Wilhelm Stekel: The life story of a pioneer psychoanalyst.* New York, NY: Liveright.

Vaillant, G. E. (1977). *Adaptation to life.* Boston, MA: Little, Brown.

Wegner, D. M. (1989). White bears and other unwanted thoughts: Suppression, obsession, and the psychology of mental control. London, UK: Guilford.

Wisman, A., & Koole, S. L. (2003) Can mortality salience promote affiliation with others who oppose one's worldview? *Journal of Personality and Social Psychology 84*(3), 511–526.

Notes

1. Freud (1919/1963), p. 48.
2. *Talking Dead* (November 9 and 23, 2014).
3. Freud (1920/1955).
4. Stekel (1950).
5. Freud (1915/1961), pp. 304–305.
6. Episode 2–10, "18 Miles Out" (February 26, 2012); issue 55 (2009).
7. Freud (1915/1963).
8. Freud, A. (1936).
9. Vaillant (1977).
10. Episode 3–15, "This Sorrowful Life" (March 24, 2013).
11. Wegner (1989).
12. Issue 13 (2004); episode 3–1, "Seed" (October 14, 2012).
13. Episode 5–10, "Them" (February 15, 2015).
14. Wisman & Koole (2003).
15. Season 5B trailer (November 30, 2014).
16. Kim et al. (2013).
17. Episode 3–1, "Seed" (October 13, 2012).
18. Metzger (2014); Vaillant (1977).
19. Issue 1 (2003).
20. Episode 5–2, "Strangers" (October 19, 2014).
21. Episode 4–11, "Claimed" (February 23, 2014).
22. Episode 5–7, "Crossed" (November 23, 2014).
23. Gantt & Burton (2013).
24. Episode 4–15, "Us" (March 23, 2014).
25. Episode 4–14, "The Grove" (March 16, 2014).
26. Diamond (2010).
27. American Psychiatric Association (1980); Horwitz & Wakefield (2007).

28. Duschinsky (2011).
29. Episode 4–3, "Isolation" (October 27, 2013).
30. Episode 5–4, "Slabtown" (November 3, 2014).
31. Episode 5–4, "Slabtown" (November 3, 2014).
32. Episode 5–8, "Coda" (November 30, 2014).
33. Issue 50 (2008); episode 4–9, "After" (February 9, 2014).
34. Episode 5–1, "No Sanctuary" (October 12, 2014).
35. Episode 4–1, "30 Days without an Accident" (October 13, 2013); again in episode 5–4.
36. Episode 2–8, "Nebraska" (February 12, 2012).
37. Savvopoulos et al. (2011).
38. Issue 53 (2008).
39. Episode 4–8, "Too Far Gone" (December 1, 2013).
40. Issue 75 (2010); episode 5–14, "Spend" (March 16, 2015).
41. Savvopoulos et al. (2011).
42. Episode 4–16, "A" (March 30, 2014).
43. American Psychiatric Association (2013).
44. Issue 48 (2008).
45. Gurstelle & Oliveira (2004).
46. Episode 2–5, "Chupacabra" (November 13, 2011).
47. Issue 41 (2007).
48. Issue 42 (2007).
49. Issue 45 (2007).
50. Episode 2–8, "Nebraska" (February 12, 2012).

· 16 ·

"Everybody Knows Their Jobs": Roles, Systems, and the Survivor Group in Your Head

Adam Davis

> **Glenn:** "You be my wingman. Jacqui stays here. Something happens, yell down to us. Get us back up here in a hurry."
> **Jacqui:** "Okay."
> **Rick:** "Okay, everybody knows their jobs."[1]

After the dead rise and civilization falls, survival for individuals depends not only on skills and knowledge but also on the group in which they find themselves. A lone person may be able to overcome one or two of the many challenges (e.g., finding supplies, fending off walkers, defending against rival survivors), but rare is the survivor who excels at all the skills necessary to make it through a typical day in the world of *The Walking Dead*.

Roles in a Group

A survivor needs to join others whose skills complement his or her own. According to the character Abraham Ford, each must "find some strong, like-minded comrades, and you stay stuck together like wet on water. We need people. The more, the better."[2] Even as skilled as the protagonist, Rick Grimes, may be, without a group of fellow survivors working together to achieve their common goals, his chances of survival would be slim. Groups of survivors are not all the same, of course, and joining the right people can make the difference between life and death. A successful group needs people who adequately fill diverse roles to respond to volatile circumstances.

Ready to explore escape options, Glenn assigns jobs to his fellow survivors: He assigns Rick and Andrea defensive roles; himself, the task of running through the sewer; Morales, assistance to Glenn; and Jacqui, lookout duties. He bases the assignments on their known strengths and abilities. For example, although Jacqui may seem underutilized as a lookout, her knowledge as a city zoning office worker plays a critical role in forming the plan of using the sewer to escape.

In this case, the group has enough individuals to address the circumstances, though the members do not know whether they all have the qualities necessary to succeed. Andrea is tasked with defending the storefront beside Rick even though she knows little about guns, as demonstrated by the fact that Rick must remind her to turn off her gun's safety so that she can fire it. She may be the best person available but is hardly the ideal candidate.

Ideally, survivor group members can shift flexibly between multiple roles. The drama therapist Robert Landy[3] notes that psychological health depends on both how many roles a person has in life (e.g., planner, protector, provider, father, friend) and how adequately that person can play those roles.[4] When a drama therapist who uses Landy's role method meets a client, the therapist often analyzes the client's *role repertoire*. Some clients have a limited access to roles (as when Carl wants to perform more mature tasks than the adults permit), some have inappropriate role selection (possibly when Rick farms while people need him in other roles), and others have roles that are underdeveloped. In families, members play more than one role.[5] A mother does not play only the mother role but also may play cook, cleaner, breadwinner, and more. Rick often plays the role of leader in his survivor group, and in his family he plays the roles of father and husband. Before Rick leaves the hospital and rejoins his family, though, Shane plays a surrogate father role for Carl, a partner role for Lori, and a leader role in their survivor group. When Rick joins the group, Shane does not shift his roles to make room for Rick's return. An overlap in group roles brings conflict that culminates in Shane's death.[6] Role flexibility is essential for a successful survivor group, with roles shifting as the needs of the group change, members leave or die, and new situations arise.

Roles in a family, as in a survivor group, can be official or unofficial. Although the group generally recognizes Rick as its official leader, Daryl as its hunter, and Dale as its mechanic, the members also play unofficial roles. Dale—like Hershel later—fills the role of the wise old man, giving advice and reminding the group members of their humanity. The children, who may officially play the role of dependents who need to be taken care of by the adults, unofficially serve as symbols of hope, reminders of why the group should keep fighting to survive.

In poorly functioning families and survivor groups, a leader who is inflexible (*role rigidity*) and has an inflated view of himself or herself (*role exaggeration*) can become the despotic Governor, pushing those in the follower roles into either subjugation or rebellion. This power imbalance divides rather than unifies. Divided groups risk reduced morale or even mutiny. When one person overfunctions in a role, another person reciprocally underfunctions to create balance.[7] If Rick plays the role of protective father to an extreme, Carl may become trapped in the reciprocal role of defenseless child as he grows into adolescence. If he never receives opportunities to develop new roles, he will not learn the valuable skills of using a weapon and defending himself, thus limiting the group's ability to be self-sustaining and adaptable for the future.

Although individual qualities are important in selecting the members of a survivor group, they may not matter if a survivor cannot form collaborative relationships with others. On an Atlanta rooftop, T-Dog watches Merle Dixon, whom Rick has handcuffed.[8] In some ways, Merle might seem ideal for a survivor group as a skilled tracker, hunter, and soldier who is able to defend the group from walkers and rival survivors alike. Unfortunately, his inability to collaborate, his impulsiveness, and his offensive personality make him an unpredictable ally at best and a traitor in waiting at worst. A successful group of survivors is more than just a collection of talented individual role players. The members also must possess qualities that enable them to collaborate with the group's other members.

Survivor Group as Survivor System

A term that family therapists use for a group of individuals is a *system*. In a system, the sum is greater than the parts. Just as individual atoms combine to create something more than they are individually, a group of individuals sharing genetic qualities become a family system and the survivors in *The Walking Dead* become a survivor system. Historically, therapists focused on events in their clients' past that have caused undesirable thoughts and behaviors in the present that prevent them from living the lives they want. If Milton, the Woodbury researcher working under the Governor in the television series, got to speak to a therapist, he might complain about his feelings of inadequacy. A traditional individual-focused therapist might work to improve Milton's self-image through positive self-talk or by looking at Milton's upbringing to find a cause for his poor self-image. This therapist may view causality as linear: Something in the past caused the current situation, and the client's task is to move forward.

A therapist considering systems, however, considers causality to be *circular*. A pattern of repeated interactions is occurring, reinforcing the presenting problem for the client. A systems therapist would look at Milton's ongoing relationships and the repeated social patterns in his life that could be perpetuating the problem. Any fan of the show could immediately point to Milton's relationships with the Governor and Merle as ongoing sources of the researcher's negative self-image. Milton behaves timidly around the Governor, who then acts aggressively toward him, which causes Milton to behave more nervously, which prompts Merle's disparaging comments. The ongoing cycle does not have a clear beginning and end, because each component in the system reinforces the others. Milton's systems-oriented therapist may attempt to break the unhealthy cycle in his relationships before working on his personal development.

In a *closed system*, the internal mechanisms that constitute the whole do not interact with anything outside the system. An example of a closed system would be a sealed greenhouse or a thermos; nothing enters or leaves the system. Survivors who

avoid outsiders and will not admit new members are attempting to create their own closed system. *Open systems*, in contrast,
mutually engage with the environment around them.[9] Most
human systems are open. Humans breathe, eat, and reproduce.
Families interact with other members of the community, and
countries trade and wage war. Survivor systems take in materi-
als from the environment as well as knowledge and sometimes
new members. Rick's group assimilates the survivor group at
the Greene farm, forming new relationships and developing a
new status quo. Being an open survivor system has its risks. A
successful survivor system needs to judge (1) when to be open
to new opportunities and resources and (2) when to stay closed
to preserve its safety. When Hershel, Rick, and Glenn venture
into town to Hatlin's Bar, they run into Dave and Tony, and
though those outsiders try to discuss merging groups and sharing resources, Rick determines that keeping the group closed is
the more intelligent option. The resulting shootout with Dave
and Tony's group validates his choice.[10]

The original system of survivors in Atlanta contains family
subsystems, which contain generational subsystems as well. Rick
and Lori are the parental subsystem within the Grimes family
system, which is inside the Atlanta Survivor Camp system.
Zooming out, groups of survivors function with one another in
a systemic way as well, interacting in cyclical patterned relationships. Systems and subsystems are surrounded by *boundaries*. A
boundary is an invisible barrier, ranging from *rigid to diffuse*, that
insulates one part of the system from another.[11] In families, the
type of parental boundary impacts the development of a child,
and in a group of survivors the boundaries around individual
families and relationships affect the larger group. The abusive
relationship between Ed and Carol Peletier, for example, is not
insulated within their marital system but spills over to affect the
Peletier family system and the larger survivor system negatively.

When Ed treats Carol abusively by the water where Andrea, Amy, Carol, and Jacqui are washing clothes, Carol is not the only one who reacts. Andrea and Shane both respond to Ed's abuse, exacerbating the situation.

Once a group of survivors develop routines and patterns of behavior, they may be hesitant to change them, especially if they seem to be working. Traditional systems theorists[12] say that systems are naturally resistant to change and that once patterns develop, the system naturally maintains the status quo; this is known as *homeostasis*. Homeostasis does not necessarily mean that the system is functioning optimally, simply that behavior has been repeated until it has become the norm. An overbearing father and a rebellious teenager may be in family therapy because the family system is perpetuating conflict instead of providing a safe and supportive atmosphere. The current homeostasis is conflict, and the family therapist will work to modify the system to establish a new homeostasis. In the context of a group of survivors, the ideal balance the system seeks to maintain is the sufficient collection of provisions for the group and the successful defense against walkers and rival survivors. Groups can achieve this homeostasis in various ways, a concept known as *equifinality*.[13] Rick's group achieves survival homeostasis at different times by building security systems and raising crops, as opposed to the survivors at Woodbury, who rely on raids of other survivor groups, and those at Terminus, who achieve homeostasis by attracting wanderers as a source of food. Though their tactics differ, the end results are similar.

Survivor systems have a narrow margin of error. If they make one mistake, like when Father Gabriel fails to lock Alexandia's gate,[14] everyone in the group could die, and so they must be receptive to continuous feedback and adjust the group accordingly. Because causality is circular and behavior patterns are repeated in a system, feedback takes the form of *feedback loops* that signal either that the system is on track and should continue functioning in the same manner or that it must adjust to correct for deviation. When walkers attack the gate at the prison, for example, the inhabitants proceed to eliminate them by striking them with weapons through the fence. No members of the system become casualties, and so the structure of the system and the behavior of its inhabitants are reinforced. Reinforcements that encourage behavior are known as *positive feedback loops*. Although positive feedback loops provide valuable information to the system, they can cause problems if they recur unchecked. For example, the positive feedback loop at the prison gives the survivors an exaggerated sense of security, leaving them unprepared for attacks by walkers and the Governor's forces from Woodbury. Their unpreparedness then results in multiple deaths and lost resources. The error-correcting mechanism in a system is a *negative feedback loop*. When a system receives negative feedback, it must regulate behavior and structure to reestablish a balance. The survivors adjust their system after the attacks by reinforcing the gates with wooden spikes, strengthening the perimeter fence, and reducing their reliance on the outside world by improving their internal ability to harvest food.

Open human systems interact with the environments in complex ways. They are adaptive[15] and self-aware. Successful survivor systems not only react to the environmental circumstances to perpetuate homeostasis but are self-aware. They predict, plan, and consciously change structure and behavior to improve their chances of survival.

For optimal chances in a zombie apocalypse, a survivor system must have role diversity, adequacy in performing roles, qualities that enable the members to form complementary relationships within the system, and receptiveness to systemic feedback. These conditions for group success within the circumstances of *The Walking Dead* are also useful as a framework for understanding

Cognitive Dissonance

Cognitive dissonance. Lilly remembers a shrink in Marietta once telling her this . . . three-dollar phrase for the games a person's mind plays on itself when faced with two or three conflicting ideas.[16]

Dissonance, the opposite of harmony, unnerves us. *Cognitive dissonance* is discomfort over inconsistencies within ourselves, when we realize that our cognitions (like the inner part of Lilly, Andrea, or Tara that recognizes the Governor's evil) are inconsistent with our actions (all the ways in which they go along with him). People often change their beliefs to make them match actions they've already taken. Placed into different roles, whether by Glenn, the Governor, or a Monroe, people can magnify their best or worst inner qualities to feel more consistent in their outward behavior. Many people follow the Governor not because they believe him; instead, some, such as Lilly and Andrea, believe him because they've followed him.

—T. L.

individual success in everyday life. Each individual has the potential to play many roles, choose which role to play at each moment on the basis of the requirements of the specific situation, and receive feedback that is based on successes and failures of the role selection. Certain situations are better suited for Rick, some for Dale, and some for Shane, Merle, or even the Governor.

The Survivor Group in Your Head

Multiplicity—the idea that an individual's psyche is composed of distinct parts—is well rooted in psychology, although from a variety of sometimes conflicting perspectives. Freud, for example, posited that the psyche is composed of the id, ego, and superego, but others disagree. Some models of psychology go a step further and, instead of simply seeing the parts of the psyche as separate and distinct, conceptualize these individual parts as distinct inner personalities functioning in systemic relationships with one another. Richard Schwartz[17] developed Internal Family Systems Therapy in response to hearing his clients refer to their internal parts as being in conflict with one another. One part of them might want to drink excessively while another part wants to remain sober. He cultivated the understanding that the parts could be considered as independent personalities within the individual, forming relationships and patterns of interaction analogous to a system of family members.

Whereas Schwartz used the model of a family to describe internal systemic functioning, the model of a survivor system also serves as useful model of a successfully functioning psyche. Imagine that everyone's individual psychological system is composed of independent personalities that function archetypically in a similar fashion to that of the characters in *The Walking Dead*. In every living person's mind are the roles of protective sheriff, innocent child, wise old man, nurturing mother, stoic Michonne, impulsive Merle, even the controlling Governor. As Schwartz makes sure to note with regard to an internal family system, each subpersonality has the goal of protecting the individual. None of them are truly destructive, even the ones that perpetually seem to sow chaos. They are, in one way or another, trying to protect the individual. In an internal survivor system, each subpersonality has the same goal; all the survivors portrayed on *The Walking Dead* seek to protect themselves from the dangers of the post-apocalyptic world in one way or another. Individuals must learn to understand their internal survivor system, seek to identify whether their inner Glenn or Rick would be the best role for a particular situation, and recognize that when their inner Merle or Governor arises, even though their methods are questionable, their goal is clear.

Surviving Together

Conditions for optimal success for a survivor group in a zombie apocalypse are a diverse, adequate, and flexible role repertoire and collaborative, complementary relationships among the members. Survivors in the group apply their skills and knowledge to multiple circumstances to the best of their abilities, and they adapt their roles from moment to moment. The members of the group must be able to build on and support one another, developing patterns of behavior and interactions that support survival, while being receptive to feedback when the system needs to adjust. If *The Walking Dead* featured these idealized groups, the audience would have little drama to enjoy.

In the everyday world, one does not need to fear walker attacks or scavenge for supplies in the ruins of Atlanta, but the conditions for success are similar. Successful people modify their behavior and relationships to meet the changing circumstances in their lives. Ideally, they choose which of their many internal roles to play, though sometimes their internal parts seem to have a mind of their own. When they choose a role (or one seems to choose itself) for a situation and the choice turns out poorly, they reflect on whether they should make the same choice or modify their behavior in the future. The survivor groups portrayed in *The Walking Dead* provide a form of research: how people can best survive a zombie apocalypse and how people can best survive the everyday world.

References

Bonansinga, J., & Kirkman, R. (2014). *The Walking Dead: Fall of the Governor part two.* New York, NY: St. Martin's Griffin.

Bowen, M. (1978). *Family therapy in clinical practice.* New York, NY: Jason Aronson.

Buckley, W. (1968). Society as a complex adaptive system. In W. Buckley (Ed.), *Modern systems research for the behavioral scientist: A sourcebook.* Chicago, IL: Aldine.

Festinger, L. (1957). *A theory of cognitive dissonance.* Stanford, CA: Stanford University Press.

Jackson, D. D. (1957). The question of family homeostasis. *The Psychiatric Quarterly Supplement, 31* (part 1), 79–90.

Landy, R. (1996). *Essays in drama therapy: The double life.* London, UK: Kingsley.

Landy, R. (2009). Role theory and the role method of drama therapy. In D. R. Johnson & R. Emunah (Eds.), *Current approaches in drama therapy* (2nd ed., pp. 65–88). Springfield, IL: Charles C Thomas.

Minuchin, S. (1974). *Families and family therapy.* Cambridge, MA: Harvard University Press.

Nichols, M. (2009). *Family therapy: Concepts and methods* (9th ed.). Boston, MA: Allyn & Bacon.

Satir, V. (1972). *Peoplemaking.* Palo Alto, CA: Science and Behavior Books.

Schwartz, R. (1995). *Internal family systems.* New York, NY: Guillotine.

Von Bertalanffy, L. (1968). *General systems theory.* New York, NY: Braziller.

Weiner, N. (1948). *Cybernetics: Or control and communication in the animal and the machine.* Cambridge, MA: MIT Press.

Notes

1. Episode 1–2, "Guts" (November 7, 2010).
2. Episode 4–11, "Claimed" (February 23, 2014).
3. Landy (1996).
4. Landy (2009).
5. Satir (1972).
6. Issue 6 (2004); episode 2–12, "Better Angels" (March 11, 2012).
7. Bowen (1978).
8. Episode 1–2, "Guts" (November 7, 2010).
9. Nichols (2009).
10. Episodes 2–8, "Nebraska," and 2–9, "Triggerfinger" (February 12 and 19, 2012).
11. Nichols (2009), p. 170.
12. Jackson (1957).
13. Von Bertalanffy (1968).
14. Episode 5–16, "Conquer (March 29, 2015).
15. Buckley (1968).
16. Bonansinga & Kirkman (2014), p. 79.
17. Schwartz (1995).

The Claimers

Jonathan Hetterly

"Seems to me like things are finally starting to
fall together. At least for guys like us."
—Joe[1]

Why hurt yourself when you can hurt other people?"[2] Joe
asks Daryl, summing up the dangerous nature of Joe's psychopathic survivor group that fans know as the Claimers.
They contrast sharply with Rick's people. Daryl, the link between
the two groups, faces his own evolving identity while navigating
his place and role within each group. The Claimers' fate, which
involves a darker turn in Rick's own character development,
raises the question of whether he and Daryl are growing in different directions as they fight their way through their world.

Primitive, Childlike Rules

Called the Claimers (by fans and those making *The Walking
Dead*) for their practice of "claiming" what is theirs—whether
person, place, or thing—the group governs in the same vein as
"calling dibs" in childhood. Calling dibs or claiming is actually done commonly among groups of men. Claiming the right
to pursue a particular woman, for example, connotes the right
to have the first chance to impress or hook up with her and
denotes that she is something to possess.

Little do Rick and Carl know that the house has been claimed (Senoia, Georgia).

Just as calling dibs fails to eliminate conflict between children, claiming does not prevent psychopathic behavior among group members. Claimers mislead, assault, and murder one another.[3] Joe's solution to Daryl's and Len's dispute over a killed rabbit is to cut the animal in half, a skewed mimicry of what King Solomon proposed to do with a baby to settle a dispute between two women claiming to be the mother.[4]

The members of Rick's group attempt to live out consistent values with one another and the outside world. The Claimers view their relationship with the outside world as open season and use deadly force as their primary method, not as a last resort, to obtain goods for survival. At some point, Joe must have realized that their group would self-destruct if they took the same approach with one another, and so he installed the one key rule—claiming right or ownership. Despite consisting of grown men, the Claimers follow a simple, almost elementary style of governing. Claiming is the method Joe hopes will allow a group of psychopaths to play together and eliminate their poor behavioral controls, violence, and violation of fellow Claimers' rights.

Identity, Community, and Belonging

The Claimers challenge Daryl to face his own identity and answer the questions "Who am I?" "Who do I belong with?" and "Why?" The group also poses the question of how much Daryl can be led into sociopathic behaviors by shared environmental factors.[5]

Daryl has been repeatedly in search of someone—whether it be Sophia, Beth, or even Merle, the brother who pounded into Daryl a belief that he was inadequate and could not make it alone. Joe accepts Daryl, and each may identify with the other on some level, starting with their mutual appreciation for crossbows.[6] Once Joe and his guys ambush Rick, Carl, and Michonne, though, Daryl recognizes that any traits and characteristics he and Joe share are superficial, outward, or outdated. The Claimers, unlike Daryl, exhibit behaviors associated with psychopathy, including violence, sexual offenses, and absence of empathy. Joe represents a less mature version of Daryl or a version of what Daryl would be if he had fallen in with the wrong group.

Character Arc and Identity Development

The Claimers highlight Daryl's long journey and transformation from a redneck, racist rebel to an integral member of a diverse group of survivors. Joe's demise at Rick's hands (or teeth) contrasts starkly with Daryl's growth.[7] Rick resorts, however justifiably, to more primal survival tactics, mirroring Joe and the group's savagery. This soon becomes evident during the main characters' escape from Terminus, when Rick wants not just to escape but also to kill everyone at Terminus, whether for revenge or for preservation.[8]

Claiming does not end with Joe's group. After psychopaths claim people, places, and things as possessions, Rick and company face cannibals claiming people for food, followed by Officer Dawn claiming people as "wards," her slaves. "He's one of mine," Dawn tells Rick regarding Noah, a ward who escaped from her. "You have no claim on him."[9]

Reference

Lykken, D. T. (1995). *The antisocial personalities.* Hillsdale, NJ: Lawrence Erlbaum.

Notes

1. Episode 4–15, "Us" (March 23, 2014).
2. Episode 4–16, "A" (March 30, 2014).
3. Episode 4–11, "Claimed" (February 23, 2014).
4. *1 Kings* 3:16–28.
5. Lykken (1995).
6. Episode 4–13, "Alone" (March 9, 2014).
7. Episode, 4–16, "A" (March 30, 2014).
8. Episode 5–1, "No Sanctuary" (October 12, 2014).
9. Episode 5–8, "Coda" (November 30, 2014).

"We didn't survive just to keep surviving," Bob assures the cynical Sasha.

Carl Gustav Jung, Abraham Maslow, Carl Rogers, C. Robert Cloninger, and others in psychology have said that people feel a deep need for *transcendence*, a need beyond other needs, a yen to go beyond the here and now. For those who keep asking and wondering what we can become, life is about more than walking. The journey itself can be lived all along the way.

By growing from an alcoholic loner who aches for a bottle to get him through the night into an idealist who sticks by friends, fosters their growth, and finds the good that can come out of every bad thing, Bob transcends circumstances. "Nightmares end," he tells Rick. "They shouldn't end who you are." Even as he lies dying, he encourages others to live.

PART FIVE

LIVING

· 17 ·

What Would You Do? Finding Meaning In Tragic Circumstances: A Bite-Sized Intro to Existential Psychology

Dana Klisanin

"Dale could get under your skin. He sure got under mine,
because he wasn't afraid to say exactly what he thought,
how he felt. That kind of honesty is rare and brave. . . .
In the end, he was talking about losing our humanity."
—Rick Grimes[1]

The *Walking Dead*, a post-apocalyptic horror story about zombies, is one of the most bizarre and popular comic books and television series in the history of either medium. How can we account for its success? *Existential psychology* may hold some answers. *The Walking Dead* is an existentialist's dream (nightmare): Nearly everyone who watches it comes away wondering what he or she would do in a similar situation. For some viewers, the show goes even further, provoking a wide range of tumultuous thoughts and feelings. One loyal fan found herself wishing for the death of Dale, a character pleading to spare the life of "a prisoner who can endanger the whole group if he gets loose." When Dale ended up being killed "in total gruesome *Walking Dead* fashion," the fan felt so terrible that she began to question her morality.[2]

Although it's extremely unlikely that we will ever confront zombie hordes, at some point in life we all face death—our own and that of our loved ones. This intersection—of life and death, of love and loss, of anxiety and despair, of our ability or inability to find meaning in life—is the subject matter of *existential philosophy* and its offspring, *existential psychology*. It is called "existential" because instead of focusing on the *essence* of human beings as other areas of psychology do, existentialists focus on *existence*. Whereas *essence* implies a static, unchanging substance, *existence* implies emerging, becoming, and changing. Existential philosophy states that we human beings have *free will* and must use it to find and create meaning in our lives, as the character Hershel Greene suggests when he says that they each have the power to choose what they risk their lives for instead of merely trying to survive without purpose. Existentialists believe that the individual must be studied as a "being-in-the-world" rather than solely from an objective or exterior point of view. Existentialism emphasizes a balance between freedom and responsibility. Some of the first existential psychologists were Ludwig Binswanger, Medard Boss, Abraham Maslow, Rollo May, and Victor Frankl.

The psychologist Rollo May (1909–1994) and the psychiatrist Viktor Frankl (1905–1997) each came extremely close to death but survived. Their respective experiences provided them with insights that shaped their approaches to psychotherapy.

May's close encounter with death came in the form of tuberculosis, a lung disease for which there was no cure at the time of his illness. May entered a sanatorium and for well over a year did not know whether he would live or die. While there, he noticed that the patients around him who passively accepted the disease tended to die, whereas those who fought against it tended to survive. He found that when he asserted his *will to live* and developed a sense of *personal responsibility* for his illness, he began to make lasting progress. May said that when our existence or values are threatened, we experience *anxiety*, but to be fully alive, we must confront our *nonbeing* or death.[3] He wasn't implying that we need to be diagnosed with a fatal illness—or battle zombies at every turn, the way Rick Grimes and the other *TWD* survivors do—but rather that through thinking about and acknowledging death, by being consciously aware of it rather than fearing it, people simultaneously become more conscious of life.

Viktor Frankl found the same truths, but his personal confrontation with death was far more horrific and thus closer to the experiences faced by Rick and the other characters in *The Walking Dead*. Instead of zombies, the horror Frankl experienced came in the form of Nazis. His father, mother, brother, and wife all died at their hands. As a prisoner in Auschwitz and other concentration camps, Frankl used his experiences later to write *Man's Search for Meaning: An Introduction to Logotherapy*. In the preface to Frankl's book, the renowned psychologist Gordon Allport asks the question that many of us ask about various characters in *The Walking Dead*: "How could he—every possession lost, every value destroyed, suffering from hunger, cold and brutality, hourly expecting extermination—find life worth preserving?"[4]

Walking these tracks, Glenn values his love for Maggie above all else (Coweta County, Georgia).

The Will to Keep Walking

The way Rick feels when he wakes up to find himself alone, without his family, in a world filled with zombies must be something like what Viktor Frankl felt when the Nazis took over Germany and began conquering Europe, rounding up Jewish citizens, and moving them first into ghettos and then to death camps. At the concentration camps, Frankl saw piles of dead bodies and rotten human flesh firsthand. Although it may seem that Rick and other characters adjust too quickly to the shocking events and circumstances, Frankl tells us that after the initial shock, he and the other prisoners quickly became numb and felt *apathy*, "the blunting of emotions and the feeling that one does not care anymore."[5] In a real-life story of rotting flesh, he tells of a prisoner who watched without disgust, horror, or pity as the "black gangrenous stumps" that once had been the toes of a twelve-year-old boy were picked off one by one with tweezers. How did Frankl continue to endure daily suffering? In the following passage, he gives us a clue:

We stumbled on in the darkness, over big stones and through large puddles, along the one road leading from the camp. The accompanying guards kept shouting at us and driving us with the butts of their rifles. Anyone with very sore feet supported himself on his neighbor's arm. Hardly a word was spoken; the icy wind did not encourage talk. Hiding his mouth behind his upturned collar, the man marching next to me whispered suddenly: "If our wives could see us now! I do hope they are better off in their camps and don't know what is happening to us."

That brought thoughts of my own wife to mind. And as we stumbled on for miles, slipping on icy spots, supporting each other time and again, dragging one another up and onward, nothing was said, but we both knew: each of us was thinking of his wife.[6]

As he made his way through the darkness, Frankl did not know if his wife was alive or dead; all he knew was that thinking of her renewed his will to live. At the beginning of *The Walking Dead*, Rick finds himself in a similar situation. When he wakes up in the hospital and then makes his way into the zombie-filled world, Rick's first thoughts are of his wife and son; he immediately makes his way home, where he hopes to find them alive. Frankl's thoughts of his wife led him to make the following discovery:

A thought transfixed me: for the first time in my life I saw the truth as it is set into song by so many poets, proclaimed as the final wisdom by so many thinkers. The truth—that love is the ultimate and the highest goal to which man can aspire. . . . I understood how a man who has nothing left in this world still may

know bliss, be it only for a brief moment, in the contemplation of his beloved. In a position of utter des-
olation, when Man cannot express himself in positive
action, when his only achievement may consist in
enduring his sufferings in the right way—an honorable way—in such a position man can, through loving
contemplation of the image he carries of his beloved,
achieve fulfillment.[7]

Just as Frankl clung to the vision of his beloved wife, Rick
clings to the hope that his wife and son are alive. He tells Morgan
Jones that he believes they must have left in time because the
family photo albums are missing. It is love that keeps Rick
moving forward. For Morgan Jones, in contrast, it is love for his
wife that has placed him in an existential dilemma. Should he
shoot her now that she has become a zombie? Can he kill the
woman he loves to save her from a fate worse than death? Is it
the right thing to do? What would Frankl tell us?

Frankl named his type of psychotherapy *logotherapy*, from the
Greek word *logos*, signifying "meaning." He described logotherapy as "focus[ing] on the meaning of human existence as well as
on man's search for such meaning." He explained his approach
as a "will to meaning" in contrast with other forms of psychotherapy, such as Freudian psychoanalysis's "pleasure principle"
(or will to pleasure) and Adlerian psychology's focus on "will to
power." It is different from psychoanalysis because it "considers
man a being whose main concern consists in fulfilling a meaning rather than in the gratification and satisfaction of drives and
instincts, or in merely reconciling the conflicting claims of id,
ego, and superego, or in the mere adaptation and adjustment to
society and environment."[8]

If we look to logotherapy for an answer to Morgan's dilemma—
that is, whether he should shoot his undead wife—Frankl would

tell us that it depends on how Morgan constructs meaning in his life. He would remind us that we do not live in a closed system but rather that we live in relationships as a being-in-the-world. In other words, when we look within ourselves, we must simultaneously recognize that we are not living in isolation—our judgments must reflect our interdependence with other people and the natural world. If Morgan constructs his meaning on the basis of his love for his wife, shooting her can be understood as a means of loving her. But there is something more than love that Morgan needs if he is to carry out this difficult action. To kill the walker that was his wife, he needs *courage*. Rollo May said, "Courage is not a virtue or value among other personal values like love or fidelity. *It is the foundation that underlies and gives reality to all other virtues and personal values. . . .*"[9] Let's look at one more example that appears both in the first issue of *The Walking Dead* and later in the first television episode. Even though the female zombie Rick encounters upon leaving the hospital poses no threat to him, just before leaving for Atlanta, he seeks her out and kills her. Rick's motivation appears to be compassion; in other words, he kills her because he wants to end her suffering.[10] Later stories may give us reason to question some of Rick's decisions and actions, but when his adventure begins, we clearly see his physical and moral courage.

Questions

This chapter posed two questions: (1) How can we account for the phenomenal success of *The Walking Dead*? and (2) How would we behave if we found ourselves in a post-apocalyptic world? Existential psychology tells us that it is through recognizing our being-in-the-world and confronting its opposite, nonbeing, that we find ourselves most fully alive. Rather than framing human beings in terms of instinctual drives and ego gratification, it asserts the primacy of free will. It tells us that we have the ability to find meaning in our lives even amid great suffering and that it is through taking personal responsibility for our lives that we embrace our freedom.

Because *The Walking Dead* is a story about survival, it speaks directly to questions of life and death, morality and meaning. On a collective level, existential psychology would suggest that while watching the characters struggle to stay alive, we are projecting our own fear of death as a way to confront it vicariously rather than directly. However, at the individual level, if the show prompts us to reflect on existential questions, we are no longer projecting our fears but instead consciously engaging with them. The show's remarkable success may well be due to its ability to speak to both types of viewers: those who harbor unconscious fears and those who are using it to prompt existential introspection.

That brings us to the second question: What would we do if we found ourselves in a post-apocalyptic world? How would we treat others? Would we betray friends and kill others to survive? Existential psychology tells us that it is impossible for anyone except you to answer that question, but before we begin patting ourselves on the back and imagining we'd take the moral high ground, let's revisit Viktor Frankl one last time. His ordeal in the concentration camps ranks among the closest approximations we have of life in a post-apocalyptic world. In the circumstances he describes, the chances are that we'd find ourselves doing things we cannot currently imagine. In a particularly poignant passage, he tells us:

> On the average, only those prisoners could keep alive
> who, after years of trekking from camp to camp, had
> lost all scruples in their fight for existence; they were

prepared to use every means, honest and otherwise, even brutal force, theft, and betrayal of their friends, in order to save themselves. We who have come back, by the aid of many lucky changes or miracles—whatever one may choose to call them—we know: the best of us did not return.[11]

Courage

In tragic circumstances, people will suffer anxiety, grief, and despair, but existential psychology tells us that if we have the courage to look for it, we can still find meaning in life.

References

Frankl, V. (1992). *Man's search for meaning: An introduction to logotherapy.* Boston, MA: Beacon.

Hilgard, E. (1987). *Psychology in America: A historical survey.* New York, NY: Harcourt Brace Jovanovich.

Howard, A. (2012). *The walking dead and existential crazy thoughts.* http://amaliehoward.com/the-walking-dead-and-existential-crazy-thoughts/.

May, R. (1972). *Power and innocence: A search for the sources of violence.* New York, NY: Norton.

May, R. (1993). *The discovery of being: Writings in existential psychology.* New York, NY: Norton.

May, R. (1994). *The courage to create.* New York, NY: Norton.

Notes

1. Episode 2–12, "Better Angels" (March 11, 2012).
2. Howard (2012).
3. May (1972).
4. Frankl (1992), p. 7.
5. Frankl (1992), p. 35.
6. Frankl (1992), p. 48.
7. Frankl (1992), p. 49.
8. Frankl (1992), pp. 108–109.
9. May (1994), p. 13; italics added.
10. Issue 1 (2003); episode 1–1, "Days Gone Bye" (October 31, 2010).
11. Frankl (1992), p. 19.

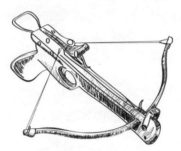

Hillbilly to Hero: The Transformation of Daryl Dixon

STEPHEN KUNIAK AND MEGAN BLINK

Beth: "You got to stay who you are, not who you were.
Places like this, you have to put away."
Daryl: "What if you can't?"
Beth: "You have to or it kills you."[1]

Many characters in *The Walking Dead* undergo transformations as they adapt to their new, harder and harsher world. The Dixon brothers, however, have already lived a tougher lifestyle than most. While Merle Dixon eventually joins the Woodbury survivors who can make use of his more belligerent approach, his "baby brother," Daryl Dixon—whose allure is as complex as his story—evolves.

At first, Daryl seems an outsider, a loner, and a loose cannon, lost in his call to adventure, but he grows into a resourceful and selfless character. His journey is fascinating and, what's more, easy to relate to. Daryl is a symbol, an example, who fits an archetype for heroes in literature, film, and religion. Fans love Daryl for the hope he instills in them for *The Walking Dead* story and also for their own life journeys. Daryl's transformation is not unlike the transformations in our own lives, though more visible with him because it is set against the backdrop of an undead apocalypse.

The ability to relate to a character was critical to the psychologist Bruno Bettelheim's[2] theory about fairy tales. Bettelheim said that fairy tales are important to us because we can learn important life lessons through their imagery. Not only is this particularly important for children, but fairy tale images are universal and therefore can be understood across cultures and ages. Tales from childhood can still inspire adults and teach values. In the same way, characters such as Daryl can show us how to become a better person despite adversity and danger.

The Hillbilly Hero's Journey

Building on the work of Carl Jung, the psychiatrist who originally proposed that all people have inherited *archetypes* (unconscious themes),[3] Joseph Campbell[4] outlined an archetypal hero that exists in all storytelling since humankind's very beginning. In considering the human psyche, Campbell was influenced strongly by Jung's archetypes of meaning. Campbell provided a model common among all heroes. This model (see the accompanying figure) outlined cornerstones of the journey as the hero receives a call to adventure and begins a resurrection quest. Although not every heroic story covers every aspect of the Hero's Journey that Campbell identified, this robust model covers a wide range of epic tales found in cultures far and wide. How does this epic journey relate to Daryl? Is he really comparable to heroes such as

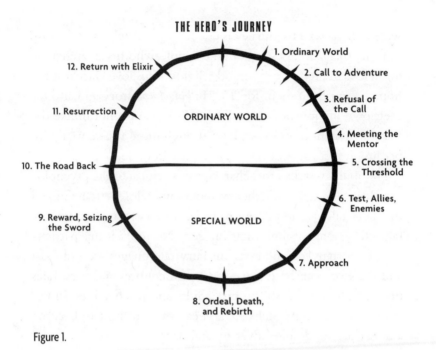

Figure 1.

King Arthur? The truth is that he's more comparable than many people might think, and those similarities hold the key to why he's so beloved.

Ordinary World

In this initial stage of the Hero's Journey, the fledgling hero appears in a raw form. We are introduced to the hero's world without any of the experiences that will play a part in shaping the transformation. Daryl reveals pieces of his humble beginnings through occasional anecdotes. This sharing is somewhat symbolic of his character evolution and his opening to other characters. His older brother, Merle, an abuser of drugs and alcohol, spends the bulk of Daryl's childhood in juvenile detention. Daryl describes his mother as an alcoholic who died in a house fire when he was young, "burnt to nothing," and his father as an abusive "dumbass" who noticed Daryl only when he was bad.[5] Daryl recounts that as a boy, he once got lost in the woods for nine days and his father never noticed he was gone.[6] Before the apocalypse, he drifted and did whatever Merle wanted: "I was nobody. Nothing. Some redneck asshole with an even bigger asshole for a brother." According to Merle, the brothers had been traveling to Atlanta for safety when they met the group, but they joined the group while planning to rob them.[7]

Call to Adventure

The Call to Adventure provides the catalyst for the hero's transformation. Circumstances that go beyond the average day-to-day experiences of the hero begin to take shape and cause the unformed protagonist to make decisions about acting differently from what would have been the status quo. The undead herald an opportunity for change. Already mentioned by group members who call him a "handful" who is unlikely to respond rationally upon learning that his brother has been left behind on a roof, Daryl first appears in the series yelling, "Son of a bitch, that's my deer,"[8] as a walker devours the animal he has shot with his crossbow. He swears, yells racial slurs, and is confrontational. His impatience and emotionality isolate him from other group members. Early in the story, he is presented as an impulsive, unpredictable hillbilly and a lone wolf in the group.

Daryl also is presented as capable and skillful. Joseph Campbell notes that the classic epic journey often includes the hero obtaining a mystical weapon as key in his development. Daryl's crossbow is practically his Excalibur in this post-apocalyptic world. The classic hero wields a weapon typically presented as unique to that hero, whether that weapon is an item (Excalibur), a powerful trait (Samson's strength), or belief (many heroes' faith) that guides the hero through his world.

The other survivors' respect and admiration for Daryl evolves as they depend on his gifts. Daryl saves T-Dog from a group of walkers by covering them both in corpses to hide from the walkers[9]—one of many times when Daryl's quick thinking saves others. When Carol's daughter, Sophia, goes missing, Daryl is quick to volunteer to lead the search, showing his hunting, tracking, and skinning skills, along with his willingness to step up. His desperation to find Sophia probably reflects his longing for someone to have searched for him in the same way when he was a child. People commonly play themes such as this from their pasts as they traverse their journeys.

Many heroes experience transformative "spirit journeys" as a part of their adventure. This experience, which gives the hero an opportunity to face and begin to put to rest past conflicts, is symbolic of the hero's struggle to let go of conflicts that hold people back in life. Alone and continuing his search for Sophia, Daryl get injured and starts hallucinating.[10] A hallucinatory Merle harasses him about his failed attempts to find Sophia. Spouting venomous comments that include calling him names such as "a joke" and a "worthless ass," Merle belittles Daryl's convictions and willingness to die to save a little girl.

Hallucination-Merle chides Daryl for joining the group, telling him he is "nothing but a freak" to the group members as they view him as "redneck trash," and asserts that they are not kin and no one but Merle will ever care about Daryl. These statements, coming from Daryl's unconscious mind, reflect his internal dialogue and relate to his self-identity. At this point, Daryl's identity within the group, his *social identity*, is evolving from a liability to an asset. Daryl has difficulty accepting this identity as he has been conditioned to believe he is "nothing." However, he begins to challenge these beliefs with statements to Merle such as "You talk a big game, but you were never there." Though Daryl has begun the transformative process, it is clear that his worst fears still haunt him and his relationships.

Refusal of the Call

The developing hero, in spite of the new circumstances, is often unsure or unwilling to step out of his previous lifestyle. We often experience the same apprehension when we know we should make a change in our lives. Even when the change is very necessary, our discomfort with the unfamiliar gives us pause.

Despite his growth, the other survivors still form expectations of Daryl that are based on his past aggressive nature. When the group captures Randall, Daryl is tasked with questioning him and beats him to obtain information.[11] He has his own beliefs about what should be done but doesn't challenge Rick's decision and test his power within the group. Since in the past he blindly followed Merle, Daryl probably still lacks confidence to stand up for what he believes. Daryl is, at this point, unwilling to accept the call to be a hero, not yet ready to challenge his conflicting beliefs about himself and take on a role in the hierarchy.

Meeting the Mentor

The rookie hero encounters a character who is able to become an instructor of sorts. The mentor is someone who believes in the hero in his early stages, often seeing something in him that no one else does. The mentor helps foster the internal strengths that are growing and developing within the new hero.

As Daryl continues his journey, he experiences another component of Campbell's heroic structure: the mentor. Despite their initial impressions of each other, Rick becomes a trusted guide and friend for Daryl. Early in the series, Daryl's willingness to give in to his anger is frequently stopped by Rick. Over time,

Daryl takes on some of these teachings and, though still a man of action, becomes much more levelheaded. As they prepare to make camp in the prison, Daryl is called out multiple times by Rick for support and is seen literally at Rick's right hand as they push through the prison doors. When two sets of keys are obtained for the prison, Rick gives one to Daryl. This symbolizes his status within the group.

Tests, Allies, Enemies

The hero will meet individuals who will help support growth and others who will seek to do the learning hero harm. Additionally, the learner will have skills and will be tested over and over. These people, experiences, and trials all mirror the same opportunities for growth we each encounter in life. The other players and occurrences in the hero's story help shape the hero into the legend that he will become.

Many heroes need individuals who can support them in understanding their conflicted nature. Carol is one of Daryl's biggest allies. Because her traumatic background relates to Daryl's upbringing and because they share past feelings of powerlessness, worthlessness, and isolation, Carol challenges his negative self-concept. She tells Daryl that he did more for Sophia than her father ever did. Despite Daryl's pulling himself away from many personal relationships, Carol continues to see his true nature. He tries to push people away by acting out in old ways, such as calling Carol a "stupid bitch" for worrying about him.[12] Rejection is less frightening than accepting his value. These doubts act as a threshold guardian or a force that stands in his way. We are often our own worst enemies in becoming the person we wish to be.

In many heroic sagas, the hero has a unique and often familial relationship with an antagonistic character. The hero is often unable to accept his relationship to the evil presence or tries to rationalize the antagonist's intentions. When Merle is found alive in Woodbury, Daryl has to face these realities. Despite Merle's actions in beating Glenn, Daryl insists on working something out with his brother. Rick pleads that he needs Daryl, and though he stands by Rick, Daryl is still conflicted. When Merle attempts to join the group after the fall of Woodbury, the group rejects him. Daryl's sense of responsibility for Merle is stronger than Rick's assertion that Daryl is part of his family now. Ultimately, his guilt over leaving his brother once before leads him to depart from the group.

Crossing the Threshold

Though Campbell's outline follows a particular order, there is no indication that every hero will follow the same steps in that order. Daryl's unique story fits better in this order. Crossing the Threshold occurs when the hero is able to accept who he or she is becoming and begins to explore his or her personal evolution.

Daryl slips back into old habits around Merle, allowing Merle to berate him and mirroring mannerisms, for example, spitting when Merle spits. After rescuing a passing group on the road, Merle attempts to rob them until Daryl threateningly holds his bow to his brother's head and saves them. Daryl's defiance of Merle is out of character in light of their past relationship. The brothers fight, and Daryl eventually asserts that he's returning to the group where he belongs. Daryl states, "I may be the one walking away, but you're the one that's leaving. Again." At this point Daryl is truly challenging his past.

Carol encourages Daryl upon his return: "Don't let him bring you down. After all, look how far you've come." Carol already has seen Daryl transforming even though he still struggles to acknowledge it for himself. He pulls himself away from Merle's influence when he sees Merle up to his old tricks, searching for alcohol and narcotics in the prison. After Merle kidnaps Michonne to deliver her to the Governor, though, Daryl still feels some responsibility for his brother and begins to search for them. Michonne tells Merle that his brother is now a well-respected member of the group, that "Rick needs Daryl," and that "Daryl has got a new family." When Daryl ultimately finds Merle, he has been killed by the Governor and has turned into a walker. Daryl weeps. He pushes Merle the walker away before finding the courage to kill him—a profound moment for Daryl as he reflects not only on the fate of his brother but also on what life without him would mean.

Daryl's entrance in season 4, when the original group and the remaining Woodbury survivors have merged as a larger group that is secure in the prison, is a stark contrast to that in season 1. Instead of dreading his arrival, the group members are eager to greet and thank him. Some shake his hand and admiringly guess what he did before the apocalypse. He is now a council member at the prison, and the community depends on him for many tasks. Daryl, ironically, is even seen deescalating fights between other members of the group. When the Governor returns to drive them from the prison, Rick looks to Daryl to help him decide what to do. Daryl Dixon has established himself as reliable, resourceful, and valuable to the group.

Ordeal, Death, and Rebirth

Heroes get challenged at the core of who they are and, if they make it through this stage, come out reforged on the other side. The ordeal puts to the test all the changes the heroes have made. They must look into themselves and shake off any of the old people they once were. This "death" of the old self allows each hero to be "reborn" as the new, legendary person he or she was always destined to become. These final experiences do not signify a complete end to the Hero's Journey. The hero will continue to be challenged and to evolve, just as we are challenged and grow as individuals. Though the evolution never truly stops, at this stage the hero's old form is almost unrecognizable in light of this newer form.

Beth evolves as a significant ally of Daryl. After they lose the prison, Daryl is beaten down. Beth observes that he seems without hope and without faith, yet every time she runs off in frustration, he is there to take her back.[13] Daryl and Beth begin to bond through discussion of past regrets and personal philosophies as they continue to seek the other members of their group. Daryl discusses his struggle to continue moving forward in the face of the guilt he feels over not having been able to stop the attack on the prison. He also discusses how the cabin where they were staying reminds him of his childhood home. The pair then burn down the house and symbolically give it the middle finger as they leave—another step in working to leave the past behind.[14]

Fate tests Daryl again when someone kidnaps Beth. In his desperation, he joins a group of renegade survivors who have harsh rules and swift justice for their members. The group's leader, Joe, continuously challenges Daryl that he is more a part of their renegade group than he wants to believe, stating, "Ain't nothing sadder than an outside cat who thinks he's an indoor cat." When Joe's group comes upon and tries to execute Rick, Michonne, and Carl, Daryl offers himself as a sacrifice. Daryl and his real friends are able to defeat Joe and his fellow psychopaths. Afterward, Rick assures Daryl that he couldn't have truly joined these cruel survivors and that Daryl, his "brother," is back where he belongs. The Hero's Journey is not a linear process. It is complicated and messy, just as life is for us. Daryl continues to navigate the path from who he was to who he wants to be.

Themes of fire continue to arise as symbols of Daryl's transformation. He is still changing and exploring who he is as a person and as a member of the group. Campbell, as was mentioned before, may indicate a particular direction for the Hero's Journey, but he doesn't state that it is universal for every

hero. It seems as though Daryl is still a work in progress on his own heroic journey. He is seeking to understand himself but still struggling with the juxtaposition of who he was and who he is becoming. This is also something most viewers can relate to on some level; we often don't show our true selves even to the ones we love for fear or rejection or fear that acknowledging our pain somehow makes it more real. Daryl tells Carol, "We ain't ashes." He is not someone who has been consumed or used up by the apocalypse; rather, he is negotiating and shedding his past self and will come out changed on the other side. Daryl has always been a survivor but it takes the apocalypse to teach him what it truly means to live.

> **Daryl:** "You said I ain't like how I was before?"
> **Carol:** "Yeah."
> **Daryl:** "How was I?"
> **Carol:** "It's like you were a kid. Now you're a man."[17]

Heroes and Hope

Daryl's evolution across the seasons of *The Walking Dead* provides an example of the power of heroes to draw us into their tales and inspire us. He has taken his trauma and his pain and channeled them into protecting others. He has learned to give love to others and accept love for himself. He has let go of his fears and begun to be reborn. He is a flawed character who, like all heroes, has become a symbol of hope. This inspires fans to make changes in their own lives. If Daryl can transform from a ruffian into a leader and protector, what can others accomplish? Walkers do not fill the real world, but the opportunity for greatness is all around. Real people from an ordinary world can underestimate their own potential. Heroes are not rare or chosen. Heroes are universal. Heroes such as Daryl are important because they give hope for something "greater" to shine from any human being.

References

Bettelheim, B. (1976). *The uses of enchantment*. Toronto, Ontario, Canada: Random House.

Campbell, J. (1949). *The hero with a thousand faces*. Princeton, NJ: Princeton University Press.

Cloitre, M., Cohen, L. R., & Koenen, K. C. (2006). *Treating survivors of childhood abuse: Psychotherapy for the interrupted life*. New York, NY: Guilford.

Jung, C. G. (1968). *The archetypes and the collective unconscious*. Princeton, NJ: Princeton University Press.

Notes

1. Episode 4–12, "Still" (March 2, 2014).
2. Bettelheim (1976).
3. Jung (1968).
4. Campbell (1949).
5. Episode 3–6, "Hounded" (November 18, 2012).
6. Episode 2–3, "Save the Last One" (October 30, 2011).
7. Episode 3–10, "Home" (February 17, 2013).
8. Episode 1–3, "Tell It to the Frogs" (November 14, 2010).
9. Episode 2–1, "What Lies Ahead" (November 13, 2011).
10. Episode 2–5, "Chupacabra" (November 11, 2011).
11. Episode 2–11, "Judge, Jury, Executioner" (March 4, 2012).
12. Episode 2–6, "Secrets" (November 27, 2011).
13. Episode 4–10, "Inmates" (February 16, 2012).
14. Episode 4–12, "Still" (March 2, 2014).
15. Cloitre et al. (2006).
16. Episode 5–6, "Consumed" (November 16, 2014).
17. Episode 5–6, "Consumed" (November 16, 2014).

Finding Your Purpose in the Zombie Apocalypse

CLAY ROUTLEDGE

"We get to start over. All of us, with each other."
—Daryl Dixon[1]

You sleep in shifts. You can't risk letting a walker sneak up on you while you slumber. It is not like it used to be, when you could just collapse at the end of a long day and drift away, forgetting your troubles. And when you are not sleeping (or trying to sleep), you must focus on immediate concerns. Hunger. You reminisce about the old days, before the walkers, when you thought you knew hunger. How naive you were. You remember that book you once read about the Great Depression in which you found people's anecdotes about hunger fascinating: the physical pain, the ever-present longing for nourishment, the nightly dreams about food. Now you understand. But food, though a source of constant distress, isn't your only or even your most pressing concern. Walkers. Death waits around every corner. Your group tries to create a place where you can all feel safe, but deep down you know safety is ultimately an illusion. If the walkers don't get you, another human may. The laws and moral conventions that once maintained some level of social harmony are long gone. But each day you start again. What choice do you have? This is the world of *The Walking Dead*, the world you would find yourself in if a zombie apocalypse occurred.

Terrifying, yet if you are like so many people, something about this scenario sounds seductive, even exciting, to you.

Humans have long been fascinated by the concept of an apocalypse. Many religions contain apocalyptic narratives or prophecies about end times. Secular apocalyptic beliefs are also common: Some believe the world as we know it will be destroyed as a result of human actions (e.g., climate change, nuclear war). Nearly half of the Americans polled by the Public Religion Research Institute reported believing that recent natural disasters are part of the "end times,"[2] and over a third of those surveyed by *National Geographic* believed an apocalyptic event similar to the one portrayed in the movie *The Day After Tomorrow* could happen in the next twenty-five years.[3]

Considering the prevalence of apocalyptic beliefs, perhaps it should not be surprising that people love apocalyptic media. In recent years, the plots of many top-grossing movies have centered on end-of-the-world scenarios such as global viral epidemics, asteroid strikes, alien invasions, and, of course, the zombie apocalypse. At the epicenter of this zombie craze is *The Walking Dead*, "the zombie movie that never ends."[4]

Post-Apocalyptic Meaning

Humans are existential animals, striving for purpose and meaning. Humans do not simply want to survive. We want to matter, to feel we are significant contributors to a meaningful world. We *need* to matter. A large body of research in psychology demonstrates that people who perceive their lives as meaningless are more likely to suffer from mental illness and addiction; they are less able to cope with stress and trauma, slower to recover from illness, and less likely to live long, productive lives compared with those who perceive their lives as being full of meaning.[5] Also, finding meaning is an important component of many mental health therapies.[6] For example, one study showed that psychotherapy more effectively improved mood and well-being if the patient displayed increased perceptions of meaning in life.[7] Things that help people perceive meaning in life include feeling that one can have an enduring impact on the world, believing that one is growing into the person he or she truly wants to be or has the potential to be, sensing that one has triumphed in the face of challenge or adversity, and experiencing close social bonds.[8] A zombie apocalypse provides an attractive opportunity for people to explore and even fantasize about each of these paths to meaning in life.

Case 1: Daryl Dixon

Consider the character Daryl Dixon. Before the zombie apocalypse, his life arguably lacks purpose or direction. Daryl grows up in an abusive household and becomes a drifter with no real goals, ambitions, or, as far as we can tell, meaningful relationships besides his troubled bond with his brother. In the aftermath of the zombie apocalypse, Daryl gets an opportunity to reinvent himself, to find new meaning and purpose. As a hunter and tracker, Daryl possesses skills that once might have made him the butt of redneck jokes but have incredible value in the new world. The apocalypse causes Daryl's social stock to skyrocket. As part of a group of survivors, he also has the opportunity to develop, for the first time, quality relationships involving mutual trust and respect—the kinds of relationships that have been shown to increase perceptions of meaning in life by making people feel truly valued.[9]

Case 2: Carol Peletier

Other characters in *The Walking Dead* take different paths to meaning, but their paths also highlight the pursuits of personal growth and triumph. Carol Peletier first appears as a soft-spoken, submissive wife lacking the will or ability to stand up to her abusive, domineering husband. Soon, though, Carol finds an inner strength as the zombie apocalypse forces her to become tough and independent. As she continues to face personal tragedy, Carol further comes into her own. As she grapples with her personal demons, she also struggles to find her own strength without losing her humanity. This balance proves difficult. With dramatic ups and downs, eventually the graphic novel version of Carol gives up and commits suicide by walker,[10] whereas the television Carol evolves into a tough as nails warrior and a reluctant leader. These divergent paths taken by the graphic novel and the television show highlight the importance of finding meaning for mental health and even survival. Research shows that those who give up on finding meaning are at risk for depression and suicide,[11] whereas those who are able to find meaning after traumatic experiences tend to become psychologically well adjusted ultimately.[12]

Case 3: Rick Grimes

The protagonist, Rick Grimes, offers a different narrative. Before the zombie apocalypse, by many standards Rick leads a life of purpose. As a law enforcement officer, he serves a vital social function. As a husband and father, he's also a family man, though his marriage is not without conflict. After the apocalypse, once Rick awakens from a coma, his life becomes focused on finding and protecting his family. He eventually finds himself in a leadership position in a group of survivors. Rick's journey is not about becoming the person he could be as much as it is about having the person he is tested. In a world that has lost its way, Rick struggles to maintain his moral compass, his compassion for others, and his belief in justice. Rick must shoulder the burden of being responsible for others, of balancing the often competing goals of keeping people safe and holding on to his humanity in an inhuman world.

Rick, like so many others, faces personal tragedy. He also is forced to make seemingly impossible choices that threaten to break his will and his sanity. Through Rick's story, fans can imagine being forced to focus on what is truly important in life: family, personal integrity, resilience in the face of despair—each of which has been shown to contribute to perceptions of meaning.[13] Rick shows viewers that one's meaning and purpose may best be revealed by hardship. In the zombie apocalypse, Rick becomes much more than a small town deputy.

These are just a few examples of how the stories of the different characters in *The Walking Dead* reflect the human struggle to find purpose and meaning. Each character has her or his own existential journey, and as fans, we get to go along for the ride. Real life is often full of mundane activities: sitting in traffic on the way to work, buying groceries, paying bills, cleaning house, arguing with our children about turning off the video games and doing their homework. Amid all these responsibilities, hassles, and distractions, it is easy to forget what it is that makes our lives feel meaningful. Indeed, daily frustrations as well as lack of meaningful stimulation can make us feel that our lives lack meaning.[14]

In a zombie apocalypse, however, things would be different. People would be forced to prioritize what is important, to hold on tightly to those they cherish the most. Materialistic concerns would largely evaporate—no more car payments, mortgages, or cell phone bills. Life would be stripped down to the basics. People would have to dig deep and live up to their true potential because everyone's contribution would matter. In the brutal and bloody struggle to survive in a world full of zombies, some people would find their true meaning and purpose.

Zombies Lack Meaning

Humans enjoy fantasizing about a zombie apocalypse in part because it allows them to imagine opportunities to find greater purpose and meaning. Again, as we've asked throughout this book, why a zombie apocalypse in particular? Any kind of apocalyptic scenario that involves survivors forging their way in a new world would offer the ingredients for meaning. What is it about zombies that captivate us?

Zombies may fascinate us because they help us confront perhaps our most basic existential fear: mortality. Humans, more than any other species, are able to contemplate the nature of mortal existence. We know that despite all efforts to survive and thrive, death is inescapable. We can exercise, eat our vegetables, wear seat belts, and get regular health screenings in an effort to live long and healthy lives, but still, we must die. Psychologists have argued that this knowledge of certain death can sometimes lead to mental problems.[15] For example, increasing the awareness of death by having people write about being mortal increases both generalized anxiety[16] and anxiety about death.[17] So what are people to do?

A large body of research in social psychology indicates that death awareness motivates people to focus on the goal of living lives that offer enduring meaning—the feeling that one is part of something or has made a contribution that will transcend the death of the physical body.[18] Sure, we endeavor to stay healthy and avoid physical harm. Why else would anyone eat broccoli or get a colonoscopy or mammogram? Critically, though, we strive to make our mark, to find enduring meaning. By living lives of meaning, we are able to attach ourselves to the *symbolic structures* (e.g., family, nation, religion) that continue to live long after we are gone. When people feel that they are part of something that transcends death (e.g., their nation and religion) or have made contributions that will allow them to live on in the memories of others, they experience a sense of meaning that in turn reduces the fear of death and promotes psychological health.[19] A life of meaning takes the sting (or at least some of it) out of death.

Zombies are physical bodies, nothing more. They lack the morals, beliefs, feelings, and goals that give human life enduring meaning. A religious person might describe zombies as meaningless because they lack souls, whereas a more secular person might call zombies meaningless because they lack minds or a true self-awareness and identity. In either case, the point is similar. The concept of zombies allows people to emphasize that the body is not what matters most. The body dies. It is transient and insignificant in the grand scheme of things.

The Walking Dead and other zombie apocalypse stories may be popular in part because they serve as reminders that living is more than just being an animated body. As humans, we do not want death to define us because we know that death is unavoidable. Therefore, we redefine what it means to exist. We focus on the aspects of ourselves that continue beyond the deaths of our fragile and always decaying bodies. Zombies exemplify this redefinition of what it means to exist. Zombies are just bodies. We believe that we are so much more.

Apocalyptic Visions

A zombie apocalypse may particularly fascinate people because the concepts of an apocalypse and zombies have great relevance to the human need for meaning. Apocalyptic thinking elevates perceptions of meaning in life. Apocalyptic visions involve

A flare near a water tower terrifies Rick's group, yet it leads to better things (Senoia, Georgia).

Apocalyptic Research

Though psychological theory and research supports the notion that apocalyptic narratives offer ways to envision new purpose and meaning, I wanted to test this possibility directly. Therefore, I conducted an experiment to see if having people entertain the idea of an apocalypse does in fact elevate perceptions of life as meaningful. In this study, I randomly assigned 90 research participants to read one of two articles. One article presented a case for a coming apocalypse, suggesting, among other things, that our planet is at increased risk of deadly viral pandemics (similar to many zombie outbreak narratives), catastrophic natural disasters, and dangerous geopolitical unrest. In short, this article served to focus participants' thoughts on the possibility that the world as they know it could come to an end soon. The participants in a control condition read an article about all the signs pointing to the death of the traditional brick-and-mortar bookstore (e.g., increased online shopping for books). The idea was to have these participants also read a passage about a change in the world but one that could not trigger apocalyptic thinking.

After reading one of the articles, all the participants completed a questionnaire that assessed the extent to which they perceived their lives as full of meaning and purpose. That is, they rated on a scale their agreement with statements indicative of meaning such as "My personal existence is purposeful and meaningful." The results from this study supported the assertion that people find thinking about an apocalypse meaningful. The participants who read the article about signs of a coming apocalypse reported significantly higher levels of perceived meaning than did the participants in the control condition who read an article about signs of the death of the traditional bookstore. The idea of an apocalypse may be scary, but it also generates perceptions of meaning in life.

themes of growth, redemption, meaningful relationships, and triumph over adversity. In addition, the concept of zombies may help people cope with one of the most potent threats to meaning (i.e., mortality) because it reminds us that life is about more than being a physical, animated body. *The Walking Dead* therefore appeals to us in part because it beautifully illustrates the human struggle to find meaning in the face of mortality. It says that our struggle matters.

References

Debats, D. L. (1996). Meaning in life: Clinical relevance and predictive power. *British Journal of Clinical Psychology, 35(4)*, 503–516.

Harlowe, L., Newcomb, M., & Bentler, P. (1986). Depression, self-derogation, substance abuse, and suicide ideation: Lack of purpose in life as a mediational factor. *Journal of Clinical Psychology, 42*, 5–21.

Heintzelman, S. J., & King, L. A. (2014). Life is pretty meaningful. *The American Psychologist, 69,* 561–574.

Hicks, J., & Routledge, C. (Eds.). (2013). *The experience of meaning in life: Classical perspectives, emerging themes, and controversies.* New York, NY: Springer.

Kashdan, T. B., & Steger, M. F. (2007). Curiosity and pathways to well-being and meaning in life: Traits, states, and everyday behaviors. *Motivation and Emotion, 31*(3), 159–173.

Kelton Research (2012). *Doomsday preppers survey* (2012). http://images.nationalgeographic. com/wpf/media-live/file/Doomsday_Preppers_Survey_-_Topline_Results.pdf.

Lambert, N. M., Stillman, T. F., Hicks, J. A., Kamble, S., Baumeister, R. F., & Fincham, F. D. (2013). To belong is to matter: Sense of belonging enhances meaning in life. *Personality and Social Psychological Bulletin, 39*(11), 1418–1427.

Markman, K. D., Proulx, T., & Lindberg, M. J. (Eds.). (2013). *The psychology of meaning.* Washington, DC: American Psychological Association.

McMillan, G. (2009, September 8). *Kirkman: TV can make the zombie movie that never ends.* http://io9.com/5353248/kirkman-tv-can-make-the-zombie-movie-that-never-ends.

Park, C. L., & Ai, A. L. (2006). Meaning making and growth: New directions for research on survivors of trauma. *Journal of Loss and Trauma: International Perspectives on Stress and Coping, 11*(5), 389–407.

Public Religion Research Institute (2014, November 21). *Believers, sympathizers, and skeptics: Why Americans are conflicted about climate change, environmental policy, and science.* http://publicreligion.org/research/2014/11/believers-sympathizers-skeptics-americans-conflicted-climate-change-environmental-policy-science/.

Routledge, C., & Juhl, J. (2010). When death thoughts turn into death fears: Purpose in life moderates the effects of mortality salience on death anxiety. *Cognition and Emotion, 24*(5), 848–854.

Routledge, C., Ostafin, B., Juhl, J., Sedikes, C., Cathey, C., & Liao, J. (2010). Adjusting to death: The effects of mortality salience and self-esteem on psychological well-being, growth motivation, and maladaptive behavior. *Journal of Personality and Social Psychology, 99*(6), 897–916.

Seligman, M. E. P., Rashid, T., & Parks, A. C. (2006). Positive psychotherapy. *American Psychologist, 61,* 774–788.

Solomon, S., Greenberg, J., & Pyszczynski, T. (1991). Terror management theory of self-esteem. In C. R. Snyder & D. Forsyth (Eds.), *Handbook of social and clinical psychology: The health perspective* (pp. 21–40). New York, NY: Pergamon.

Solomon, S., Greenberg, J., & Pyszczynski, T. (2004). The cultural animal: Twenty years of terror management theory and research. In J. Greenberg, S. L., Koole, & T. Pyszczynski (Eds.), *Handbook of experimental existential psychology* (pp. 13–34). New York, NY: Guilford.

Notes

1. Episode 5–2, "Strangers" (October 19, 2014).
2. Public Religion Research Institute (2014).
3. Kelton Research (2012).
4. McMillan (2009).
5. Heintzelman & King (2014).
6. Seligman et al. (2006).
7. Debats (1996).
8. Hicks & Routledge (2013).
9. Lambert et al. (2013).
10. Issues 41–42 (2007).

11. Harlowe et al. (1986).
12. Park & Ai (2006).
13. Markman et al. (2013).
14. Kashdan & Steger (2007).
15. Solomon et al. (1991).
16. Routledge et al. (2010).
17. Routledge & Juhl (2010).
18. Solomon et al. (2004).
19. Solomon et al. (2004).

Negan

TRAVIS LANGLEY

*"Negan rules by fear or by manipulating people into
thinking he's the only thing keeping them alive.
They worship him. For him, it's all about ego."*
—Paul "Jesus" Monroe[1]

"Power is the ultimate aphrodisiac."
— diplomat Henry Kissinger[2]

Stronger, smarter, saner" and more in control than the Governor according to creator Robert Kirkman,[3] the man known as Negan ("KNEE-gan") wages a war worse than anything Woodbury's leader ever manages.

The Saviors, Negan's band of over a hundred survivors, eliminate walkers surrounding communities and demand half of those communities' rations in return, whether the communities welcome this arrangement or not. When people resist, when Negan feels the Saviors have been shortchanged, his men kill to make a point. Negan even orders a man to stab a friend for fear of what the Saviors will do to them all.[4]

"He's a character who clearly is thriving after this apocalypse," says the actor Andrew J. West (Gareth).[5] "It sounds like he's happy this happened. It seems that way, the way he lives his life and treats people. You'd have to be a sadist, I think, in order to enjoy or appreciate a world like that, but if you're a guy like

Negan who doesn't really have empathy or really care about other people, you might do pretty well."

How does Negan rank on the dark tetrad, that checklist for evil?

Psychopathy: He is callous and short on empathy even though he denies it. His post-apocalyptic actions are antisocial by most people's standards, although probably not by his own because as he sees it, he sets the standards. He makes the rules. Negan is more of a *high-functioning psychopath*,[6] the kind who might have put his boldness to great use as a pre-apocalyptic firefighter, soldier, surgeon, reporter, civil servant, or master chef.[7]

Machiavellianism: Unlike the deceitful Governor, Negan tells the truth as he sees it. Still, he believes in ruling through fear, intimidation, and other forms of manipulation. He therefore exhibits a different set of Machiavellian attitudes.

Narcissism: Ego can get in the way of his better judgment. Negan's a bully. Vain, selfish, and not prone to noticing the real damage he's causing even to himself, he knows his way is best and anything else is idiotic. To be sure, though, he accomplishes much during the post-apocalypse. Thus, although some degree of his egotism seems lifelong, recent circumstances may have inflated his ego.

Sadism: No matter how often Negan says he does not enjoy cruelty, his actions suggest otherwise: his creativity in devising new ways to hurt people, his thin smile when picking punishments, and the severity of his cruel and unusual punishments. Using an iron to burn half of a man's face off goes beyond making a point. Negan's "big picture" goals, though, are not about hurting people. He perceives his brutality as a tool for the greater good. Even so, saying that his bloody bat "Lucille" loves bashing heads reflects his own glee.

As to whether Negan is evil or how much, there is no simple answer. He shows potential for insight that the Governor never achieves and Claimer Joe never would want. At the climax of their war, he finally, really hears Rick's message. "I've had it all wrong," Negan realizes. "I've been acting like a hungry dog, hoarding supplies, pushing others away. For safety, for my people."[8] An epiphany washes over him: Instead of building a rigid system in which survivors can exist if they do what he wants, he should have applied his resources and skills toward a far greater goal: reestablishing civilization itself. They can create a new way of life.

References

Barker, E. (2014, March 21). *Which professions have the most psychopaths? The fewest?* http://time.com/32647/which-professions-have-the-most-psychopaths-the-fewest/.

Kirkman, R. (2014, March 19). *I'm Robert Kirkman, creator of The Walking Dead.* AMA!https://www.topiama.com/r/2359/im-robert-kirkman-creator-of-the-walking-dead-ama.

Kraft, J. (1973, October 28). Secretary Henry. *New York Times Magazine,* 63.

Pensador, R. (2011, September 10). *Why "high-functioning" psychopaths rule the world.* http://www.dailykos.com/story/2011/09/10/1015320/-Why-High-Functioning-Psychopaths-Rule-The-World#.

Notes

1. Issue 114 (2013).
2. Kraft (1973).
3. Kirkman (2014).
4. Issue 95 (2012).
5. Personal communication (February 14, 2015).
6. Pensador (2011).
7. Barker (2014).
8. Issue 126 (2014).

The Whisperers

Travis Langley

"People wearing dead people's faces!"
—Morgan Jones[1]

"It isn't what they say about you, it's what they whisper."
—actor Errol Flynn[2]

A survivor named Marco, while hunkering down to hide, hears words whispered among passing walkers. He panics and abandons an injured friend. "There were whispers and I was afraid," he says, lying terrified in the infirmary after another man, Dante, finds him. Rick says, "The guy has clearly lost his mind."[3] Dante soon encounters these talking walkers himself. Talkers kill his companions. Dante kills talkers and then stands in shock: "They were talking." But once he spies a seam on the back of one body's head, he discovers that these were living humans wearing costumes made from corpse skins. Another corpse-costumed survivor arrives to point a shotgun and say, "Don't move."[4]

These are the Whisperers. Similarly to the way Rick, Glenn, and others have moved safely among walkers by wearing zombie gore,[5] the Whisperers wear human skin—possibly from walkers, possibly from people skinned alive or those who died without turning. The dead accept them. The living fear them. Dante's captor warns, "You came into our land. Killed our kind. Now we explore your land, learn about your people. You will see many of us. You will know us. You will fear us."[6]

A mask has might. When donning these disguises to affect others both dead and alive, the Whisperers may not have anticipated how it would affect themselves. A disguise can be liberating. Face paint or a feathered mask at Mardi Gras can help unleash hedonistic partying. Behind an avatar, the online anonymity can let one user share feelings too intimate to disclose in person or turn someone else into a troublemaking troll.[7] Anonymity in any form can lower inhibitions (*disinhibition*) by insulating a person against consequences or reducing consciousness of oneself as an individual (*deindividuation*[8]). Many situations deindividuate people—among them, getting lost in a crowd. Whisperers start out wearing corpse skins in order to get lost in walker crowds.

A costume, a uniform, or any other outfit affects the way people act, think, and feel. For example, sports players wearing black uniforms get more penalties for aggressiveness compared with the players on other teams and even compared with themselves when they don't wear black.[9] The Whisperers don't just disguise themselves as walkers. They play the part. They are *role-playing*: adopting and acting out roles that can have personalities, motives, and actions different from their own. Continuously playing a role can be a tricky thing. Police officers who go deep undercover for long periods may have trouble defining themselves after a while.[10]

The Whisperers come to identify with walkers. They walk among the walkers for safety. Then, in time, they walk with the walkers for company. "The skin makes the dead leave us alone," a Whisperer named Lydia explains. "We travel with them. They protect us, and we protect them."[11]

References

Festinger, L., Pepitone, A., & Newcomb, T. (1952). Some consequences of deindividuation in a group. *Journal of Personality and Social Psychology, 47,* 382–389.

Frank, M. G. (1988). The dark side of self- and social perception: Black uniforms and aggression in professional sports. *Journal of Personality and Social Psychology, 54*(1), 74–85.

Girodo, M., & Deck, T. (2002). Dissociative-type identity disturbances in undercover agents: Socio-cognitive factors behind false-identity appearances and reenactments. *Social Behavior and Personality, 30*(7), 631–644.

Hollenbaugh, E. E., & Everett, M. K. (2013). The effects of anonymity on self-disclosure in blogs: An application of the online disinhibition effect. *Journal of Computer-Mediated Communication, 18*(3), 283–302.

Love, K. G., Vinson, J., Tolsma, J., & Kaufmann, G. (2008). Symptoms of undercover police officers: A comparison of officers currently, formerly, and without undercover experience. *International Journal of Stress Management, 15*(2), 136–152.

Suler, J. (2004). The online disinhibition effect. *CyberPsychology & Behavior, 7*(3), 321–326.

Notes

1. Episode 3–12, "Clear" (March 3, 2013).
2. http://www.brainyquote.com/quotes/quotes/e/errolflynn125391.html.
3. Issue 130 (2014).
4. Issue 132 (2014).
5. Issue 4 (2004); Episode 1–2, "Guts" (November 7, 2010).
6. Issue 133 (2014).
7. Hollenbaugh & Everett (2013); Suler (2004).
8. Festinger et al. (1952).
9. Frank (1988).
10. Girodo & Deck (2002); Love et al. (2008).
11. Issue 135 (2014).

• FINAL WORD •

Thriving

*F*ight the dead, fear the living.

The tagline sounds cynical. Is *The Walking Dead* overall a pessimistic story or an optimistic one? Is there hope?

> **Andrew J. West (Gareth):** Absolutely, I think it is hopeful. And honest, too, because you do see so many different sides of humanity, but it's hopeful because you spend most of your time with good people who are still good in spite of this world in which they live. So I think in that sense, it's definitely optimistic and hopeful.[1]

Good people, West says. "Intriguing, believable characters whom people care about," John Russo calls them in this book's foreword. Paradoxical as it might seem, the characters' flaws and mistakes make it easier for us to hope for them and for them to inspire us. If they can keep trying to do the right thing, so can we. So can other people we meet in this life. The fact that they're fictional gives us greater freedom to connect to them, no strings attached. We want heroes, but in this cynical age when social media and 24/7 news announce living heroes' every mistake, we need Sheriff Rick Grimes, not Dudley Do-Right, to show us that imperfect people can keep trying to do the right thing.

Heroism is about standing up when it's hard, even dangerous, and it can cost us a lot. Heroes persist. "Never give up!" we expect them to say, and yet heroism is also about coming back from a fall. Descending into a dark place can bestow new respect for the light. "I wanted to die for what I'd lost," Tyreese tells Noah, "and later, I was there for Judith when she needed me. And that wouldn't have happened if I'd just given up, if I hadn't chosen to live."[2]

"The world we knew is gone, but keeping our humanity? That's a choice," Dale says,[3] and many others echo his concern along the way. What does that really mean, though? Empathy, sympathy, looking out for others? It's not cold practicality. Rick considers killing Randall at the farm but does not. He considers turning Michonne over to the Governor but does not. Why? Because either act would be inhuman. Existence means more than surviving. Throughout the dark tetrad, that four-part model of evil we've used to examine *The Walking Dead*'s top troublemakers throughout this book, we see selfish motivations behind exploitative actions. The hero can be tempted and sometimes may fall, but he or she keeps coming back. Others see heroism in Rick Grimes where he does not. Even when Rick thinks he can betray Michonne, everyone else has faith that he will not.

"I believe in Rick Grimes,"[4] Maggie declares during a later conflict against a more rational villain, and she's not alone. We— the readers, viewers, game players, and cosplayers—believe in *them*. Individually, some will fail, we know, but we have faith in the greater group. Like our hope for humanity, we want people to endeavor to do more right than wrong.

After these characters lose the farm and the prison, after they face Claimers and cannibals and hospital cops, after they suffer loss upon loss but before they finally reach a safe zone, a community where they can live, a different tagline appears, one with an inherent promise that no matter how much there is to dread, life can become better and bigger:

Beyond fear, find hope.[5]

Behind even a dreary setting, the sun will still rise (Grantville, Georgia).

We would not fear for these characters so strongly if we did not hope for them as well. They keep going without knowing for certain what will happen—and so do we. When situations seem darkest, we can looks for signs that things will brighten. In the darkness, every light stands out. We hope for hope, and that keeps us going until we find it. We can do more than survive. We can thrive.

Notes

1. Personal communication (January 10, 2015).
2. Episode 5–9, "What Happened and What's Going On" (February 8, 2015).
3. Episode 2–11, "Judge, Jury, Executioner" (March 3, 2012).
4. Issue 118 (2013).
5. Season 5B trailer (November 30, 2014).

Travis Langley, PhD, editor of *Star Wars Psychology: Dark Side of the Mind* and *The Walking Dead Psychology: Psych of the Living Dead*, is a psychology professor who teaches courses on crime, media, and mental illness at Henderson State University. He received a bachelor's degree from Hendrix College and graduate degrees in psychology from Tulane University in New Orleans. Dr. Langley regularly speaks on media and heroism at conventions and universities. *Necessary Evil: Super-Villains of DC Comics* and other films have featured him as an expert interviewee, and the documentary *Legends of the Knight* spotlighted how he uses fiction to teach real psychology. He authored the acclaimed book *Batman and Psychology: A Dark and Stormy Knight*. *Psychology Today* carries his blog, "Beyond Heroes and Villains."

Follow him as @Superherologist on Twitter, where he ranks among the ten most popular psychologists. You can also keep up with him and the rest of this book's authors through **Facebook. com/ThePsychGeeks**.

Close-quarters weapon of choice: a long crowbar—quiet, unlikely to get stuck in an undead skull, and practical for other things. Walkers and locked doors, beware!

• ABOUT THE CONTRIBUTORS •

John C. Blanchar, MA, is a doctoral candidate in social psychology and a National Science Foundation Graduate Research Fellow at the University of Arkansas. His research investigates status quo preference, defense, and change and the social-cognitive processes underlying political and religious ideology.

Megan Blink, MEd, NCC, is a practicing mental health therapist who works with children, adolescents, and families. She cofounded the Geek and Gamer Counseling Alliance, a nonprofit organization dedicated to research, education, and wellness services for the geek and gamer community. Megan seeks to use her training, creativity, and passion for games and geek culture to "level up" her clients and their mental health treatment.

Colt J. Blunt, PsyD, LP, has worked as a forensic examiner throughout his career and serves as a guest lecturer and trainer for a number of organizations and educational institutions. Colt claims to possess a number of skills he believes make him a key member of any post-apocalyptic society, such as being a black belt martial artist who will gladly fix your car, build you a rifle, and brew you a delicious beer. Consider voting for him as Woodbury's next Governor.

Josué Cardona, MS, is a licensed clinical psycho-therapist and entrepreneur. He is a tech, language, and culture expert, with an emphasis on geek culture. He is a frequent speaker at popular culture and professional conventions and is the founder of GeekTherapy.com.

Adam Davis holds a master's in education with a specialization in drama therapy from Antioch University Seattle. A lifelong geek and game enthusiast, he founded Wheelhouse Workshop, an organization that uses role-playing games to help neurodiverse teenagers build social skills. He teaches literacy in Seattle and in his spare time likes to play board games and cook.

William Blake Erickson, MA, is a doctoral candidate and researcher at the University of Arkansas. His research interests include eyewitness memory, face recognition, and the impact of stress on memory. He has published in journals such as *Applied Cognitive Psychology, Psychonomic Bulletin and Review*, and *Journal of Police and Criminal Psychology*.

Frank Gaskill, PhD, is a cofounder of Southeast Psych, one of the largest private practices in the United States. He coauthored *Max Gamer: Aspie Superhero* and *How We Built Our Dream Practice: Innovative Ideas for Building Yours*. Dr. Gaskill special-izes in parenting, Asperger's, and the way technology affects children, teens, and families. He lives with his wife, Liz, and his children, Olivia and Maddox, in Charlotte, NC. Follow him on twitter (@drfgaskill).

 **Jennifer Golbeck**, associate professor in the College of Information Studies at the University of Maryland, studies human-computer interaction, social media, and how computer models can discover psychological traits and other personal attributes by analyzing what we share online. *Psychology Today* carries Jennifer's blog, "Your Online Secrets," and she has written for the print magazine as well. She has a PhD from the University of Maryland and SB and SM degrees from the University of Chicago.

 **Alan Kistler** (@SizzlerKistler) is the author of the *New York Times* best seller *Doctor Who: A History*. He is an actor, writer, and professional geek consultant who often lectures and writes about the history of superheroes, pop culture, and science fiction, with a focus on representation, feminism, and morality. He is a character in multiple *Star Trek* novels and a host for the online shows *Crazy Sexy Geeks* and *Fortress of Awesome*.

 Dana Klisanin, PhD, is a psychologist, futurist, and author. Her interdisciplinary research examines the impact of media and digital technologies on the mythic and moral dimensions of humanity. Dana's pioneering research includes the areas of integral media, digital altruism, the cyberhero archetype, and collaborative heroism. The American Psychological Association's Division of Media Psychology awarded her the 2012 Early Career Award for Scientific Achievement in Media Psychology. Dana is the CEO of Evolutionary Guidance Media R&D, Inc., where she is currently designing and developing *Cyberhero League*, a twenty-first-century scoutlike gaming adventure. *BBC, Time,*

USA Today, and other media outlets have featured her research, and *Psychology Today* carries her blog. Dana serves on the board of the World Futures Study Federation and is the director of the MindLab at c3: Center for Conscious Creativity.

Stephen Kuniak, PhD, NCC, is a licensed professional counselor providing mental health services and clinical supervision and an adjunct faculty member at Westmoreland County Community College. A cofounder of the Geek and Gamer Counseling Alliance, he has frequently appeared at conventions and has been interviewed about geek and gamer counseling. Steve's dissertation, using data gathered at PAX East, explored cultural aspects and psychological features of gamers.

Martin Lloyd, PhD, LP, received a doctorate in clinical psychology from the University of Minnesota. He has worked in various prisons and high-security hospitals, including the United States Medical Center for Federal Prisoners and Patton State Hospital. He practices as a forensic psychologist in Minnesota and occasionally teaches forensic psychology at Gustavus Adolphus College.

Stephanie Norman completed a bachelor's degree in both biology and kinesiology at the University of Victoria, which provided her with insight into the body at the subcellular and systemic levels. The topic of zombies naturally attracted Stephanie as it provided an extreme but enlightening example of human behavior in the face of internal adversity. She wrote an essay that served as the seed that grew into her chapter in this book.

Patrick O'Connor, PsyD, is the creator of Comicspedia, an online tool that assists therapists in bringing comic books into therapy. He teaches at the Chicago School of Professional Psychology, where he debuted the course "Geek Culture in Therapy," in which students discover how geek culture plays a role in our understanding of ourselves and others and how its artifacts are the vehicles through which we develop this understanding.

Katherine Ramsland, PhD, has published fifty-eight books (including *The Mind of a Murderer, The Forensic Science of Criminal Minds,* and *Darkest Waters*) and over 1,000 articles, focusing on extreme offenders. She is a professor and the director for the master of arts in criminal justice program at DeSales University, where she teaches forensic psychology. She writes a blog for *Psychology Today*, "Shadow Boxing," and is a frequent consultant on crime documentaries.

Clay Routledge, PhD, is a social psychologist and associate professor at North Dakota State University. A leading expert on the psychology of meaning, he has published over seventy-five scientific papers or chapters, coedited a book on the psychology of meaning, and authored the book *Nostalgia: A Psychological Resource*. CBS News, the *New York Times*, and many other media outlets have featured his work. Dr. Routledge writes an online column for *Psychology Today*, "More Than Mortal," and has served as a guest blogger for *Scientific American*.

 **Billy San Juan** received a PsyD in 2014 and is currently working toward a license in clinical psychology. Dr. San Juan has spoken on panels at San Diego Comic-Con, WonderCon, and Stan Lee's Comikaze Expo, and he is a judge for *Magic: The Gathering*. Read his thoughts and insights at Facebook.com/Billicent and on Twitter (@billi_sense).

 Janina Scarlet, PhD, is a licensed clinical psychologist, scientist, and full-time geek. She uses Superhero Therapy to help clients with anxiety, depression, chronic pain, and PTSD at the Center for Stress and Anxiety Management, the Veterans Medical Research Foundation, and Sharp Memorial Hospital. A professor at Alliant International University, San Diego, Dr. Scarlet is the author of the book *Superhero Therapy*. She can be reached via her website at superhero-therapy.com or on Twitter (@shadowquill).

 **Steven C. Schlozman,** MD, is an assistant professor of psychiatry at Harvard Medical School and a staff child psychiatrist at Massachusetts General Hospital. These aspects of his career matter a great deal to his mother. Additionally (and wonderfully still important to his mother), Steve has written short fiction as well as the novel *The Zombie Autopsies: Secret Notebooks from the Apocalypse*. George Romero has optioned this novel and written the screenplay adapting the book for film. Steven also teaches a course on horror in literature and film to Harvard undergraduates, though it is not clear how much more of this avocational dabbling his medical bosses will tolerate. We'll see.

 **Lara Taylor** holds a master's degree in counseling psychology as well as a certificate in traumatology from Holy Names University. She is the creator of TherapeuticCode.com and a contributing editor at GeekTherapy.com.

 **Dave Verhaagen**, PhD, is the author or coauthor of seven books, including *Parenting the Millennial Generation* and *Therapy with Young Men*. He serves as the creative director for Southeast Psych Presents.

 **Mara Wood** is a school psychology doctoral student. Her research focus is the educational application of comic books and their therapeutic use with children and adolescents. She has presented research on transportation and identification with comic book characters at the Comics Arts Conference. She is a regular contributor for *Talking Comics*, is a co-host of *The Missfits* podcast, and writes about psychology, comics, books, and *Dungeons & Dragons* on her blog, marawoodblog.com. You can find her on twitter as @MegaMaraMon.

 E. Paul Zehr, PhD, is a professor, author, and martial artist at the University of Victoria, where he teaches in the neuroscience, kinesiology, and Island Medical programs. His pop-sci books include *Becoming Batman, Inventing Iron Man, Project Superhero*, and *Enhancing our Evolution with Science and Technology*. *Maxim*, CNN, NPR, and others have interviewed him for his diverse expertise. Paul writes for *Psychology Today, Scientific American*, and *Digital Journal*.

Special Contributors

These individuals helped our chapter authors liven things up: Jonathan Hetterly and Katrina Hill wrote some of the special features (case files, sidebars), and Nick Langley contributed illustrations to the book.

Jonathan Hetterly, MA, LPC, is in full-time private practice at Southeast Psych in Charlotte, North Carolina. He works with teenage and young adult males and specializes in treating substance abuse, addiction, and failure to launch struggles. Jonathan approaches counseling primarily through cognitive-behavioral therapy (CBT).

Katrina Hill is a lover of all things action. Her book *Action Movie Freak* is a guidebook to the best action films. She writes for *CraveOnline* and *Arcade Sushi* and created the web series *Geeks and Gamers Anonymous (GAGA)*. Katrina has interviewed most of *The Walking Dead*'s main cast members and moderated for the Dixons (Reedus and Rooker) at Austin Comic Con; Norman Reedus had been a contest judge for her website, *ActionFlickChick.com*. Follow her on Twitter (@ActionChick) or Facebook (Action Flick Chick).

Nick Langley, a graphic design BFA, has presented on many panels at conventions such as San Diego Comic-Con International and WonderCon on topics ranging from the economy of web comics to the psychology of superheroes. His professional works include contributions to Namco-Bandai's *Dig Dug* anniversary web comic, artwork for RocketLlama.com and

ActionFlickChick.com, and illustrations for *The Geek Handbook,*
The Geek Handbook 2.0, and *Batman and Psychology: A Dark and*
Stormy Knight. He founded *The Workday Comic,* a project that
involved collaborating with many artists such as David Mack
(*Kabuki, Daredevil*).

John Russo co-created *Night of the Living Dead* with George
Romero. Russo invented the Living Dead as we know them,
the flesh-eating ghouls people later called zombies, when he
came up with the idea for the people attacking the film's farmhouse to be the recently deceased. His sequel novel, *Return of the*
Living Dead, spawned a movie series that bears little resemblance
to his book. Those films introduced the zombies that famously
groan, "Brains!" John has written much more for film and print,
including comic books such as *Escape of the Living Dead.* His
academic endeavors include co-founding the John Russo Movie
Making Program at Dubois Business College.